The God That the Poor Seek compels readers to do something profound when exploring the nexus of faith and poverty: assume a posture of sincere listening. Too often global discourses on extreme poverty involve the nonpoor talking on behalf of the poor and informing them about their own realities. Regrettably, this is a pitfall for many Christians; we tend to package the experiences of the poor to fit conventional frameworks rather than allowing their voices to illuminate our understandings of God's redemptive pursuit of humanity. Even something as deeply personal as faith conversion is largely explained in terms that are actually foreign to the poor. This book speaks directly to the issue by urging readers to consider, even discover, a nuanced way of comprehending the world of the poor and the nature of God. Rupen Das blends a survey of conversion theory with empirical research from Majority World contexts to provide a comprehensive study about how the poor encounter Christ. The result is innovative insights into the kingdom of God and the ways it is transforming hearts and changing lives. Though there is nothing fundamentally different about the poor, Das keenly demonstrates that there is something acutely unique. With thoughtful recognition of this uniqueness, *The God That the Poor Seek* helps reveal more fully the truth of God's unrelenting nearness, compassion, and hope within a world of chronic human suffering.

Brent Hamoud
Programs Coordinator,
Arab Baptist Theological Seminary, Beirut, Lebanon

The voices of the poor are recorded on these pages, if you would hear them. Rupen Das is an authentic advocate for the poor and marginalized. His many years of service among them have given him a keen insight into the cares, burdens, and motivations of the disadvantaged.

Chris Todd
Pastor and Missionary,
National Evangelical Synod of Syria and Lebanon

The heart of *The God That the Poor Seek* is the testimonies of the marginalized poor in their own voices and their journey to allegiance to God through Jesus Christ. To understand this journey, Rupen Das through scholarly research has documented the history and development of the dynamics of conversion and contextualization and presented them in a very accessible way. This book will open your eyes to the many and varied ways in which people begin to follow

Jesus and help you understand the worldview of those whose life experience is very different from your own. This is a must-own book because it is full of surprises: amazing discoveries and insights, inspiring testimonies, and depth of understanding of the world in which the marginalized poor live.

Don Bartel
Associate Field Director,
US Navigators

Having lived for a number of years and served the church in "The City of Joy," Kolkata, India, and encountering people living on the streets day in and day out, I was anxiously looking forward to Dr. Rupen Das's book *The God That the Poor Seek.* He has done thorough research on the subject of the poor from both the liberal and evangelical perspectives. I quote: "Research has shown a clear connection between poverty and spirituality"; and "Poverty is multidimensional and has certain unique characteristics." He explores the different ramifications of the word "conversion" from the evangelical perspective beginning from the Acts of the Apostles and the early church fathers to the follow-up related to the subject of "conversion" at the New Delhi Assembly of the World Council of Churches. He deals in detail with the understanding of the word "contextualization." The real-life stories of the poor and their relationship with Christ seals the validity of this excellent scholarly work. This book transports us from our comfortable world to the realities that confront the poor resulting in their encounter with Jesus Christ.

Rev. Dr. Robert Cunville
President, United Bible Societies
Associate Evangelist, The Billy Graham Evangelistic Association

Rupen Das's thorough theological reflection with a social scientific analysis brilliantly explores the brokenness of the poor in seeing through their eyes, feeling their hearts, respecting their reflections, and comprehending the dynamics of their decisions to follow Christ in their ongoing struggle to experience lives anew. This is a must-read book to understand the significance of Jesus's proclamation of good news to the poor.

Rev. Suraj Komaravalli, PhD
India Team Leader,
Canadian Baptist Ministries

Here's yet another compelling book! With careful scholarship and personal experience, Rupen Das establishes the transcending power of the gospel in the lived realities of cultures and human experiences. This book skillfully portrays the profound interplay of culture and theology, the simple yet incredible faith of the poor, and the radical impact of the gospel. The voices of the poor, including the Indian slum dwellers, provide us with contagious insights of theologizing in context. This book realizes new hope and direction in theological education and mission.

Jessy Jaison, PhD
Director of Research & Advancement,
New India Bible Seminary, Kerala, India

Rupen Das's study on the conversion of the poor demonstrates the need to listen to them and understand their religious and socioeconomic contexts to know the reasons why they turn to Christ. It further shows that the typical evangelical assumption that conversion is a cognitive process which begins with the conviction of sin and need for forgiveness, followed by turning to Christ as Savior, rarely applies to the poor from non-Christian religious backgrounds. This study therefore is a serious corrective to any oversimplification of the reasons behind Christian conversion, a powerful aid to those seeking to reach the poor with the gospel, and a most useful contribution to the literature on practical contextualization in mission. I recommend it warmly.

Hwa Yung, DMiss
Bishop Emeritus,
The Methodist Church of Malaysia

This book meets a great need in the field of missiology, especially with regards to contextualization of the gospel among the poor. While much of the literature on poverty and the poor is written by authors who are outsiders to the community, Das wisely calls us to listen to the poor themselves: people who struggle daily with powerlessness, vulnerability, isolation, and weakness. Herein are authentic and honest voices of the poor, who amidst their hopelessness abandoned their deities, followed Christ, and encountered the living God. Das not only empowers them to be "heard to speech" but reflects on these powerful stories in light of the broader literature on contextualization, guiding the wider church to more intentional faith responses in God's kingdom among us.

Yau Man Siew, PhD
Associate Professor of Practical Theology,
Tyndale Seminary at Tyndale University, Toronto, Canada

An utterly captivating book about the deep longings of poor people from two completely different contexts on why they were attracted to Christ and decided to follow him. Based on phenomenological traditions of research inquiry, Rupen Das faithfully communicates the stories and lived experiences of Syrian refugees in Lebanon and slum dwellers in Bangalore, India, on their conversion journeys to Christianity and analyzes them in light of rich missiological literature and practices. Das shows that for the poor, conversion is not about believing the gospel truth proclamation at a given point of time, divorced from their contexts. Instead it is a process consisting of encounters with Christ in their lived realities, and decisions and choices over a period of time, along with a growing understanding of who Christ is and faith in his attributes such as love and power which are manifest in their lives. This book raises a number of questions and considerations for mission organizations and Christian NGOs as they seek to partner with local churches and serve the poor and the marginalized in meeting their physical and spiritual needs in an integrated manner. This is a must-read book for every student and practitioner who is committed to a holistic understanding of mission among the poor which breaks down the divisions between the physical, social, and spiritual aspects of their lives and instead sees them as a coherent whole.

Jaisankar Sarma, PhD
Adjunct Faculty, Transformational Development,
Fuller Theological Seminary, Pasadena, California, USA
Vice President, Hope Walks

We commend the research and analysis of Rupen Das in *The God That the Poor Seek*. Das brings decades of work among the poor to his work. He challenges the assumption that the Christian gospel is primarily about the "management of sin" and the prospect of eternal life. He shows that people in situations of desperate poverty are moved to faith by the message that God loves them and is concerned about the painful and dehumanizing factors that make their lives uncertain and even dangerous. The stories of Jesus give substance to the message that the gospel is good news for the poor. We were particularly moved by the life experiences of Christians in India and Lebanon who live in the context of poverty and who find faith to be transformative.

Gordon King, DMin
Adjunct Faculty, Ambrose University, Calgary, Alberta, Canada
Author of *Seed Falling on Good Soil*

If you want to understand the moral of Jesus's call to his church, "lift up your eyes and look on the fields, that they are white for harvest," here is a book that opens it up to you. Rupen Das has done that, and what a blessed harvest! Read it here – a gem of Christian testimony that you'll have trouble putting down.

Rosangela Jarjour
General Secretary,
Fellowship of Middle East Evangelical Churches

"Do poor people become Christians just because you give them something?" I often get asked this question as I travel around the world. Rupen Das very expertly answers this question, and the answer will surprise you. This book provides excellent background studies, many examples and stories from work among Syrian refugees and Indian slums, and good theological and missiological discussion on the subject. But the greatest value of this book for me is an exhortation to "listen to the poor." The church around the world will be more blessed, more effective, and very productive among the poor if we just develop this one gift. All of us are indebted to Rupen Das for highlighting this in *The God That the Poor Seek*.

Moses Parmar
Program Director, Evangelical Fellowship of India

Rupen Das has asked a profound question. Western evangelicalism may say that "Jesus is the answer," but the unstated assumption is that everyone from every culture is asking the same question. Jesus indeed bids us to follow him and offers the abundant life, but Das probes more deeply, asking how cultural background shapes our understanding of what abundant life means. Through often profoundly moving interactions with new Christians in two non-Western cultures, all living in poverty, he asks: What deep need did Jesus meet for you which brought you to faith? These men and especially women share what an utter about-face in life direction – conversion to Christ – meant for them. The answers are surprising. Western evangelicals may think that conversion for the Majority World's poor should look like "The Four Spiritual Laws." But secularism has its own rigid preconceptions, proposing panaceas of class vengeance, or economic and political power. Das instead shows us the importance of actually talking with the poor themselves. They share with him their search for inner joy, confidence about their eternal future, domestic reconciliation, and peace with God to replace fear and rebellion. Anyone who aspires to effective cross-cultural evangelism will profit from reading this thought-provoking book to learn from these case studies the importance of approaching those from other cultures in order to understand their deepest needs and how the gospel will be good news to them.

Steven Van Dyck
Executive Director,
Langham Partnership Canada

Once again Rupen Das is calling followers of Jesus to informed vision and compassionate engagement. This book moves his readers to be rooted in the full scope of God's purposes in Christ, not only through Scripture but through a deep understanding of the realities of brothers and sisters living with poverty. His book is full of accessible, applicable content that acts as the context for the reader to hear more clearly and purposefully the voices and stories of the poor. Das develops the central theme of conversion and holds it in the dual light of scriptural analysis and real-life experience in order to make clear the need to understand our own potential biases and blind spots both intellectually and experientially. The principles and frameworks that Das develops through his research leave the reader with a humility and hunger to truly listen to the lives of others and to share a gospel that is real and constantly transformational both for the one who is sharing and for the one who receives.

Sandra Ryan
Pastor of Global Mission,
The Peoples Church, Toronto, Canada

How easy it is for so many of us to take up the practice of theologizing about the poor rather than first hearing the responses to Christ from the poor. Das directs our attention to the voices and witness of the poor showing us why they value and follow the God who meets them in their struggles, God with us. *The God That the Poor Seek* makes it clear that those of us who want to know and speak about Christ do well to imitate this God and to follow the Holy One into the fray of the lives of the poor. Das has followed this path and as a result gives us theology that matters in a world of economic disparities and injustice.

Tim Dickau, DMin
Teacher, The Center for Missional Leadership
Former Pastor, Grandview Church, East Vancouver, Canada

Rupen Das has produced a winner with *The God That the Poor Seek*! He has done a very thorough job in tackling very complex issues. I believe his analysis of context, conversion, and the poor will prove to be a gift to the global church in this COVID-19 world, and even beyond the pandemic, as we all wrestle with the injustices around the world that have been highlighted by the pandemic. I have read a number of books about the poor, and most of the time, they are us speaking for the poor. In this book, Rupen Das has amplified the voices of the poor and allowed us to hear firsthand from them. He is helping the poor find their voices and express for themselves their hopes and dreams. His "whole gospel" approach is refreshing! I will certainly be promoting this book as much as I can!

Peter Tarantal
Associate International Director, OM International
Chair, Majority World Christian Leaders Conversation

Rupen Das has written a book that provides a window into the church in the Majority World which is growing exponentially in the contexts of religious pluralism, poverty, and sociopolitical systems that inflict oppression. Das challenges the reader to understand that there can never be a "cultureless" presentation of the gospel. We all come with cultural assumptions when seeking to engage the gospel in different cultural contexts. Through his research and biblical exposition, Das helps the church of the Global North to see the world and the gospel through the eyes of the poor and disenfranchised. Das encourages the development of a listening posture rather than imposing a Western formulaic presentation of the gospel. This listening, he believes, will go a long way in discovering how the poor experience the transcendent reality of an all-powerful, loving God.

Robert Cousins, DMin
Cross-Cultural Mission Consultant
Former Director, Tyndale Intercultural Ministry Centre,
Tyndale University, Toronto, Canada

The God That the Poor Seek

The God That the Poor Seek

Conversion, Context, and the World of the Vulnerable

Rupen Das

Langham

GLOBAL LIBRARY

Published 2022 by Langham Global Library
An imprint of Langham Publishing
www.langhampublishing.org

Langham Publishing and its imprints are a ministry of Langham Partnership

Langham Partnership
PO Box 296, Carlisle, Cumbria, CA3 9WZ, UK
www.langham.org

ISBNs:
978-1-83973-273-7 Print
978-1-83973-615-5 ePub
978-1-83973-616-2 Mobi
978-1-83973-617-9 PDF

British Library Cataloguing-in-Publication Data
A catalogue record for this book is available from the British Library

ISBN: 978-1-83973-273-7

Cover photo © Rupen Das

Cover & Book Design: projectluz.com

The LORD is trustworthy in all he promises
and faithful in all he does.
The LORD upholds all who fall
and lifts up all who are bowed down.
The eyes of all look to you,
and you give them their food at the proper time.
You open your hand
and satisfy the desires of every living thing.
The LORD is righteous in all his ways
and faithful in all he does.
The LORD is near to all who call on him,
to all who call on him in truth.
Psalm 145:13–18

Contents

Acronyms

COME	Christian Outreach for Mission and Evangelism Trust
HH	households
HU	homogeneous unit
HUP	homogeneous unit principle
IAMS	International Association of Mission Studies
LSESD	Lebanese Society for Education and Social Development
MDG	Millennium Development Goals
NGO	nongovernmental organization
NIV	New International Version
PRA	participatory rural appraisal
SES	socioeconomic status
TEF	Theological Education Fund
UN	United Nations
WCC	World Council of Churches
WEA	World Evangelical Alliance

Non-English Words

Bhajan — Spiritual songs (Hindi and other Indian languages)

Bhakti — Devotion to a god (Hindi and other Indian languages)

Campesino — Peasant in Latin America (Spanish)

Coolie — Day laborer (Hindi and other Indian languages)

Ethne — Nations, ethnic or people groups (Greek)

Mala — A flower garland used in Hindu worship as well as to honor guests (Hindi and other Indian languages)

Pistis — Commonly translated as "faith" or "believe" (Greek)

Puja — Worship rituals and celebrations in Hinduism (Indian languages)

Satsangh — Gathering for the truth (Hindi/Sanskrit)

Shangdi — The High God (Chinese)

Shari'a — Islamic canonical law based on the teachings of the Qur'an and the traditions of the Prophet (Hadith and Sunna), prescribing both religious and secular duties and sometimes retributive penalties for lawbreaking. It has generally been supplemented by legislation adapted to the conditions of the day, though the manner in which it should be applied in modern states is a subject of dispute between Islamic fundamentalists and modernists (Arabic)

Shen — Generic term to refer to God (Chinese)

Shubh — Turning, repentance, rejecting the vices of the culture and "coming to one's senses" (Hebrew)

Takbir — The Islamic proclamation *Allahu Akbar* meaning God is great (Arabic)

Acknowledgements

A number of people assisted in recording the stories of conversion and faith in this book. I am grateful to Lily Malki, Samar Khoury, Chris Todd, and Suzy Schenkel Lahoud in Lebanon, and Joshua Mahadev with COME ministry and Rev. K. Vasudevan in Bangalore, India, for identifying the participants and recording the stories. Rev. Jihad Haddad, Naji Daoud, and Rev. Dr. Hikmat Kashouh in Lebanon facilitated access to many of the refugees in their churches and areas of ministry.

I am indebted to two friends who have stimulated my thinking over the years. Dr. Gary Nelson, formerly the president of Tyndale University, provided me with an academic home and all that it entails. Dr. Gordon King has, over the years, been a sounding board for ideas and insights as we journeyed together on so many occasions through a troubled world trying to make sense of it.

I am deeply grateful to Vivian Doub, Mark Arnold, and the team at Langham for their interest and guiding this book to completion. Without their encouragement over a number of book projects in the past few years, this present book would not have been possible. I am indebted to Nelly Safari who brought her rich experience in publishing as the director for Scripture resources at the Canadian Bible Society to do an initial edit of the manuscript.

My wife, Mamta, provided me the time and mental space to focus on the research and writing, while undergirding me with prayer. I can never fully express my gratitude.

Many people seeded thoughts and provided feedback as I tried to think through many of the issues discussed in this book. They are more than I can list here. I acknowledge their invaluable investment over many years.

My prayer for you as you read this book is from St. Irenaeus:

> I appeal to you, Lord, God of Abraham, God of Isaac, God of Jacob and Israel, You the Father of our Lord Jesus Christ. Infinitely merciful as you are, it is your will that we should learn to know you. You made heaven and earth, you rule supreme over all that is. You are the true, the only God; there is no other god above you. Through our Lord Jesus Christ . . . and the gifts of the Holy Spirit,

grant that all who read what I have written here may know you, because you alone are God.[1]

Soli Deo Gloria!
Rupen Das
Mississauga, Canada 2021

---

1. Irenaeus quoted in A. G. Hamman and W. Mitchell, eds., *Early Christian Prayers* (Chicago: Henry Regnery Company, 1961), 30–31.

Foreword

"What did Jesus come to do?" Take a minute. How do you answer this question?

I typically ask this question to the students on the first day of my "Gospel, Church, and Culture" class at the seminary.

"To seek and save the lost."

"To save people from their sins."

"To give eternal life."

After receiving answers like these on that first day of class, I then describe my own journey of faith. I reveal that I did not come to Jesus with a deep sense of my sinfulness and rebellion. For me, this sense came much later in my faith journey.

From students whose box of appropriation is transactional, focused on the personal salvation and eternal life continuum, there is immediate push back. They are not aware that they are culturally bound in their perspective. They fear for "my salvation," and some even wonder if I am apostate. But this is my story. I came to faith not because of being convicted with my sin, but with a deep sense of the pointlessness of my life and a profound need for purpose and meaning. It culminated in the discovery of the person of Jesus Christ, an adventure of faith through living the good news the kingdom offers. I have never doubted that decision even in the darkest times of my life.

It can be threatening to discover that others appropriate faith in ways different than one's own experience. Carlos Cardoza-Orlandi points this out when he writes:

> Many Christians assume that their Christianity is normative and pure; they are blind to the interplay between the gospel and their culture(s), the way in which their faith is shaped by the context where they live. There is not "pure" faith, and mission is always shaped by the context. Hence the Christian faith is always a contextualized faith, and their contextualized faith is also what Christians share in the missional endeavour.[1]

---

1. Cardoza-Orlandi, *Mission: An Essential Guide*, 14.

However, that each of our encounters with the gospel is unique is a truth worth celebrating. It speaks to its wideness, its attractiveness, and its boundlessness.

I have had the privilege of serving as president of Tyndale Seminary in Toronto, Canada, for the last ten years. This large trans-denominational seminary located in what is considered to be one of the most multicultural cities in the world is a mirror of that reality all around it. Over sixty people groups gather in classes in which people with Anglo-Saxon roots such as mine are the exception rather than the norm. The faces of the faculty, staff, and students reflect a variety of racial heritages, ethnic backgrounds, and cultural differences.

In this place of diversity, the Christian faith is appropriated, understood, and lived out in unique and different ways. The diversity makes for challenging yet incredibly enriching conversation. It requires a deep and intentional posture of listening, a posture that is not always a place in which we like to locate ourselves. To miss this is to miss the amazing thing Jesus has done.

Rupen has not missed what Jesus has done. Rupen has seen it firsthand in the lives of people in very different contexts than mine. He shares his experience as one who has been a listener and a companion to so many people living marginalized lives in various contexts around the world. His attentiveness emerges from his curiosity and his thoughtfulness that as a former colleague and an ongoing friend, I have always admired.

Rupen reminds us that the message of Jesus can be translated into any one of our cultures. For us to understand the gospel most deeply, we will need to attend to those who see it differently than we do. A Latin American woman living in the barrios of Lima will bring a perspective on a particular passage of Scripture that will fill in the blanks of my understanding. She will also talk about a very different conversion experience that you or I may have had. An Arab Christian living in Lebanon as a minority person will do the same. Many Turkish Christians were first attracted to the gospel through dreams. Together they and so many others give us a deeper understanding of how incredibly revolutionary this good news of Jesus really is.

So, what did Jesus come to do? The Gospel writers are clear: Jesus came to preach the good news of the kingdom to all people in all places.

Matthew tells us, "Jesus went throughout Galilee, teaching in their synagogues, proclaiming the good news of the kingdom" (Matt 4:23).

Mark in his youthful enthusiasm reports Jesus declaring, "The kingdom of God has come near. Repent and believe the good news!" (Mark 1:15).

With a clear sense of what the mission of Jesus is about, Luke quotes Jesus saying, "I must proclaim the good news of the kingdom of God to the other towns also, because that is why I was sent" (Luke 4:43).

Rupen reminds us that the gospel has an unlimited translatability that we are called to embrace. It crosses cultures and socioeconomic barriers. If we are humble enough and willing to take the posture of a listener, we will discover that our little box is not big enough for the gospel that has taken hold of our lives.

Rupen does this by introducing us to the intimate stories of some of the poor he has shared life with as they encounter Christ. Rupen introduces us to the writings of Stephen Bevans and Roger Schroeder and quotes them as writing, "If the church is to be in mission, to be in mission is to be responsive to the demands of the gospel in particular contexts, to be continually 'reinventing' itself as it struggles with and approaches new situations, new places, new cultures, and new questions."[2] This book is focused on the poor, but it carries a transcendence to all contexts and experiences. However, its value is found in the introduction Rupen gives us to how the poor encounter God revealed in Christ and what is the good news for which they search.

My hope is that in the reading of this book, in the richness of its solid research framework, even the most skeptical will come to know what Rupen is pointing to – a revolutionary gospel that points to a way of living that is radical enough to embrace and change the whole world! A gospel that is not only good news to the poor but to all who seek him.

Dr. Gary Nelson
Former President of Tyndale University, Toronto, Canada
Author of *Borderland Churches* and *Leading in DisOrienting Times*

---

2. Bevans and Schroeder, *Constants in Context*, 31.

Preface

The *missio Dei,* in which the church participates, is not just about helping the poor but about following Christ and discovering that those whom one is called to serve also have something to give.[1]

Fr. Daniel Groody, missiologist

My writings have always had a context. They are rarely mere academic explorations of an interesting topic. They emerge out of my own struggles to understand the world we live in and what it means to follow Christ in such a world. There were two streams of personal experiences that converged, resulting in questions for which I had to find answers.

The issue of poverty and a concern for the poor has been a part of my personal spiritual journey for a long time. As a young adult, as my faith deepened, I was involved with ministries that focused almost exclusively on the eternal dimensions of life and ignored the realities of living in a broken world. The question that haunted me was whether God was really concerned for the poor, the injustices that enslaved the marginalized, and the violence and conflicts that destroyed lives and societies. Study, research, conversations, life experiences, and reflection over decades culminated in the publication of *Compassion and the Mission of God: Revealing the Invisible Kingdom* and *Strangers in the Kingdom: Refugees, Migrants and the Stateless.*[2] The question that I asked and tried to answer was, *why* does God care for the poor, the marginalized, and the displaced?

The answer I found was in Jürgen Moltmann's writings as he draws on Rabbi Abraham Heschel's concept of the *pathos of God.*[3] God is not cold, dispassionate, and distant, somehow unconnected with the human experience. Instead, he is someone who feels deeply. This *pathos* is not what Moltmann calls "irrational human emotions," but describes a God who is affected by events, human actions, and suffering in history. Moltmann writes, "He [God]

---

1. Groody, *Crossing the Divide,* 26–27.

2. Das, *Compassion and the Mission of God*; and Das and Hamoud, *Strangers in the Kingdom.*

3. Heschel's discussion on the pathos of God is from *The Prophets* (New York: Harper & Row, 1962).

is affected by them because he is interested in his creation, his people."[4] The world is not the way God intended it to be. But because God is Creator, he is moved to redeem and restore brokenness when he sees the destructive effects of evil on all of his creation. This *pathos* was the compassion that motivated Jesus in his ministry.[5] The *pathos* of God is contrasted with the *apatheia* of the gods that Judaism and early Christianity encountered in the religions of the ancient world. *Apatheia* was the inability of the gods to feel compassion or sorrow about the human condition and be influenced by what happened to human beings.

Having gotten a glimpse of how God feels about human beings and his creation, *I often wondered what the poor, the victims of human trafficking and abuse, and the refugees think about God.* I often find myself reacting with anger at the injustices I see, realizing that this is not the way God intended this world to be. However, because of my position of privilege, I have not been able to see the world through the eyes of those who are victims of evil. I do not understand why they would even turn to a God who seemingly has betrayed them and ignored their destitution and desperation.

As these questions continued to play in the background, in my work I would often hear the poor talk about their faith. Their ability to survive in the face of seemingly insurmountable challenges was something that I have admired. It seemed to me that their resilience is rooted in a worldview expressed through their faith and spirituality that is very different than mine. Listening to their life experiences and the simplicity of their faith pushed me beyond my safe and comfortable religious traditions and practices to seek the reality of God through Jesus Christ, who is known as *Immanuel*, in the daily affairs and challenges of my own life.

The second stream of experience started with a Muslim student of mine in one of my postgraduate international development classes. One day in a private conversation, he spoke about some personal challenges he was facing and then narrated a dream that he had had. He said that a few nights before, Jesus had appeared to him in a dream, told him what to do about his problem,

---

4. Moltmann, *Crucified God*, 270.

5. D. Preman Niles explains that the Greek word for compassion is *splanchnizomai* and literally means, "to be moved in the inward parts." It connotes a strong physical and emotional reaction, "a gut-wrenching response." It is the idea of *pathos.* He says that the word *splanchnizomai* only occurs in the Gospels and is only used to describe Jesus's reactions. "It is used . . . to describe the attitude of Jesus to people defined as the [multitudes] and the action that ensues from that attitude." Niles, *From East and West*, 79.

and then simply said, "Follow me." He said that he woke up and then woke up his wife and told her he was going to follow Jesus.

Nothing in my years of ministry and of studying the Bible provided me a framework to understand his experience. He did not respond to a gospel presentation. He was not asked to make a decision or pray a prayer. Something about his encounter with Christ was so profound that he would have tears in his eyes every time he spoke about what had happened – even years later.

Over the years as I listened to the stories of the poor and those from non-Christian backgrounds, I heard similar experiences. It opened a Pandora's box for me of trying to understand how God works in the lives of people to reconcile and restore them to himself – how conversion actually happens.

As both of these streams converged, they raised questions about the God that the poor seek and about how conversions happen. These questions led to the genesis of this book.

1

Introduction

Theology is an act of repentant humility. . . . This act exists in the fact that in theology the Church seeks again and again to examine itself critically as it asks itself what it means and implies to be a Church among men.[1]

Karl Barth

The church, which had its origins on the margins of the Roman Empire and of Roman society, breathed new life into the Jewish idea that the Creator God dwells among his people. He cared for them, provided for their needs, comforted them in times of crisis, and gave them eternal hope when they faced death. This idea was so revolutionary that it intrigued people who were not yet part of the faith community that worshiped Jesus Christ. Early church historian Alan Kreider writes, "Rumors that God was present in Christian gatherings may have also attracted outsiders to investigate Christianity."[2]

As I encountered people in many parts of the world who were poor and were turning to worship Christ, I saw something in their new-found faith that had echoes of the life of the early church and had been pushed to the margins of my thinking in the midst of theological studies, research, writing, and ministry: God is not distant but is deeply involved in human lives and history. He answers all who call on him in the name of Jesus.

The Missing Piece in Understanding the World of the Poor

Through my years of working in international development and humanitarian assistance, I have noticed that the poor in the Majority World approach

---

1. Barth, *God in Action*, 44.
2. Kreider, *Patient Ferment of the Early Church*, 109.

God very differently than most of us who either live in the Western world or are among the privileged in the Majority World. In my conversations with the poor who have become followers of Christ, I also sensed that they were encountering Christ in ways that were different from what traditional Christian and evangelical[3] theology and recent missional practice constituted as conversion. In the midst of their destitution and suffering, what the poor expected from God when they turned to him surprised me. I expected them to want liberation, freedom, and a pathway to a middle-class lifestyle; but what they yearned for was something quite different. While we are beginning to understand the socioeconomic world of those living in poverty, we really don't yet understand the spirituality of the poor.

It is this intuition or clue that sparked the desire for further investigation. I realized very early on that this investigation would require a paradigm shift in me to understand the dynamics of conversion to Christ among the poor.[4] In order for this shift to happen, I needed to lay aside my worldview's preconceived notions about poverty and the poor, the anecdotal stories as to why the poor were attracted to religion, and then try to see God and his work of redemption through the eyes of some of the poor themselves. This book is about conversion in the contexts of the poor.

The issue of poverty and the poor has become part of the global political agenda as seen through initiatives such as the Millennium Development Goals (MDGs) and the Sustainable Development Goals (SDGs);[5] critical discussions

---

3. Historically, the mainline Protestant denominations in the Middle East were known as the Protestant Evangelical churches. In Europe, Martin Luther referred to the *evangelische Kirche* (evangelical church) to distinguish Protestants from the Catholic Church. "Evangelical" is difficult to define. The National Association of Evangelicals (NAE) defines "evangelical" as follows: "The term 'evangelical' comes from the Greek word *euangelion*, meaning 'the good news' or the 'gospel.' Thus, the evangelical faith focuses on the 'good news' of salvation brought to sinners by Jesus Christ." National Association of Evangelicals, "What Is an Evangelical?" Roger Olsen states that "*evangelicalism is not a movement or group but a spiritual-theological ethos* marked by David Bebbington's four hallmarks (Biblicism, conversionism, crucicentrism, activism) plus a deep respect for orthodox Christianity as expressed by the earliest Christian creeds and councils and by the Protestant reformers." Roger E. Olsen, "What Is an 'Evangelical' and Does It Matter?" (emphasis original).

4. Leslie Newbigin writes that in science and religion, innovation is the result not so much of new facts, but of paradigm shifts which are acts of imagination or intuition. This shift provides a clue which then gives rise to advances in knowledge. Newbigin, *Gospel in a Pluralistic Society*, 5.

5. MDGs were not just a one-off, time-bound initiative that ended in September 2015. On 25 September 2015, 193 countries adopted the United Nations' new Sustainable Development Goals (SDGs) to build on the impact of the MDGs.

on the roots of terrorism, violence, and crime;[6] the ethics of international trade;[7] and the question of the obligation of rich nations toward poorer countries.[8] While there has been an increasing focus on how to address the social, political, and economic dimensions of poverty, understanding the spiritual realities of the poor, how they relate to God, and why they seek Christ have received comparatively less attention.

A concern for the poor has always been an integral part of most religions. Religious texts refer to the poor rather than poverty. Obligations as dictated by their religious tradition are their prescription to respond to human needs in the community.[9] This emphasis on the poor has not escaped the church. The early church responded to the needs of refugees, the poor, and others on the margins of society.[10] Addressing poverty has been part of the doctrine and practice of the Roman Catholic Church over the centuries through the ministries of its various monastic orders, religious societies, and communities. In 1891, Pope Leo XIII addressed the issue of labor and capital, which is regarded as the first encyclical of Catholic social teaching.[11] Vatican II (1962–65) provided "a theological atmosphere characterized by greater freedom and creativity"[12] within which the issues of injustice and poverty were also discussed. Pope Paul VI addressed issues such as the impact of colonialism and the growing disparity between the rich and the poor, and stressed the need for justice and social and economic development. He wrote, "It is true that colonizing nations were sometimes concerned with nothing save their own interests, their own power and their own prestige; their departure left the economy of these countries in precarious imbalance."[13] He went on to address how social and economic development should be approached.

---

6. Abadie, "Poverty, Political Freedom, and the Roots of Terrorism," 50–66; Krueger and Malečková, "Education, Poverty and Terrorism," 119–44.

7. Bhagwati and Srinivasan, "Trade and Poverty in the Poor Countries," 180–83.

8. Grenier, "Jubilee 2000: Laying the Foundations for a Social Movement," 86–108.

9. Das and Brackney, eds., *Poverty and the Poor in the World Religions*; Das, *Poor and Poverty in Islam*.

10. Brueggemann, "How the Early Church Practiced Charity"; Brown, *Poverty and Leadership in the Later Roman Empire*; Brown, *Through the Eye of a Needle*.

11. Leo XIII, "Rerum Novarum: Encyclical of Pope Leo XIII on Capital and Labour," 592–651.

12. Boff and Boff, *Introducing Liberation Theology*, 69.

13. Pope Paul VI, "Populorum Progressio: Encyclical of Pope Paul VI on the Development of Peoples: 26th March 1967," 7.

The development we speak of here cannot be restricted to economic growth alone. To be authentic, it must be well rounded; it must foster the development of each man and of the whole man. As an eminent specialist on this question has rightly said: "We cannot allow economics to be separated from human realities, nor development from the civilization in which it takes place. What counts for us is man – each individual man, each human group, and humanity as a whole."[14]

By the 1960s, *how* poverty should be addressed became a controversial issue with the emergence of liberation theology.[15] The election of Pope Francis in 2013 and his emphasis on social justice has brought the issues of global poverty and injustice into the mainstreams of Catholic discourse again.[16]

The social issues related to poverty and the poor were not always part of the modern Protestant missionary movement which emerged in the late 1700s. It was not until the Liverpool Missionary Conference in 1860 that the impact of poverty was addressed with the first medical missionary being commissioned and the decision made that education (anything beyond literacy) could also be part of the missionary mandate.[17] The succeeding missionary conferences of that period[18] occasionally discussed social issues.[19] However, with the advent of the social gospel in the late nineteenth and early twentieth centuries, with its focus on social progress, issues related to poverty and the poor began to dominate the agenda of mission agencies.

Regardless of this lack of focus on social issues in missional strategies until the mid-1800s, in 1865 William Booth (1829–1912), a former Methodist minister in England, started working with the "undesirables" of society in London. These included morphine and other drug addicts, prostitutes, and

---

14. Pope Paul VI, "Populorum Progressio," 14. These remarks were further elaborated on in Hollenbach, "Gaudium et Spes (1965)," 266–314; Pope Paul VI, "Evangelica Testuficatio: On the Renewal of the Religious Life According to the Teaching of the Second Vatican Council," 1–20.

15. Hesselgrave and Rommen, *Contextualization*, 87. Liberation theology was not the only driver within the Roman Catholic Church in bringing the issues of poverty and social change to the forefront in recent times.

16. Stan Chu Ilo, "Poverty and Economic Justice in Pope Francis," 38–56; Tan, "Pope Francis's Preferential Option," 58–66.

17. The Secretaries to the Conference, ed., *Conference on Missions Held in 1860 at Liverpool*.

18. London 1878 and 1888, New York 1900, and Edinburgh 1910.

19. The Secretaries to the Conference, ed., *Proceedings of the General Conference on Foreign Missions*; Johnston, ed., *Report of the Centenary Conference*; Askew, "The 1888 London Centenary Missions Conference," 113–18; Askew, "The New York 1900 Ecumenical Missionary Conference," 146–50; *The World Missionary Conference, 1910.*

alcoholics. Industrialization in Britain had created significant social problems, and a large section of the population was either unemployed or living in very poor and unhealthy conditions. Booth felt that the church had a responsibility to show the love of Christ to the poor and marginalized in tangible ways.

Because of the theological tensions between the fundamentalists who were dispensationalists and the proponents of the social gospel who ultimately were rooted in liberal theology,[20] evangelicals did not address the issues of the poor and poverty until much later. However, there were dispensationalists who were involved with social reforms between the 1870s and the 1920s. These included A. J. Gordon, Arthur T. Pierson, William Bell Riley, and John Roach Straton, among others.[21] A few decades later, one of the few evangelicals who wrote about the need to also address social issues was Carl F. H. Henry, who in his 1947 book *The Uneasy Conscience of Modern Fundamentalism*[22] challenged the indifference of the fundamentalists and evangelicals. It was only at the 1966 Wheaton Congress on the Church's Worldwide Mission, followed by the 1973 Chicago Declaration of Evangelical Social Concern, culminating with the Lausanne International Congress on World Evangelization in 1974, that many evangelicals recognized social responsibility and social justice as part of the mission of the church.[23] The resulting focus was to move beyond charity toward stressing the need for social justice and improving the socioeconomic and political status of the poor and marginalized.

As churches, mission agencies, and Christian organizations focused on understanding and responding to the sociopolitical and economic needs of the poor, the paradigm was of the nonpoor and outsiders to the context analyzing the realities of the poor and the dynamics of poverty. Much has been written by them about their understanding of poverty and their proposed strategies for

---

20. For a short review of the tensions, see Das, *Compassion and the Mission of God*, 105–34.

21. Timothy Webber at Denver Seminary in his survey of American premillennialism summarizes the range of attitudes toward social change. "Some premillennialists condemned all reform efforts as unsuitable for those who expected Christ momentarily; but others believed that until Christ does appear, Christians should engage in certain kinds of reform activity and do whatever possible to slow down the inevitable decline and breakdown of the social order." Webber, *Living in the Shadow of the Second Coming*, 83.

22. Henry, *Uneasy Conscience of Modern Fundamentalism*.

23. Though the Lausanne 1974 Covenant was approved by the conference, there were evangelicals led by Peter Wagner, Donald MacGavran, and Ralph Winters who opposed the inclusion of social responsibility as part of the mandate of the Great Commission. Houston, "Story of the Lausanne Covenant"; Hunt, "History of the Lausanne Movement, 1974–2010," 81–84.

addressing the needs of the poor.[24] The poor were the objects of their charity and subjects to be studied and empowered.

By the 1960s and 1970s, there was a strong reaction against this paternalistic approach. The British academic and development practitioner Robert Chambers stressed that the realities of poverty need to be defined by the poor themselves and not by outsiders imposing their own conceptual frameworks and agendas. Chambers' contention was that assessing and addressing poverty at the community level should not just be a top-down process implemented by the government or any external agency, but that people in communities need to be at the center of the process and involved throughout.[25] Paulo Freire, the Brazilian educator and philosopher, wrote in *Pedagogy of the Oppressed* that the poor having a voice is a fundamental part of empowerment in liberation theology. He refers to this empowerment as *conscientization*, which is the process by which a person "[learns] to perceive social, political, and economic contradictions, and to take action against the oppressive elements of reality."[26] The attempt of liberation theologians to systematize and interpret the longings of the poor and their biblical reflections from within their socioeconomic

---

24. Much has been written in recent years about poverty and how to address it from a Christian perspective. Some of the key publications are Christian, *God of the Empty-Handed*; Farmer, *Pathologies of Power*; Nancy Maeker and Peter Rognes, *Ending Poverty: A 20/20 Vision. A Guide for Individuals and Congregations,* Lutheran Voices (Minneapolis: Augsburg, 2006). Christopher Heuertz and Christine Pohl, *Friendship at the Margins: Discovering Mutuality in Service and Mission*, Resources for Reconciliation (Downers Grove: IVP Books, 2010); Shane Claiborne, Jonathan Wilson-Hartgrove, and Scott Bessenecker, *Living Mission: The Vision and Voices of New Friars* (Downers Grove: InterVarsity, 2010); Scott Bessenecker, *The New Friars: The Emerging Movement Serving the World's Poor* (Downers Grove: IVP Books, 2010); Eric Swanson and Sam Williams, *To Transform a City: Whole Church, Whole Gospel, Whole City* (Grand Rapids: Zondervan, 2010); Bryant Myers, *Walking with the Poor: Principles and Practices of Transformational Development* (Maryknoll: Orbis, 2011); Robert Lupton, *Toxic Charity: How Churches and Charities Hurt Those They Help (and How to Reverse It)* (New York: HarperOne, 2012); Ash Baker, *Slum Life Rising: How to Enflesh Hope within a New Urban World* (Amazon Digital Services Inc., 24 May 2012); Tim Chester, *Good News to the Poor: Social Involvement and the Gospel* (Wheaton, Crossway, 2013); Gary Anderson, *Charity: The Place of the Poor in the Biblical Tradition* (New Haven: Yale University Press, 2013); Ben Lowe and Ajith Fernando, *Doing Good without Giving Up: Sustaining Social Action in a World That's Hard to Change* (Downers Grove: IVP Books, 2014); Steve Corbett and Brian Fikkert, *When Helping Hurts: How to Alleviate Poverty Without Hurting the Poor . . . and Yourself* (Chicago: Moody, 2014); Brian Fikkert and Russell Mask, *From Dependence to Dignity: How to Alleviate Poverty through Church-Centered Microfinance* (Grand Rapids: Zondervan, 2015); Mez McConnell and Mike McKinley, *Church in Hard Places: How the Local Church Brings Life to the Poor and Needy*, 9Marks (Wheaton: Crossway, 2016); T. Aaron Smith and Viv Grigg, *Thriving in the City: A Guide for Sustainable Incarnational Ministry Among the Urban Poor* (Pomona: Servant Partners, 2016).

25. Robert Chambers, *Whose Reality Counts?*, 46.

26. Freire, *Pedagogy of the Oppressed*, 19.

realities was one of the earliest efforts to enable the poor to speak about their spirituality and spiritual priorities.[27]

What has been missing in both the literature on the spirituality of the poor and in missional practice is an understanding of how and why the poor choose to worship Jesus Christ. What do the poor themselves have to say as to what attracts them to Christ and the gospel? A growing number of Majority World and Western missiologists are writing about how conversion in different cultural and religious contexts may vary from the standardized approaches used by Western mission agencies.[28] Recent research has shown that the poor tend to be more religious than the nonpoor.[29] However, there is very little empirical research on how the poor in the Majority World encounter Christ as articulated by the poor themselves.

This Book

This book is about the stories of some of the poor as they encountered Christ. The stories stand on their own merit and require no justification. The book would be complete even if only the stories that the poor told about their experiences of the living God were recorded. In order to respect the integrity of the poor and their stories of conversion, two chapters (5 and 6) record these stories as told by the poor themselves without any commentary. But the question is this: where would these stories and experiences reside within missiological thinking? In order to answer this question, conversion and the importance of contexts and contextualization are the two lenses through which the stories of the poor will be interpreted for missiological purposes. Missiologists Stephen Bevans and Roger Schroeder write, "If the church is to be in mission, to be in mission is to be responsive to the demands of the gospel in particular contexts, to be continually 'reinventing' itself as it struggles with and approaches new situations, new places, new cultures, and new questions."[30] This book about how some of the poor encounter God revealed in Christ

---

27. An example of the process is in Cardenal, *Gospel in Solentiname.*

28. Iyadurai, *Transformative Religious Experience*; Hilderbrand, "What Led Thai Buddhist Background Believers," 400–415; Garrison, *Wind in the House of Islam*; G. Smith, *Transforming Conversion*; Woodberry and Shubin, "Why I Chose Jesus"; J. Woodberry, Shubin, and Marks, "Why Muslims Follow Jesus."

29. Crabtree, "Religiosity Highest in World's Poorest Nations"; Rees, "Is Personal Insecurity a Cause," 1–26; Schieman, "Socioeconomic Status and Beliefs," 25–51.

30. Bevans and Schroeder, *Constants in Context*, 31.

provides a window into how this God relates to those who live on the margins of society and what is the good news that they seek.

In order to understand how the poor encounter the living God and choose to follow Christ, it is important to look at how conversion has been understood throughout church history and how it was practiced by Christian mission agencies. Chapter 2 will look at the question of conversion and how conversion happens so as to later use conversion as a window into the spiritual lives of the poor.

Chapter 3 tackles the fundamental issue of whether context and culture have an influence on how and why conversion happens. Contextualization in Christian mission has been based on an anthropological understanding of society and culture. Until recently there had been no acknowledgement that economic status influences the culture of a community. This is particularly true when considering the perceptions of who God is and the spiritual priorities and expectations of people. Research has shown a clear connection between poverty and spirituality. So, is there a culture or cultures of poverty that needs to be considered when trying to understand the conversion experiences and spirituality of the poor?

A review of the literature on poverty and the poor, both secular and Christian, reveals that most of the authors are the nonpoor who are outsiders to the community and who record what they observe and understand. This work is influenced by their worldview, values, experiences, and agendas. Where are the voices of the poor describing what it is to be poor? The challenge is that the language the poor use does not fit into the neat conceptual frameworks of the academics and theologians. What is heard is translated conceptually into a format that the researcher, theologian, or government administrator can make sense of and use. Chapter 4 explores whether it is possible to actually hear the voices of the poor.

Chapters 5 and 6 are some of the voices of the poor as they speak about *how* they encountered the living God, *why* they chose to abandon the deities they had worshiped and follow Christ, and *what* is their understanding of who this living God is. Each chapter begins with a description of the context the poor in that chapter live in and from within which they speak, which provides context to what they say and why they say it.

Chapter 7 puts the voices of the poor recorded in chapters 5 and 6 into the context of the literature and missional experience regarding conversion and contextualization documented in chapters 2 and 3. What do the poor who are on the margins of the global church have to say about the dynamics of believing in Christ and how God relates to those who are not in the mainstreams of society? Chapter 8 looks at what we learn from the stories of the poor.

Understanding Poverty Provides Context for the Faith of the Poor

To understand the faith and spirituality of the poor, it is important to understand the poverty that causes their despair, which then gives birth to their faith and in some strange way nurtures it. Theologian Daniel Migliore highlights the fact that a particular context will shape a person's understanding of who Christ is and how he helps them.[31] So what is the poverty that the poor experience? This question is discussed further in chapter 3 under the section on cultures of poverty.

Poverty is multidimensional and has certain unique characteristics. Measuring it solely by income, living and working conditions, health conditions, or any other single indicator (monetary or otherwise) does a disservice to the poor and really does not help understand their desperation. The United Nations (UN) provides the most widely accepted and comprehensive definition of poverty:

> [Poverty] means lack of basic capacity to participate effectively in society. It means not having enough to feed and clothe a family, not having a school or clinic to go to, not having the land on which to grow one's food or a job to earn one's living, not having access to credit. It means insecurity, powerlessness and exclusion of individuals, households, and communities. It means susceptibility to violence, and it often implies living in marginal or fragile environments, without access to clean water or sanitation.[32]

Because of its multidimensionality, poverty impacts every aspect of a person's life, family, and community. As will be noted later in chapter 3, poverty has a negative effect on the physical, psychological, and social dimensions of a person.

The complexity of poverty had not been studied until the past century. The theoretical term "poverty" was not common in sacred religious texts or oral traditions. Instead they refer to the "poor" or to a state of "ill-being," as in the tribal societies of Africa and the First Nations in Canada. There are very

---

31. Migliore, *Faith Seeking Understanding*, 197.

32. UNESCO, "Statement of Commitment for Action to Eradicate Poverty Adopted by Administrative Committee on Coordination."

rich traditions in the world religions of responding to human need in one's own community,[33] and the Bible consistently refers to the poor.[34] Gustavo Gutiérrez writes,

> Poverty is a central theme in both the Old and New Testaments. It is treated both briefly and profoundly; it describes social situations and expresses spiritual experiences communicated only with difficulty; it defines personal attitudes, a whole people's attitude before God, and the relationships of people with each other . . . [it] is a scandalous condition inimical to human dignity and therefore contrary to the will of God.[35]

It was not until the twentieth century that empirical studies using specific measurements and definitions were used to identify those living in poverty. Some of the most significant developments in understanding poverty were through the work of Robert Chambers. Poverty is not only multidimensional, but he stressed that the realities of poverty need to be defined by the poor themselves and not by outsiders imposing their own frameworks and agendas.[36] His tools of participatory rural appraisal (PRA) provide those living in poverty with the opportunity to define their own reality and to express their needs.[37]

Chambers' model of poverty identifies five interrelated dimensions based on the poor defining their own reality. According to this model, the profile of poverty will vary between communities, as one dimension may be more prevalent than others. In all likelihood, the poor often experience all five dimensions to varying degrees. Each dimension influences the others, resulting in a web of entanglement or a "cluster of disadvantages."[38]

---

33. See Brackney and Das, eds., *Poor and Poverty in the World's Religions*. Also see Das, *Poor and Poverty in Islam*.

34. The Old Testament uses at least ten Hebrew words that denote different kinds of poverty. The Hebrew terms are *ebhyon* (needy, poor); *dal* (lean, poor, weak); *dallah* (poverty, weakness); *chelekah* (adjectival); *machsor* (one that lacks); *misken* (poor, useful); *aneh* (humble, poor); *ani* (poor, oppressed); *rush* (poor, impoverished); *chelkaim* (afflicted); *yarash* (to become impoverished); and *nouk* (to become low or poor). The words *ani* and *ebhyon* frequently denote the godly poor who are servants of YHWH; *ani* also may denote Israel as a nation in its low estate. The Greek terms used in the New Testament are *penes* (a poor man); *penichros* (very poor); and *ptochos* (trembling, poor). For a detailed discussion of a biblical understanding of poverty see Das, *Compassion and the Mission of God*, 43–92.

35. Gutiérrez, *Theology of Liberation*, 165.

36. Chambers, *Whose Reality Counts?*, 46.

37. See Narayanasamy, *Participatory Rural Appraisal*.

38. Chambers, *Whose Reality Counts*, 103–39.

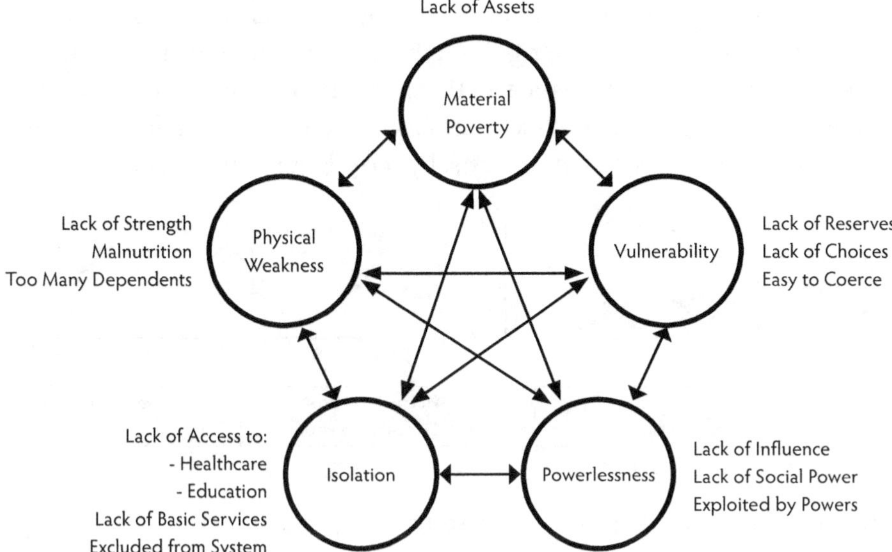

Figure 1.1 Dimensions of Poverty[39]

Poverty is not visible in just one form, nor do the poor experience it in any one particular way. Life circumstances and the context within which the poor live may push them in or out of poverty. People may also experience different types of poverty, and the severity may vary. There are three degrees of *severity* of poverty: extreme (absolute), moderate, and relative poverty. Extreme poverty is a situation in which households are unable to meet their basic needs for food and water, health care and education, and shelter and clothing, which ultimately affect their ability to survive. These are people who are destitute. Those living in extreme poverty are marginalized from mainstream society and are unable to access services and benefits that would enable them to improve the quality of their life and their socioeconomic status. Moderate poverty is when basic needs are met, but just barely, whereas relative poverty is "a household income level below a given proportion of the average national income."[40]

Poverty can also be classified according to the *length of time*. Some people may live the majority of their lives in poverty, while others move in and out of poverty at various times. According to this system of classification, poverty can be categorized as transitory poverty, chronic poverty, generational poverty, and event-based poverty. Generational poverty is also sometimes referred to as

---

39. Adapted from Chambers, *Rural Development*, 110.

40. Sachs, *End of Poverty*, 20.

traditional poverty and often encompasses groups that are customarily viewed as being poor, such as certain tribal or ethnic groups or residents of slums.[41] Event-based poverty refers to the fact that people may be pushed into poverty through a series of events such as conflicts, forced displacement (refugees), loss of family members, failed harvests, hyperinflation, divorce, etc.

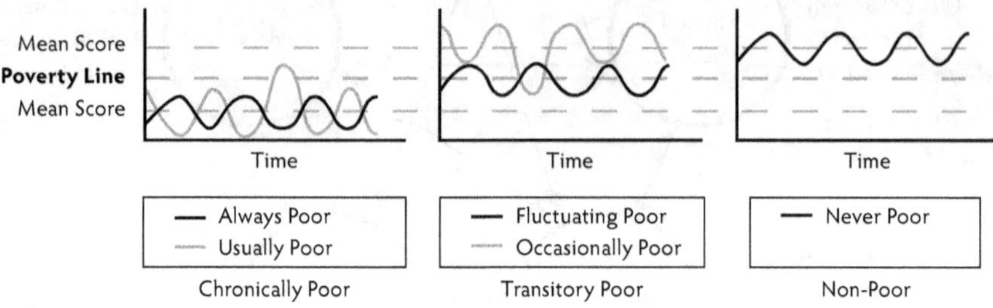

Figure 1.2 The Fluctuating Nature of Poverty[42]

Chronic poverty usually lasts throughout the lifetime of a person and may also be generational. The lives of people living in chronic poverty are often characterized by insecure and low-paid employment, health problems, and extremely poor living conditions. They are likely to suffer from social discrimination and die preventable deaths.[43] This type of poverty is found in all regions of the world and is particularly prevalent among the elderly and people with disabilities in economically underdeveloped contexts. People in such contexts are least likely to have assets and capacities that they can use to mitigate or improve their situations. The Chronic Poverty Research Centre notes that this type of poverty is particularly difficult to undo and analysis of the underlying causes is necessary in any response.[44]

This book will try to listen to the voices of those who live in chronic poverty (slum dwellers) as well as those who are experiencing event-based poverty – refugees who had recently been displaced. Does poverty influence who they perceive God to be and what their expectations are of a deity?

---

41. The perception that tribal groups and residents of slums are poor may not always be accurate. For example, there is significant evidence that many residents of slums may be middle class (economically) but are forced to live in slums because of the unavailability of affordable housing in many urban areas. Sinha and Sinha, *Ecology and Quality of Life in Urban Slums*, 99.

42. Adapted from Chronic Poverty Research Center, *Chronic Poverty Report 2004–05*, 12.

43. These and other criteria are referred to as the "social determinant of health in poverty."

44. Chronic Poverty Research Center, *Chronic Poverty Report 2004–05*.

Missiologist Allen Yeh provides a wide-ranging overview of the present state of mission as he reviews the proceedings of five of the latest mission conferences – Tokyo 2010, Edinburgh 2010, Cape Town 2010, Boston 2010, and CLADE V (San Jose 2012). His summary of the key missiological issues of this present era are the following: evangelism, frontier missions, ecumenism, post-Christian populations, reconciliation, postmodernities, contextualization, post colonialism, technology, holistic mission, and creation care, among other issues.[45] This list is helpful in positioning this book within the wider discussions on mission, specifically evangelism, contextualization, and holistic mission, at this point in time.

---

45. Yeh, *Polycentric Misssiology*.

2

Conversion as a Window into the Spiritual Lives of the Poor

The language of conversion is necessarily informed by experience – the experience of the church and particularly the experience of those who come to faith in Christ. . . . We attend to conversion narratives and recognize that these are a witness to the way in which the Spirit brings people into a transforming encounter with Christ.[1]

Gordon T. Smith

The Question about Conversion[2]

There are a number of ways of gaining insight into the spirituality of those living in poverty. Liberation theology's process of conscientization enables the poor to reflect on their circumstances through the filter of Scripture in order to respond to God's work in their lives and in their community. Their reflections are indications of who they know God to be and how he responds to human need. The rituals, spiritual disciplines, and use of religious texts by a community provide another window into how people relate to God or the deities they worship. These disciplines not only enable them to express their faith, but also to find the support they lean on during difficult times. Often a life-changing event like a spiritual conversion will highlight why a person seeks God. There has to be a reason why a person makes a radical decision to change whom they worship. Understanding conversion experiences provides

---

1. G. Smith, *Transforming Conversion*, 20.

2. A modified and shortened version of part of this chapter was published in Das, "Becoming a Follower of Christ," 21–40.

insights into the struggles and challenges of their everyday lives and exposes their vulnerabilities, which then provides the context for why they seek God.

This book will use the history of conversion as a paradigm to explore what attracts some of the poor to Christ. Gordon Smith, in reviewing the factors that affect the understanding of conversion, writes about how the recent conversion experiences of Hindus and Muslims are influencing the evangelical discussion on conversion.

> As evangelical witness has led to the conversion of Hindus and Muslims, there has been an increasing willingness to ask, for example, not "how *should* a Muslim become a Christian" but how *does* it actually happen: What is the character of their experience and how can we appreciate this without having to superimpose the categories of revivalism on their faith journey?[3]

It is this latter question that is explored in this book.

The present-day literature on conversion in Christian mission and church life is mainly from the 1990s and the early 2000s and is primarily connected with the issues of contextualization. The more recent literature on conversion has been on insider movements and conversions from the major religions such as Islam, Hinduism, Buddhism, etc. There is limited literature on the dynamics of conversion in missional practice. Though the American psychologist and philosopher William James explored the issue of religious conversion as early as 1902, conversion has only been studied periodically from a social science perspective since 1981.

This chapter will first look at conversion from a social science perspective and then at the literature about how conversion has been understood and practiced historically in mission and by churches. It will only discuss the sociological and anthropological dimensions of conversion briefly where appropriate, because they provide insights into the process of conversion. While most Christian denominations believe that repentance from sin and believing in the atoning death and resurrection of Jesus Christ are foundational to being a Christian, how one comes to the point of repentance and believing, and then how one is initiated into the church (i.e. how the conversion experience is confirmed) vary considerably. An historical understanding of conversion may provide models or insights that may help explain what attracts the poor to the gospel and the process by which they come to follow Christ.

---

3. Smith, "Conversion and Redemption," 211.

Conversion in the Social Sciences

Conversion has now entered the general vocabulary of social sciences where it seems to mean any sort of transition or rite of passage. However, each academic discipline analyzes conversion from within their own theoretical framework, and there are very few multidisciplinary studies on conversion which include theology or look at conversion from other religions to Christianity.[4]

William James provides one of the earliest definitions of conversion. He states that conversion is a psychological phenomenon and is not necessarily limited to Christianity. In 1902, he writes in his now famous Gifford Lectures, *The Varieties of Religious Experience*, "Conversion is a process, gradual or sudden, by which a self, hitherto divided and consciously wrong, inferior and unhappy, becomes unified and consciously right, superior and happy, through an establishment of a right relationship with the object of the religious sentiment."[5] Anthropologist Arnold van Gennep in his book *Rites of Passage* describes the circumcision ritual among Muslims, the "rite of separation" among Hindus, and the "departure from childhood" of the Taoist and Confucianists as conversions.[6] Some psychologists see conversion as a form of acute psychosis.[7]

Meredith McGuire writes about how conversion has been understood sociologically. Conversion is "a transformation of one's self concurrent with a transformation of one's basic meaning system, [which] changes the sense of who one is and how one belongs in the social system."[8] She identifies the different aspects of conversion. The social component relates to interaction with people in one's circle of relationship and the changes that ensue. The psychological component deals with changes in values and attitudes, as well as the emotional and affective aspects of conversion. The ideational component is the "simple set of beliefs that both justify the new meaning system and negate the former one." They are rarely well-thought-out philosophical or theological ideas.[9]

---

4. Iyadurai, *Transformative Religious Experience*, 16. See also Rambo and Farhadian, eds., *Oxford Handbook of Religious Conversion*, which is probably the most recent and most comprehensive publication with interdisciplinary perspectives on religious conversions.

5. James, *Varieties of Religious Experience*, 168.

6. van Gennep, *Rites of Passage* (Chicago: University of Chicago Press, 1961).

7. Glasser, "An International Perspective," 23. Other secular scholars who have written about conversion are Alfred Clair Underwood, *Conversion: Christian and Non-Christian: A Comparative and Psychological Study* (1925, reprint Abington; New York: Routledge, 2018), and Karl F. Morrison, *Understanding Conversion*, Page-Barbour Lecture Series (Charlottesville: University of Virginia Press, 1992).

8. McGuire, *Religion: The Social Context*, 73.

9. McGuire, *Religion: The Social Context*, 77.

Many social science researchers have developed models that reflect the various stages in the process of conversion. Sociologists John Lofland and Norman Skonovd, both at the University of California, identified six "conversion motifs" with which to classify the influences on the convert's subjective experience: intellectual, mystical, experimental, affectional, revivalist, and coercive.[10] In their study of conversion experiences of young people in the United States, they state that conversion experiences vary and are complex, with an interim stage between a convert's old and new faiths which often causes a crisis.[11]

C. J. Bauer also identified a seven-stage model.[12] J. V. Downton identifies a ten-stage conversion process.[13] Anthropologist R. A. Tippett describes a seven-stage process.[14] While each of the stages is a period of time, the decision is a moment in time. Thus in Tippett's model, conversion is both a process and an event. Batson, Schoenrade, and Ventis developed a four-stage model.[15] They based their model on an existential crisis which is then resolved to gain a new vision and a new life. This transformation is possible because the new vision originates "from a transcendent realm outside oneself."[16] They built their model with insights from William James and Kelly Bulkeley, who claim that a realm beyond the conscious mind is where the interaction with the divine occurs, and this is often mediated through mystical states of consciousness.[17]

Lewis Rambo, research professor of psychology and religion, states that conversion takes place within a dynamic context and includes social, cultural, religious, and personal dimensions. According to Rambo, the

---

10. Lofland and Skonovd, "Conversion Motifs," 373–85.

11. Lofland and Skonovd, 373–85.

12. Bauer's seven stages are indifference, dissatisfaction with self, new understanding, beginning of changes, sudden conversion experience, sense of new being, and the beginning of the path of transformation. Bauer, "Conversion: From Puritanism to Revivalism," 227–43.

13. Downton's stages are disillusionment, seeking spiritual solutions, determination to move forward, personal futility, contact with the religious community, accepting the claims, initiation, surrender, intensification, and gradual modification. Downton, "Evolutionary Theory of Spiritual Conversion and Commitment," 381–96.

14. Tippett's stages are the period of awareness, point of realization, period of decision, point of encounter, period of incorporation, point of consummation or confirmation, and period of maturity. Tippett, "Cultural Anthropology of Conversion," 192–205.

15. The four stages of Batson, Schoenrade, and Ventis are existential crisis, self-surrender, new vision, and new life. Batson, Schoenrade, and Ventis, *Religion and the Individual*.

16. Batson, Schoenrade, and Ventis, 104.

17. James, *Varieties of Religious Experience*; Bulkeley, *Visions of the Night*.

process of conversion is crisis, quest, encounter, interaction, commitment, and consequences.[18] He describes conversion as

> a process of religious change that takes place in a dynamic force field of people, events, ideologies, institutions, expectations, and experiences. It is assumed that a) conversion is a process, rather than a single event; b) conversion is contextual and cannot be extricated from the fabric of relationships, process and ideologies which provide the matrix for religious change; and c) factors involved in the conversion process are multiple, interactive, and cumulative. While there are unique aspects of particular conversions, it is also assumed that there are broad descriptions of conversion that are useful in the comparison and assessment of conversion theories.[19]

Henri Gooren, an anthropologist, identifies different aspects of the conversion experience and describes five types of religious affiliation, with conversion being one.[20] He also identifies five groups of factors that influence conversion. These are personality factors, social factors, institutional factors dealing with the religious organization, cultural factors including political and economic, and contingency factors. This last group may include random meetings with a missionary, stressful situations, or acutely felt personal crises. Pentecostals call these divine interventions or providence.[21]

What social scientists highlight is that conversion is a process; that it involves the total being, impacting social relationships, the emotional, psychological, and the intellectual; and that it arises from circumstances or crises in life. Cultural, socioeconomic, political, and religious factors may also influence the process and decision. Finally, some acknowledge that a mystical element may be involved.

---

18. Rambo, *Understanding Religious Conversion*, 168–69.

19. Rambo, "Conversion: Toward a Holistic Model of Religious Change," 48.

20. Pre-affiliation – describes the worldview and social context of potential members of a group; Affiliation – refers to church membership which is not necessarily a central part of their identity; Conversion – radical change of one's worldview and identity; Confession – core membership, describing a high level of participation in a new religious group and strong missionary attitude toward nongroup members; and Disaffiliation – lack of involvement in an organized religious group. Gooren, "Conversion Narratives," 94.

21. Gooren, 94.

Biblical Foundations

The term "conversion" is a foundational concept in the history of mission and in evangelical theology. It would seem that it is a word rooted in Scripture. However, the word "conversion" was coined by Jonathan Edwards to refer to decisions made for Christ at the revival meetings he held in the early 1700s. It then became an integral part of the language to describe some of the practices of nineteenth century American evangelicalism.[22]

There is a difference between a convert and a proselyte. The origin of the term "proselyte" is the Greek language and refers to heathens and Gentiles becoming Jews.[23] Proselytes are changing their religious beliefs, joining a new faith, and as a result changing their social location. According to theologian Ernst von Dobschutz, the original Greek term *proselytos* is not found in the writings of the classical authors, but in the Septuagint. It seems to have been borrowed from colloquial speech as the equivalent for the Hebrew word *ger*, meaning stranger, someone who is not a Jew.[24]

The words "conversion" and "proselytism" have often been used interchangeably. Missiologist Andrew Walls writes that the word "conversion" has been used either as an "external act of religious change" or as a "critical internal religious change in persons."[25] He makes a distinction between a convert and proselyte. Referring to the book of Acts, Walls states that the Jews who responded to the gospel were not joining a religious movement or a sect within Judaism but were converts affiliated with Jesus Christ. The new Gentile believers were not required to become Jews and thus were not proselytes, but as converts, their identity, loyalty, and obedience was now exclusively to Christ.[26] While proselytism is an act of changing one's religious affiliation (and thus one's social location), conversion signifies an internal human dynamic,[27] which may have implications with regards to one's religious affiliation and social location.[28] So both Jewish and Gentile followers of Christ are converts and not proselytes.

---

22. Hill, "Entering the Kingdom: Then and Now," 1.

23. Harper, "Proselyte."

24. von Dobschutz, "Proselytes." *Proselytos* occurs seventy-eight times in the Septuagint as a translation for *ger* and four times in the New Testament.

25. Walls, "Converts or Proselytes?," 2.

26. Walls, 2–5.

27. Conversion as understood from Scripture (regardless of Christian tradition) is an experience that is much deeper and more profound, impacting the whole individual and is not just about joining a different religious group.

28. As mentioned, this study will not look at the theological dimensions of conversion. In Protestant theology, the issues regarding conversion address who does the converting (God or human beings), how long does it take (is it instantaneous or is it a process), and whether

Because of the varying and sometimes confusing understanding of what conversion is, Joshua Iyadurai instead refers to it as a "transformative religious experience." He explains,

> This knowledge gained is not a rational understanding of religious truths. This knowledge is possible only through direct experience of God, which cannot be imparted or articulated in verifiable philosophical propositions. This knowledge is given to converts at the divine-human encounter despite their antagonism against Christianity.[29]

The concept of conversion is not unique to early Christianity. Greek Epicureans, Cynics, and Stoics demanded a type of conversion, a moral transformation brought about by education and a rational way of living. Like the Old Testament Hebrew word *shubh*, the language of the Greek philosophers was also one of turning, repentance, rejecting the vices of the culture, and "coming to one's senses." By the time of Paul, the Greek word *epistrephei* became the Christian term for conversion. Both *epistrophe* and *metanoia* were translated as *conversio* (a turning over) in Latin, and then later entered the English language as "conversion."[30]

The literature indicates that the concept of conversion is rooted in Greek and Hebrew words. Three concepts are at the heart of the concept of conversion. These are "to turn," "to repent," and "to be born again." Other words also have a bearing upon the concept of conversion such as "to believe" and "to confess."[31] The first concept is the Greek word *epistrepho* which means to turn, and has connotations of change of mind and heart and of turning physically. George Carey, the former Archbishop of Canterbury, states that in the Septuagint it conveys the meaning of turning toward something or someone, such where the people of Judah are accused of turning away from Yahweh toward evil.[32] In the New Testament, the theological concept is understood as turning to God (away from the idols). Half of the thirty-six times the word is used in the New

---

conversion is only individual or whether it can be corporate – such as a family, clan, or tribe converting at the same time.

29. Iyadurai, *Transformative Religious Experience*, 21.

30. Kling, "Conversion to Christianity," 599–600.

31. Carey, "Biblical Perspective," 11.

32. Carey, 12.

Testament, it is used to theologically mean conversion, such as in 2 Corinthians 3:16, "But whenever anyone turns to the Lord, the veil is taken away."[33]

The second Greek word connected to conversion is *metanoia*, which means to think again, to have second thoughts, to repent.[34] The implication is the need to change direction. John the Baptist preached *metanoia* when he urged people to turn from their old life of sinful living, to "Repent and believe in the good news!" (Mark 1:15). Peter at Pentecost preached, "repent and be baptized" (Acts 2:38). In Acts 3:19 and 26:20, the idea of repentance and turning appear together.[35]

The various biblical writers refer to repentance and entering the kingdom of God (Synoptic Gospels), repentance and turning to God (Acts), and justification by faith and sonship (Paul). George Carey adds the third concept describing conversion – new birth. The term "born again" (John 3:16)[36] is used primarily in the New Testament, but the ideas of renewal and regeneration are found throughout the Old and New Testaments. Carey writes that Ezekiel (36:24–28), Jeremiah (31:31–34), and Joel (2:28–30) all refer to the coming of the Messiah and renewal by God's Spirit. In the New Testament, Titus 3:5 refers to the renewal by the Holy Spirit.[37]

Old Testament scholar Christopher Wright summarizes the biblical understanding of conversion by stating that there is continuity between the Old Testament, where Israel is repeatedly called to return to God, and the New Testament context. He states that the nature of conversion in the New Testament is the radical rejection and displacement of all other gods, allegiance to Christ, inclusion in the community of God's people, and a radical ethical transformation.[38] Wright provides an interesting insight into the motivation of Gentiles seeking the God of the Jews in the Old Testament. At the dedication of the temple recorded in 1 Kings 8:41–43, Solomon describes what attracts the Gentiles to the living God.

---

33. Some other references in the New Testament are in Acts 14:15 where Paul urges people to turn from "worthless things to the living God" and in Acts 26:17–18 where the commission given to the apostles is to turn people "from darkness to light and from the power of Satan to God." Carey, 12–13.

34. The Hebrew word used in the Old Testament is *shub*, meaning to turn, return, bring back, restore. "Shub, 7725," *Strong's Concordance*. A related word is *niham*, meaning to be sorry or to regret.

35. Carey, "Biblical Perspective," 11.

36. The apostle John in his writings often refers to being born anew or being born from above: John 1:13; 3:5–6, 8; 1 John 2:29; 3:9; 4:7; 5:1, 4, 18.

37. Carey, "Biblical Perspective," 13–14.

38. Wright, "Implications of Conversion," 18–19.

> As for the foreigner who does not belong to your people Israel but has come from a distant land because of your name – for they will hear of your great name and your mighty hand and your outstretched arm – when they come and pray toward this temple, then hear from heaven, your dwelling place. Do whatever the foreigner asks of you, so that all the peoples of the earth may know your name and fear you, as do your own people Israel, and may know that this house I have built bears your Name.

The Gentiles hear about God's character and his power and want to experience it firsthand. Solomon beseeches God to answer their prayers, as a result of which God's name would be known throughout the earth. Wright concludes, "This text is remarkable in its very anticipation that such things would happen – that is, that foreigners would be so attracted to the power and presence of this God, Yahweh the God of Israel, that they would come from afar to pray for his blessing."[39]

There is a growing consensus among many Old and New Testament scholars that any theology of conversion and redemption cannot be based on individual verses but must be rooted in the "full scope of God's purposes in Christ," a biblical narrative that starts with a vision of God's righteousness in the Old Testament which then finds expression in the New Testament. Such a theology of conversion not only encompasses time (past, present, and future dimensions of conversion), but also has individual, corporate, and cosmic dimensions.[40]

Ecumenical Understandings of Conversion

Christian denominations have different understandings of conversion which are reflected not only in their theology but also in their traditions. New Testament scholar Scott McKnight writes that there are three orientations to conversion: socialization, liturgical acts, and personal decision. He goes on to point out that each is aligned with factions (denominations) within the church and each is "allergic" to the others.[41] Richard Peace, professor of

---

39. Wright, 18.

40. Smith, "Conversion and Redemption," 209–20. Old and New Testament scholars adding to this discussion are James Dunn, Gordon Fee, N. T. Wright, and Christopher Wright, among others.

41. McKnight, *Turning to Jesus*, 1–2.

evangelism, uses these three orientations to look at the missiological challenges each provides.[42]

According to Peace, conversion through a *personal decision* is central to evangelical tradition and theology. According to this tradition, one cannot be considered a Christian unless they are converted through an experience that is sudden, that can be dated, and is an encounter of some sort – with truth, with Jesus, or with conviction of sin. The strength of this orientation is its simplicity and functionality. It provides a clear process of how to believe and what to believe in order to become a Christian. The Pentecostal view of conversion is similar to the traditional evangelical view, but they tend to be much more intense. Conversion involves an encounter, an experience, and a decision. Peace states that the Pentecostal experience also tends to be accompanied by signs of God's power to indicate that he is present and active in their lives.[43]

The second orientation is conversion by *socialization*. Many churches see Christian conversion as a process of nurture and socialization rather than a decision. In denominations where infant baptism is practiced, the decision made later by the individual affirming the commitment that the parents had made has more to do with alignment with the beliefs of the community.

The final orientation is the use of *liturgical acts* to signify conversion. This orientation is practiced by Catholic,[44] Anglican, and Orthodox churches. While there is some overlap with the socialization process, liturgical acts such as baptism and partaking in the Eucharist for the first time are official rites of passage and initiation into the church. Children born within Catholic families do not need to be converted as they have been baptized as children; but they undergo confirmation and other rites of passage. Adult converts from other faiths or Christian traditions to Catholicism undergo instruction and baptism before they can take the sacraments. Conversion does not seem to be part of the "functional vocabulary" of the Orthodox Church. Peace quotes Russian

---

42. Peace, "Conflicting Understandings of Christian Conversion," 8–10.

43. Peace makes an interesting observation that "power evangelism" as taught by John Wimber is a potent force in the two-thirds world, as people are attracted to the power and reality of God's presence.

44. There is considerable literature on the Catholic understanding of conversion. Some key sources are Walter Conn, ed., *Christian Conversion: A Developmental Interpretation of Autonomy and Surrender* (Mahwah, NJ: Paulist Press, 1986); Bernard Lonergan, *Grace and Freedom: Operative Grace in the Thought of St. Thomas Aquinas* (New York: Herder & Herder, 1971); and three books by Donald Gelpi, SJ: *Charism and Sacrament: A Theology of Christian Conversion* (Mahwah, NJ: Paulist Press, 1976); *The Conversion Experience: A Reflective Process for RCIA Participants and Others* (Mahwah, NJ: Paulist Press, 1988); and *Committed Worship: A Sacramental Theology for Converting Christians* (Collegeville, MN.: Liturgical Press, 1993).

Orthodox theologian and philosopher Aleksei Khomiakov, "No one is saved alone. He who is saved is saved in the Church, as a member of her and in union with all her other members."[45] Conversion is equated with joining the church. Both Catholic and Orthodox theologians are rooted in the teachings of the church fathers. They refer back to Origen of Alexandria in the third century who wrote, "Let no one fool himself; outside of this house, i.e. outside of the Church, no one is saved; for if someone goes outside, he becomes responsible for his own death."[46] They also refer to the dictum attributed to Cyprian, the Bishop of Carthage, also in the third century, "*extra ecclesiam nulla salus*," meaning outside the church there is no salvation.[47]

Any ecumenical review of the understanding of conversion would be lacking if the soteriology of liberation theology and its understanding of conversion were not referenced because of the impact and influence of liberation theology in denominations beyond the Catholic Church.[48] The experience of salvation is central in Gustavo Gutiérrez's theology of liberation.[49] He writes, "The theology of liberation is a theology of salvation in the concrete, historical and political conditions of our day."[50] He is critical of the existing theologies as being insufficient in their understanding of God's salvation because they ignored the realities of the world and refers to these theologies as having "the absence of a profound and lucid reflection on the theme of salvation."[51] For Gutiérrez, the church's mission involves the "annunciation" of the good news of liberation and the "denunciation" of the structures and situations that are roadblocks to human freedom and development.[52]

Gutiérrez and the other liberation theologians are deeply influenced by the teachings of Irenaeus, the Bishop of Lyon, an early church father. Irenaeus

---

45. Aleksei Khomiakov quoted in Peace, "Conflicting Understandings of Christian Conversion," 10–11.

46. Origen, *Homilies on Joshua*, 3, 5, in Patrologiae Curus Completus, Series Gracea, ed. J. P. Migne, 12, 841f. as quoted in Teasedale, *Catholicism in Dialogue*, 84.

47. Cyprian quoted in Bevans and Schroeder, *Constants in Context*, 40. "Augustine's strong argument for the holiness of the church would later be developed into the belief that salvation itself is equated with membership in the church. In other words, we see the beginnings of the 'ecclesiasticization' of *salvation*." Bevans and Schroeder, 132, emphasis original.

48. There is no one corpus of literature identified as liberation theology, and there are many different perspectives. In this section, only Gustavo Gutiérrez's perspective will be referred as indicative of liberation theology's understanding of conversion.

49. Murray, "Liberation for Communion in the Soteriology of Gustavo Gutiérrez," 51.

50. Gutiérrez, *Power of the Poor in History*, 63.

51. Gutiérrez, *Theology of Liberation*.

52. Gutiérrez, 265–72.

believed that history is not just a faithful narrative of the past but that "despite sin, God as Father and Shepherd continues mercifully to lead and guide humanity throughout history. God sent Jesus to free humanity from Satan's clutches and so to make possible continued growth, until at the End all will be recapitulated to him."[53] This is why liberation theologians Leonardo Boff and Jon Sobrino start with the historical Jesus, where he lived and the people he met in everyday life, so many of whom lived in misery. For Boff, Sobrino, and Gutiérrez, Christ's divinity was a given. Instead they focus on the implications of Irenaeus' writings that God is involved in history through the incarnation of his Son and the working of the Holy Spirit.

Because God's work was in and through human history in the death and resurrection of Christ, salvation is not only about eternity, but also imbedded in human realities. For Gutiérrez, salvation is communal in nature. He writes it is "conversion to the neighbour."[54] Catholic social activist Joyce Murray writes that Gutiérrez makes "the soteriological point that human beings are called to meet God insofar as they constitute a community."[55] Stott quotes Gutiérrez, "man is saved if he opens himself to God and to others, even if he is not clearly aware that he is doing so."[56]

Because Gutiérrez's context was predominantly Catholic, he does not address the issue of conversion and of non-Catholics joining the faith. Instead, he talks about spirituality and communion with God. However as Murray points out, the spirituality that Gutiérrez refers to is ecclesiological and communal in nature and not individualistic.[57] Gutiérrez writes in *We Drink from Our Own Wells*, "The following of Jesus is not, purely, or primarily, an individual matter but a collective adventure. The journey of the people of

---

53. Bevans and Schroeder summarize Irenaeus's understanding of history in *Constants in Context*, 62.

54. Gutiérrez, *Theology of Liberation*, 194.

55. Murray, "Liberation for Communion," 52. Murray further writes,

> [Gutiérrez] reasoned that a communal praxis of liberation is necessary in the face of structural injustice and the collective dimension of oppression; poor communities are agents of transformation as they affirm life in the midst of death; liberating social praxis requires solidarity understood as transformative action with and for the poor, and individuals are invited to move beyond isolating individualism and join in solidarity in the building of a new society; and finally there is an integral link between the gratuitous love for the poor on God's part and ours, and solidarity in the search for the social justice that restores communion.

Murray, 53.

56. Gutiérrez, quoted in Stott, *Christian Mission in the Modern World*, 141.

57. Murray, "Liberation for Communion in the Soteriology of Gustavo Gutiérrez," 57.

God is set in motion by a direct encounter with the Lord but an encounter in community: '*We* have found the Messiah.'"[58] While Gutiérrez writes that salvation is "God's gift of definitive life to God's children,"[59] he clarifies this statement by saying that "salvation [is] the communion of human beings with God and among themselves."[60] One of Gutiérrez's major contributions to the ecumenical community is this understanding of the communal and holistic nature of God's salvation. The communal aspects resonate with the teachings of the Orthodox Church that salvation is found in the church.[61]

There is no one Christian tradition that encompasses a full understanding of conversion. Peace summarizes the situation as follows:

> No single view captures fully the nature of conversion. All views contribute important parts to a holistic understanding of conversion and hence of evangelism. Holistic evangelism will invite people into the kingdom of God. It will invite them to turn to Jesus in repentance and faith in the context of the community of God's people, which has worship and the sacraments at its center. Such evangelism will invite nominal Christians to become active followers of Jesus. It will engage genuine seekers as they explore the issues that will move them forward in their pilgrimages. It will not settle for cultural faith. It will have as its goal the genuine conversion of others, even as the evangelists themselves continue their own conversion process.[62]

Unlike proselytism, conversion is a process of radical transformation of the individual. "*Metanoia* must be combined with *pistis* (faith) in order to bring about *epistrophe* (as in the summary in Mark 1:15 of Jesus' message)."[63] Conversions are often seen as the result of churches and mission agencies doing evangelism and church planting, and where it concerns people who do not as yet follow Christ. Christopher Wright provides balance to this perspective when he writes:

> Any missiological reflection on conversion must wrestle with this issue of the continuous need of God's people for radical

---

58. Gutiérrez, *We Drink from Our Own Wells*, 42.

59. Gutiérrez, *Theology of Liberation*, xxxix.

60. Gutiérrez, *Truth Shall Make You Free*, 12.

61. Peace, "Conflicting Understandings of Christian Conversion," 10.

62. Peace, 12.

63. Peace, 8.

conversion themselves, rather than being seen only as the agent of the conversion of others. It is often pointed out that the so-called conversion of Cornelius, for example, was just as much (and necessarily) the conversion of Peter, or the conversion of the Ninevites and the (unsuccessful) conversion of Jonah.[64]

World Council of Churches

The World Council of Churches (WCC) in many ways reflects the spiritual and theological realities of its member churches. In recent decades, the understanding of conversion, so central to evangelical theology and historical missional practice, has been questioned as to its necessity in a modernizing and religiously pluralistic world.

At the founding Assembly of the WCC in Amsterdam in 1948, there was an unequivocal call for evangelism. The assembly's understanding of conversion was articulated when they stated that the church is given the privilege, "of making Christ known so that each is confronted with the necessity of a personal decision, Yes or No."[65] However, by the 1960s there was a need to respond to the growing secularization of Western society, and the feeling was that evangelism was not the appropriate strategy. Earlier in 1952 at the International Missionary Council (IMC) at Willingen, Germany, the term "conversion" did not appear in any of the final reports. David Jenkins at the WCC (later Bishop of Durham) wrote, "Mission is the activity of God, not the conversion of men to belief, or the recruiting of men into the ranks of the saved."[66] The WCC rejected endorsing any particular type of conversion experience. Instead they urged the churches to let the focus be on Jesus – "the unique example of sacrificial personal concern and social service," which was summarized in the slogan "Doing justice and loving mercy."[67]

The Third Assembly of the WCC in New Delhi in 1961 was a turning point in the discussions on conversion. Orthodox Churches joined, ending the distinctly Protestant character of the WCC. Because of what they felt was "unethical proselytism" by evangelical churches and mission agencies in Orthodox majority countries, the Orthodox representatives heavily influenced the discussion on missions, evangelism, and conversion, especially the report

---

64. Wright, "Implications of Conversion," 14.
65. Glasser, "Conciliar Debate," 84.
66. David Jenkins quoted in Glasser, 85.
67. Glasser, 86.

Christian Witness, Proselytism, and Religious Liberty in the Setting of the World Council of Churches.[68] Evangelism and proselytism became synonymous.[69]

One of the outcomes of the New Delhi Assembly was the establishment of the Commission for World Mission and Evangelism. Their objective was to "further the proclamation to the whole world of the Gospel of Jesus Christ, the end that all may believe in Him and be saved."[70] The first meeting of the commission in 1963 in Mexico City did not live up to its stated expectations. Because of the influence of Asian theologians working in religiously pluralistic contexts, there was talk of the Cosmic Christ penetrating all cultures and religions and that Christ was already at work in secular history, beyond the confines of the church. This view became evident in the publication of *The Theology of the Christian Mission* in 1961, in which none of the twenty-seven contributors dealt with the issue of conversion.[71] The new words were "dialogue" and "Christian presence." Glasser summarizes what conversion was understood by the WCC to be: "Conversion must be defined in terms of a person's response to the needs of the world, rather than in the traditional language of turning to Christ in repentance and faith. The evidence of its reality must be expressed in action for social change and the advancement of human community."[72]

The divergence between the WCC and the evangelical community reached a peak at the Fourth Assembly of the WCC in Uppsala, Sweden, in 1968. Earlier, the Second Vatican Council (1962–65), which had been concerned about diminishing missionary activity, stated in its final documents on the essentialness of conversion that "men must be called to faith and conversion."[73] Missiologist Donald McGavran, siding with the statement of Vatican II, challenged the WCC Assembly to not "betray the two billion" who had not heard by not sharing the gospel with them.[74] Unfortunately, the overall thrust

---

68. World Council of Churches, "Revised Report of the Commission on 'Christian Witness,'" 79–89.

69. Glasser, "Conciliar Debate," 86–87.

70. Commission for World Mission and Evangelism, quoted in Glasser, 88.

71. Anderson, ed., *Theology of the Christian Mission.* Even though noted evangelical scholars such as Harold Lindsell at Fuller and Bishop Lesslie Newbigin contributed, with well-known theologians such as Karl Barth and Paul Tillich, among others, none discussed conversion.

72. Glasser, "Conciliar Debate," 89.

73. Pope Paul VI, "Constitution on the Sacred Liturgy SACROSANCTUM CONCILIUM, No. 9."

74. McGavran, "Will Uppsala Betray the Two Billion?" 233–41.

of the Fourth Assembly was silence on the issue of conversion and the task of bringing people to faith in Jesus Christ.[75]

There has been significant dialogue between the WCC and the evangelicals since. German missiologist Peter Beyerhaus at the University of Tübingen in 1970 brought together a sizeable number of German theologians and church leaders to draft what came to be known as the Frankfurt Declaration.[76] Glasser writes that it was a "straightforward though hardline exposure of the World Council of Churches' reduction of the Christian mission to secular humanism."[77] At the 1972–73 World Mission Conference in Bangkok, a sizable number of delegates challenged the WCC's position on evangelism. At the 1974 meeting of the Faith and Order Commission of the WCC, the two hundred theologians from diverse church traditions with concern and humility openly discussed the implications of the 1966 Wheaton Declaration and the just concluded 1974 Lausanne Consultation.[78] There has been significant dialogue since. Through the efforts of Uruguayan theologian Emilio Castro, this dialogue culminated in a document entitled "Mission and Evangelism: An Ecumenical Affirmation" which was approved by the Central Committee of the WCC in 1982,[79] in which the WCC spelled out the relationship between conversion and "doing justice and loving mercy."[80] Important evangelical voices contributed to this discussion such as Hong Kong Baptist missiologist Raymond Fung as well as Orlando Costas and René Padilla.

---

75. However, in the pre-Assembly text of the final report, conversion is specifically mentioned as "a personal reorientation towards God" and then adds, "but this must be understood individualistically." The reactions of the leaders of the WCC to McGavran were not gracious. Eugene Smith, the executive secretary, USA of the WCC, wrote, "There is nausea, widespread and justified, about the kind of evangelism which calls a man to the altar and tells him he has met Christ, but sends him out with segregationist racial attitudes unchallenged and unchanged." WCC report and Eugene Smith quoted in Glasser, "Conciliar Debate," 91.

76. Beyerhaus, et. al., "Frankfurt Declaration on the Fundamental Crisis in Mission."

77. Glasser, "Conciliar Debate," 91.

78. Glasser, 92–94.

79. World Council of Churches, Commission on World Mission and Evangelism, "Mission and Evangelism: An Ecumenical Affirmation," 65–71. Key statement, "The Church is sent into the world to call people and nations to repentance, to announce forgiveness of sin and a new beginning in relations with God and with neighbours through Jesus Christ. This evangelistic calling has a new urgency today." "Mission and Evangelism," 65.

80. "Mission and Evangelism," quoted in Glasser, "Conciliar Debate," 94–96.

Historical Understanding and Practice of Conversion in Christian Mission

How has conversion been understood and practiced by the church historically? Are there models and practices that explain the phenomena of conversion, especially of those from non-Christian traditions? Gordon Smith writes that over the past generation, evangelical theologians have started engaging theologically with Christians from other theological traditions with their own historical understanding and practice of conversion. This engagement is enriching the evangelical understanding of conversion and redemption.[81] Such a historical perspective is important for this book as it seeks to analyze the conversion experiences of the poor. Are the conversion experiences of some of the poor a completely new phenomenon, or do they have historical precedence?

Conversion During the First Christian Centuries

While conversion is not a biblical term, the concept of coming to faith by believing is an integral part of the Old and New Testaments. Gordon Smith writes that the idea of conversion in the Old Testament was a "call to the nations to acknowledge that Yahweh and Yahweh alone is God and is thus the Creator."[82] Only he is worthy of worship. Christopher Wright clarifies the idea of conversion in the Old Testament when he says that the Hebrew word *shub* used to identify repentance and conversion is more often associated with ancient Israel than to the non-covenant nations.[83] In contrast, he states that the equivalent Greek word *epistrepho* used in the New Testament is more commonly used for the conversion of nonbelievers.[84]

The Gospels also contain conversion narratives, and these are primarily of people responding to the preaching of Jesus and choosing to become his disciples. These narratives include (among others) the call to the disciples

---

81. Smith, "Conversion and Redemption."

82. Smith, *Transforming Conversion*, 43.

83. However, Wright states that while in the Old Testament repentance and conversion resulting in blessings was a call to Israel, Jer 18, the book of Jonah, Isa 2:1–5, 19, and Mic 4:1–5 all attest to the fact that God made the same offer to the nations also.

> Not only, then, will these ancient enemies of Israel be the beneficiaries of the Abrahamic covenant (that is, they will receive the explicit blessing of Yahweh), but also they will become the agents of Abraham's blessing – they will share in the task of being "a blessing on the earth." The converted become the converting; the blessed become the blessers.

Wright, "Implications of Conversion," 14–15.

84. Wright, 14, 19.

in Luke 5, to the rich young ruler in Luke 18, and to Zacchaeus in Luke 19. Some responded, while others did not.[85] In the book of Acts, Pentecost adds a further dimension to the conversion experience, highlighting the work of God the Holy Spirit in the process.[86]

The very early church, because of its Jewishness, was not very concerned with inviting Gentiles to join the community of God's people. As Andrew Walls points out, the Gentiles who came – Cornelius, the Samaritans, and the Ethiopian eunuch – did so because of "providential nudges" rather than any policy of evangelism. Conversion was still understood as repentance, a turning away from sin in the light of the kingdom of God – as John the Baptist had preached. The call for repentance (conversion) was for the Jews, and they continued to focus on "messianic renewal and restoration of Israel."[87]

This focus changed with the execution of Stephen and scattering of the mainly Hellenistic Jewish followers of Christ that resulted.[88] Most took shelter in Jewish communities in the places they went and proclaimed Jesus as Messiah. However, those mainly from Libya and Cyprus arriving in Antioch began talking to the Greeks (Gentiles) about Jesus.[89] Because the Greeks had no understanding of the Messiah, the Hope of Israel, evangelism required not only a linguistic translation but also a conceptual translation. This is where they presented Jesus as *kyrios* – Lord – something that the Greeks understood, since that was the title used for the divinities of the cults.[90]

As the Greeks responded to Jesus as the Lord who is to be worshiped, there was a need to rethink their status. Were they to become proselytes – Gentiles becoming Jews – or was there another way of describing their experience and decision? The Council of Jerusalem mentioned in Acts 15 and Galatians 2 resolved the issue by stating that Gentiles (not just Greeks) did not have to become proselytes and keep the Jewish laws. Though the word is not used in Scripture, the concept of the "convert" was introduced. Walls describes the emergence of the convert model in Paul's writings in Galatian 2.

---

85. Smith, *Transforming Conversion*, 44.

86. Besides the conversion experiences of thousands on the day of Pentecost, there are six other conversion experiences in Acts. These are the conversion of the Ethiopian eunuch (8:26–40), of the apostle Paul (9:1–19; 22:6–16; 26:12–18), Cornelius (10), of Lydia (16:14–15), of the Philippian jailer (16:25–31), and finally of many Corinthians (18:1–8). Smith, *Transforming Conversion*, 44–47.

87. Walls, "Converts or Proselytes?," 4.

88. Bevans and Schroeder, *Constants in Context*, 18–21.

89. Acts 6:8–8:1; 11:19–20.

90. Walls, "Converts or Proselytes?," 4.

It is not just disagreement – it is white-hot indignation. His [Paul's] emotions are so strong as to strain his syntax, and his language becomes so robust that some English versions translate rather coyly. Paul will not allow it even as an option for people brought up as Hellenistic pagans to adopt, on coming to Christ, the lifestyle of very good, devout, observant Jewish believers. The followers of Jesus are not proselytes. They are converts.[91]

Moving beyond the biblical witness, early church historian Alan Kreider summarizes the range of perspectives of various scholars as they have looked at the issue of conversion in the early church.[92] Some scholars described conversion as a change in the beliefs of an individual and the soul of the person being reoriented.[93] Others understood the communal dimensions of conversion and see it as a resocialization, moving from their old community defined by ethnicity or nationality, into a new community.[94] For some, conversion was the encounter of potential converts with supernatural power,[95] while for others, there was a ritualistic dimension of conversion.[96] One scholar studying Augustine's approach to conversion describes it as a journey that is

---

91. Walls, 5. Walls concludes his discussion on what is conversion by saying,

> nor is conversion a case of adding something new to what is already there, a new set of beliefs and values to supplement and refine those already in place. Conversion requires something much more radical. It is less about content than about *direction*. It involves turning the whole personality with its social, cultural, and religious inheritance toward Christ, opening it up to him. It is about turning *what is already there*. Christ is formed among the elements of the preconversion life as he is received by faith there. And as the Gospel crosses cultural frontiers, many things, as the apostles and elders at Jerusalem realized, are open-ended and unpredictable. The realization would be unbearable but for one thing: the knowledge that new believers receive the Holy Spirit. In the Acts 15 account, it was the fact that God, who knows the heart, had given the Holy Spirit to the Gentiles as well as to the apostolic company; that reality clinched the matter for Peter (Acts 15:8). The Hellenistic way of Christian living would be constructed under the guidance of the Holy Spirit. In a very profound sense conversion is the work of the Holy Spirit in the church.

Walls, 6, emphasis original.

92. Kreider, *The Change of Conversion and the Origin of Christendom*, xiii-xviii.

93. Kurt Aland, *Uber Den Glaubenswechsel in Der Geschichte Des Christentums* (Berlin: Topelmann, 1961). Arthur Darby Nock, *Conversion* (Oxford: Clarendon Press, 1933).

94. Wayne A. Meeks, *The Origins Of Christian Morality: The First Two Centuries* (New Haven, CT: Yale University Press, 1993).

95. Ramsay MacCullen, "Two Types of Conversion to Early Christianity," *Vigiliae Christianae*, no. 37 (1983): 174–92.

96. Thomas Finn, *From Death to Rebirth: Ritual and Conversion in Antiquity* (Mahwah, NJ: Paulist Press, 1977).

lifelong, communal in nature, and required of all.[97] Kreider summarizes all of these views; because of the pagan backgrounds, conversion in the early church involved not just a change in beliefs but also in belonging, behavior, and values.[98]

The new Christian congregations in the decades following the events in the Gospels were fairly open and welcoming communities. However, this changed around AD 60 as persecution started. Kreider points out that for the early Christians at this time, openly proclaiming their faith would have gotten them and their congregations into "deathly difficulty." The only times when public statements about their faith were made was in amphitheaters as they were executed.[99] Christian worship, participation in the Lord's Supper, and communal gatherings were no longer open to anyone because of the fear of spies and the threat of betrayal. This caution gradually changed the process of conversion.

Kreider writes about what attracted many to Christianity in the early centuries. "Rumors that God was present in Christian gatherings may have also attracted outsiders to investigate Christianity."[100] While this may have been the initial attraction, ancient historian and classicist Robin Lane Fox writes that conversion in the early church was a process and not just a supernatural encounter.

> To believe that Christians were fully won by the sight of a wonder or an exorcism is to shorten a long process and ultimately to misjudge the extreme canniness of Mediterranean men. . . . Whereas pagan cults won adherents, Christianity aimed, and contrived, to win converts. It won them by conviction and persuasion, long and detailed sequels to the initial proof that faith could work.[101]

For the early church, conversion was not a moment or event, but a journey, a pilgrimage, an extended period of intentional formation. While the process may have varied from place to place, there were basically four stages.[102] In

---

97. William Harmless, *Augustine and the Catechumenate* (Collegeville: Liturgical Press, 1995).

98. Alan Kreider, *The Change of Conversion and the Origin of Christendom*, xv.

99. Kreider, 13–14.

100. Kreider, *Patient Ferment of the Early Church*, 109.

101. Fox, *Pagans and Christians*, 330.

102. Kreider, *The Change of Conversion and the Origin of Christendom*, 21–22. Kreider states that the earliest source mentioning the stages of conversion is the *Apostolic Tradition*, presumed to be the work of Hippolytus of Rome and dated around AD 215 (others date this

the first stage of evangelism, contact with the potential believer was informal and was dependent on each person's experience. This contact culminated in those who were attracted to Christianity approaching the church leaders and requesting instruction. The candidate was examined by the church leaders, and if they approved, the candidate was allowed to move to stage two as a "catechumen." This title signified that the candidate was committed to the journey of conversion, having left old values, allegiances, and relationships behind. While candidates were no longer pagans, they were not yet members of the Christian community either. They received instruction, and the focus was on reshaping their behavior. Once significant change was attested by the church leadership, candidates could then move to stage three, one of enlightenment and where the teaching focused on belief. Besides teaching, the candidates also received exorcisms and other spiritual preparation culminating in baptism. After baptism they belonged to the Christian community and could participate in the prayers and the Eucharist. Often a stage four was added, where the mysteries of baptism and the Eucharist were explained.[103]

The conversion of Emperor Constantine and the Edict of Milan in AD 313 decriminalized and legalized Christianity. Though Constantine had a life-transforming experience at the Battle of the Milvian Bridge in 312, he remained unbaptized and uncatechized, yet was considered a Christian. It was only toward the end of his life in 337 when he realized that he was gravely ill that Constantine approached the church leaders to become a Christian in the prescribed and accepted manner. While the process and rigor of his formation may not have been similar to other catechumens, he submitted to it and was finally initiated according to the prescribed rites of exorcism, baptism, and anointing.[104]

The conversion of Constantine is significant because for the first time, a person "somehow was a Christian" (in name only) without having undergone any test of their behavior, beliefs, or faith, and not becoming part of a Christian

---

work to around AD 375–400). It is a source of information about early church life and liturgy in the third century. Kreider, 21.

103. Kreider, *Change of Conversion*, 22. What is interesting is that in spite of the challenging process of becoming a Christian, by the time of Constantine in AD 312, already 10 percent of the population in the Roman Empire belonged to the Christian church. This meant that over the previous three centuries, the number of Christians grew at the average rate of 40 percent per decade. Kreider quoting historian Rodney Stark, 10.

104. Kreider, 35–37.

community or participating in any of the liturgical acts.[105] With persecution ending as early as AD 258, church membership grew rapidly, and Christians were no longer a beleaguered minority but a recognized part of the society. By the end of the fourth century, the emperors succeeding Constantine offered powerful incentives for conversion to Christianity.[106] Christianity became an attractive option.

With the coming of Christendom, how people became Christians and were initiated into the church changed. The catechetical process became shorter[107] as less was taught, and there was less supervision by the church leaders. By the end of the fourth century, most of the catechumens were not being catechized. Kreider describes them as a "large, amorphous group of unbaptized 'Christians' hesitating and temporizing, deferring the time when they would be willing to submit themselves to the rigors of conversion."[108] The focus now shifted to converting "Christians."[109] As most of the population professed to be "Christians," the focus of recruitment to the church was on baptizing infants, whom preachers would later remind of the promises made on their behalf by parents and sponsors.[110]

---

105. Kreider quotes Constantine informing the bishops during his catechetical process that he had long "thirsted and prayed that [he] might receive the salvation which is in God . . . [and] be numbered henceforth among the flock of the people of God." Kreider, 36.

106. Kreider quotes historian Sir Henry Butterfield referring to the incentives as "inducements and compulsions." Kreider, 39. The inducements included immunity for church leaders from onerous public duties, enrichment of churches, the advancement of the careers of civil servants who had become Christians, and the respectability that came from adhering to the emperor's religion. The compulsions included the banning of groups considered heretical because they deviated from the prescribed norm, for known pagans to get work in the imperial establishment, and an edict which stated that only professing Christians could be hired by the imperial armies and civil service.

107. Catechism was reduced from a three-year process to a ten-day event just before Easter. Smith, *Transforming Conversion*, 57.

108. Kreider, *Change of Conversion*, 41.

109. Pastors and church leaders developed a new genre of sermons containing threats and appeal. Christian initiation rites became more theatrical. Kreider quotes Paul Bradshaw, a specialist in the early history of Christian liturgy, in saying that they produced "a powerful emotional and psychological impression upon the candidates in the hope of bringing about their conversion." Kreider, 42.

110. Kreider, 94. It became illegal to deprive infants of baptism. However, this varied across the regions of the empire, as did the ages at which children were baptized.

The Middle Ages to Wesley and the Holiness Movement

Pastors and leaders now preached for the need of conversion, to turn from all that taints one in the world and keeps one from a total devotion to Christ, though the reality was that few could do it, even if they wanted to. In the sixth century, Caesarius of Arles in Gaul writes about young married couples wondering how they could abandon everything and change their lifestyle. However, though he believed that conversion was for all Christians, it was a requirement for clergy.[111] As a result, starting in the sixth century right through the Middle Ages in the Latin West, the primary meaning of "conversion" was a person seeking a vocation in the religious or monastic life, turning from the life of the world to God.[112]

With this change in the understanding of conversion in the Middle Ages, the monastery became a place of conversion in the midst of the evils and compromises of the world. This conversion would be experienced in a community that was seeking conversion daily in the midst of the chores and routines of life, and in solitude. Historian James Muldoon says that there was a spectrum in the understanding of conversion in the Middle Ages. It could be a Christian moving from one level of spirituality to another, a lay person entering a monastery, or a monk or nun seeking a higher level of spiritual development.[113]

As much as the early Reformers, especially Martin Luther and John Calvin, wrote about going back to a biblical understanding of salvation, they wrote surprisingly little about a theology of conversion.[114] Smith states that for the early Reformers, the experience of justification did not consist of one defining

---

111. Caesarius stipulated that no lay person could be ordained until a year had passed since their conversion. He writes that for monks and nuns, conversion did not have to do with a change in beliefs but a change in belonging and behavior. Kreider, 81–82.

112. Walls, "Converts or Proselytes?," 2.

113. Muldoon, "Introduction: Conversion of Europe," 1.

114. Regarding Calvin's soteriology, J. Todd Billings, professor of reformed theology, writes,

> But there is also a shorter answer to that question, as Calvin himself describes the "sum of the gospel" as the "newness of life" and "free reconciliation," which "are conferred on us by Christ, and both are attained by us through faith." [*Institutes* 3:3:1] To draw from elsewhere in his writing to expand this summary, the gospel is the double grace of justification and sanctification accessed through union with Christ by the Spirit, received through the instrument of faith.

Billings, "John Calvin's Soteriology," 428. Calvin adds the critical need for repentance. Repentance almost seems synonymous with conversion. The title of book 3, chapter 3 of *Institutes* is "Our Regeneration by Faith: A Discourse on Repentance." Repentance meant a turning from the "flesh" and self-reliance to turning to a true dependence on God. Calvin, *Institutes of the Christian Religion*.

moment. Instead it was a process as one learned more of what it means to live by faith.[115] The link between conversion as a momentary event and justification would develop later with Puritan and evangelical thought.

The Radical Reformation, in reaction to fifteenth- and sixteenth-century Catholicism, provided an alternate trajectory for the development of theology and practice to that of the Magisterial Reformation. The Anabaptists emphasized the role of preaching the word, turning away from sins, and taking up a new life. These elements resulted in "new birth."[116] Some scholars have argued that for Anabaptists, conversion was a crisis encounter with God, which resulted in radical personal change.[117] The Anabaptists' focus was more on the regeneration that comes through the conversion experience. They believed that their new faith was expressed in good works, and they criticized the other Reformation groups for not emphasizing the need for behavior change.[118]

The modern evangelical understanding of conversion has its root in the Puritans and Jonathan Edwards (and to a certain degree the Anabaptists).[119] Drawing deeply from the theology of the Reformation, they believed that salvation is by the grace of God and that it is supernatural in origin. It was Edwards who formulated a doctrine of conversion. He wrote in 1740:

> The doctrine of conversion, or the new birth, is one of the great and fundamental doctrines of the Christian religion . . . because [conversion] is by Christ's express declaration absolutely necessary to their salvation. Thus, the voice of reason, Scripture and

Luther in his sermon "Day of Christ's Ascension into Heaven" states what he believed to be the gospel. "What is the Gospel? It is these words, which the Lord speaks: 'He that believeth and is baptized shall be saved.' For, 'if it is by grace,' says St. Paul, Romans 11:6, 'it is no more of works: otherwise grace is no more grace.' I cannot say that God owes me a reward, but I must confess that he has given it to me entirely as a free gift." Luther, "Sermons of Martin Luther – Day of Christ's Ascension into Heaven."

115. Smith, *Transforming Conversion*, 63. This is an interesting comment because both Luther and Calvin describe a defining moment in their own salvation, the point at which their spiritual journeys changed.

116. Mennonite theologian Harold Bender writes that for Conrad Grebel, baptism was not the point at which conversion happens. "The sinner is converted by the preaching of the Word, that is, he is brought thereby to the point where he will turn from his sins, abandon them completely and take up a new life. This conversion is a new birth." Bender, quoted in Ediger, "Conversion in Anabaptist and Mennonite History," 17.

117. Loewen, "Socialization and Conversion in the Ongoing Church," 235–51.

118. Smith, *Transforming Conversion*, 72.

119. Mullens provides a fairly detailed review and analysis of the emergence of conversion as a religious experience in the United States. Mullens, *Chance of Salvation*.

> experience, and the testimony of the best of men all do concur in
> it, that there must be such a thing as conversion.[120]

Edwards believed in the possibility and necessity of conversion and that conversion was the only way that spiritual transformation would occur. His belief was rooted in the Puritan conviction of the predicament of human sin and that divine grace offers the solution. "For them a personal radical conversion is a benchmark of authentic religious experience. It is the indispensable first experience of all genuine Christians."[121] They believed that without a conversion experience, there is no assurance that a person knows the salvation of God. However, the Puritans believed that Christian conversion is a protracted process, with various stages or moments.

In England, John Wesley drew from his Puritan roots,[122] which nurtured a deep commitment toward holiness. This commitment would be central to Wesley's understanding of conversion. For Wesley, conversion is a true encounter with the living God that transforms an individual, resulting in holiness in all areas of life. Because of his focus on human responsibility as a response to God's initiative, and also because of his own experience of a moment in 1738 at Aldersgate when he felt his "heart strangely warmed," conversion for Wesley was an experience in a moment of time which started the journey toward holiness.[123]

Conversion for evangelical and Pentecostal churches was the Puritan ideal of an individualized conversion. Though there were awakenings and revivals with a significant emotionalism, by the Second Awakening in the early 1800s, the conversion model of repentance, accepting Jesus Christ as one's personal Savior, and baptism by full immersion were consolidated into the Holiness Movement. With the rise of Pentecostalism in the 1900s, this model became standard practice in their churches, too. The distinctiveness of the early Pentecostal churches was that praying, singing, and speaking in

---

120. Jonathan Edwards, "The Reality of Conversion (1740)," in *The Sermons of Jonathan Edwards: A Reader*, ed. Wilson H. Kimnach, Kenneth P. Minkema, and Douglas A. Sweeney (New Haven, CT: Yale University Press, 1999), 83, quoted in Smith, *Transforming Conversion*, 68.

121. Edwards quoted in Smith, 69.

122. Wesley's parents were Puritan dissenters, and the family's devotional reading included Puritans such as Richard Baxter and John Bunyan. Smith, *Transforming Conversion*, 71.

123. Smith, 76. Within the Wesleyan and Methodist movements, there was a second experience that complemented conversion. They believed that this experience would enable sanctification and that Christian perfection was possible as it would deliver them from the power of sin. Those from more Presbyterian backgrounds, such as D. L. Moody and R. A. Torrey, believed that the baptism of the Holy Spirit is an empowering for service. However, this second experience could not be considered a conversion experience.

unknown tongues were the main markers of the conversion experience. For some Pentecostals, these markers were given at the moment of conversion, while for others, they were part of a second experience.[124] They believed that the Holy Spirit in some measure is in the new Christian, but may not be dwelling there "in power."[125]

Modern Missions and Conversion from Other Religions

Since the late 1700s, modern missions working in religiously pluralistic contexts have used a variation of the pattern that the early church had used with regard to the conversion of non-Christians. Enquirers would receive instruction, and the sincerity of their decision to become a Christian would be discerned before they were baptized and initiated into the church. The period of instruction varied depending on the policies of the mission agency and the religious context.

In more recent times, the approach to conversion based on repentance and accepting Christ as personal Savior as a punctiliar event, instead of systematic "catechetical" instruction, is more commonly used, whether in mass evangelism events such as those of Billy Graham, in evangelistic preaching in churches, or in personal evangelism. This conversion was sometimes attested by baptism by immersion. For evangelicals, the method did not vary whether the potential enquirer was a nominal Christian, from a secular background, or from another religion.

However, encounters with other religions, in particular Islam, Buddhism, and Hinduism, is showing that people can encounter Christ in ways that are very different than the traditional evangelical model of conversion.[126] Missiologist Dudley Woodberry and his colleagues have extensively researched

---

124. Gooren, "Conversion Narratives," 96–99.

125. Smith, *Transforming Conversion*, 76–78. There was a growing divide between those who believed that the "second blessing" was empowerment for service (Finney, Moody, and Torrey) and those who believed it was sanctification (those from a Wesleyan heritage). A third stream believed that the experience was for "the higher Christian life" or the "deeper Christian life" (William Boardman, A. B. Simpson). This second blessing was not just for sanctification and empowerment, but for the experience of Christ himself. Smith, 78.

126. A Muslim convert to Christianity ibn Warraq (pen name) points out: "A Muslim abandoning his faith for humanism or atheism is likely to give rational explanations why belief in any of the tenets of Islam is no longer intellectually tenable, and his reasons would differ substantially from a Muslim who converted to Christianity." Ibn Warraq, *Leaving Islam: Apostates Speak Out*, 91.

how and why Muslims leave Islam and embrace Christianity.[127] He notes a number of influences. The first is that the Muslims saw a lived-out faith in Christians – in the loving relationships in Christian marriages, treatment of women as equals, a simple lifestyle, respecting local customs of not drinking alcohol or eating pork, and not touching people from the opposite sex. They were particularly attracted to the person, life, and teachings of Jesus. "Nearly half of all Muslims who have made a shift of faith allegiance have affirmed that the love of God was a critical key in their decision."[128]

The second influence was the experience of answered prayer, healing, and the supernatural intervention of God. Closely related to this influence was deliverance from demonic power in the contexts of widespread prevalence of folk Islam. Missionary Christy Wilson mentions that Muslims love to discuss and argue issues. Yet when healing or supernatural experiences occur, they are much more open to Christ.[129]

The third influence was dissatisfaction with the kind of Islam they had experienced, especially the fact that they perceived their religion as emphasizing God's punishment more than his love. Many were also repulsed by religiously motivated violence and the imposition of Islamic law. The fourth and final influence was dreams and visions that played a role in the conversion of many.[130] These elements were more decisive than intellectual arguments. Muslims often come to faith in Christ without having a full understanding of the gospel and all its implications.[131]

Kelly Hilderbrand, who conducted research on Buddhist converts to Christianity, listed three factors that contributed to their conversion – an encounter with the supernatural, contact with Christians, and dissatisfaction or incongruence with their traditional faith.[132] These results are comparable to those of Woodberry. Joshua Iyadurai, analyzing the conversion narratives

---

127. Between 1991 and 2007, Woodberry interviewed 750 Muslims from thirty countries and fifty ethnic groups who had decided to follow Christ. He then ranked the relative importance of influences on Muslims to choose to follow Christ. Woodberry, Shubin, and Marks, "Why Muslims Follow Jesus: The Results of a Recent Survey of Converts from Islam."

128. Woodberry and Shubin, "Why I Chose Jesus."

129. Wilson, "Muslims Who Came to Christ."

130. Woodberry, Shubin, and Marks, "Why Muslims Follow Jesus." Pieter Pikkert confirms their findings and looks at various other sources. He cites the work of Miriam Adeney among Muslim women and says that the key "milestones" along the journey for Muslim women were the Christian Scriptures, spiritual power encounters, the love of Christians, sex and beauty issues, and social justice. Pieter Pikkert, "Protestant Missionaries to the Middle East," 42.

131. Garrison, *Wind in the House of Islam*, 235.

132. Hilderbrand, "What Led Thai Buddhist Background Believers," 400–415.

of people from mainly Hindu backgrounds, had similar findings, with emphasis on the supernatural. The converts spoke about visions, dreams, mystical experiences, miracles, and answers to prayer as being critical in their transformative conversion experience.[133]

The research on converts from all three religions shows that for most, conversion was a process punctuated with spiritual encounters and a series of decisions, rather than a single crisis event. South African missiologist Pieter Pikkert summarizes:

> There was usually more than a single factor which led to their eventual conversion . . . there tended to be one specific thing which stopped them in their tracks and caused them to examine Christianity in a new light. This event then led them to embark on their sometimes complex, diverse spiritual journeys – in the course of which they often received encouragement at critical junctions – until they made their solemn decision to embrace the Christ of Christianity.[134]

Recent missional experience shows that becoming part of a community of Christ-followers is an important aspect of the conversion process. Both the word of God and Christian fellowship enable the converts to understand their supernatural encounters and to grow in their understanding of salvation. These new relationships are even more important as many converts from non-Christian backgrounds are rejected by their own community. Belonging to a Christian community helps them to survive as individuals and to continue to grow in their new identity.[135] What is also becoming increasingly clear from these conversion experiences is that the converts respond to the person of Christ rather than only to information on the work of Christ. In the light of this, "conversion is ultimately an experience of Christ that is mediated by the Word on one hand, and the Christian community on the other, and this coming to faith cannot be choreographed."[136] Smith writes elsewhere that there is a growing appreciation that conversion is a complex experience, emphasizing the role of the Spirit.

---

133. Iyadurai, *Transformative Religious Experience*.

134. Pikkert, "Protestant Missionaries to the Middle East," 271.

135. See Das, "Refugees: Exploring Theological and Missiological Foundations," 33–37; Das, "Impact of the Local Church Showing Compassion," 43–50.

136. Smith, *Transforming Conversion*, 85.

The power or energy of this experience is one of immediate encounter with the risen Christ – rather than principles or laws – and this experience is choreographed by the Spirit rather than evangelistic techniques. Evangelicals are reappropriating the heritage of the Reformation with its emphasis on the means of grace, and thereby affirming the priority of the Spirit's work in religious experience.[137]

Conversion within Evangelical Soteriology

Theologian John Webster at Oxford writes that, "Evangelical soteriology covers a great deal more ground than some dominant strands of contemporary evangelicalism are disposed to believe."[138] The traditional evangelical understanding of conversion is of an event or decision. It contains the language of revivalism, as Gordon Smith writes, "Conversion was viewed to be a punctiliar experience: persons could specify with confidence and assurance the time and place of their conversion, by reference, as often as not, to the moment when they prayed what was typically called 'the sinner's prayer.'"[139] While this view has been prevalent in missional practice, the literature over the past couple of decades acknowledges a wider understanding of salvation and the gospel that states that the goal or end (*telos*) of God's work of salvation is the restoration of all of creation and the return of God's anointed King, and not just individual souls destined for heaven.[140] Salvation and the restoration of *imago Dei* are inseparable.[141] Professor of theology Jonathan Wilson describes

---

137. Smith, "Conversion and Redemption."

138. Webster, "What's Evangelical about Evangelical Soteriology?," 179. Traditionally Western (Northern) soteriology has been construed as follows: (1) mystical theory – the Orthodox understanding of salvation and later Friedrich Schleiermacher's; (2) ransom theory – "an offering for sin" of Athanasius, Origen, Irenaeus, Martin Luther, and Karl Barth; (3) satisfaction theory – the juridical view of Cyprian, Gregory the Great, Ambrose, Augustine, and Anselm of Canterbury; (4) penal substitutionary theory – held by Calvin, J. I. Packer, and Donald G. Bloesch; (5) moral example theory – held by Peter Abelard, Friedrich Schleiermacher, and Horace Bushnell; and (6) participatory soteriology – held by James F. McGrath, Mark M. Mattison, Marcus J. Borg, and John Dominic Crossan. Gene L. Green, Stephen T. Pardue, and K. K. Yeo, eds., *So Great a Salvation*, 2.

139. Smith, "Conversion and Redemption," 210.

140. Stackhouse, ed., *What Does It Mean to Be Saved?* See also Davidson and Rae, eds., *God of Salvation.*

141. Referring to the restoration of *imago Dei*, Webster writes, "It is the central motif in ensuring the co-inheritance of creation and redemption; it offers a means of emphasizing that salvation concerns the restoration of human fellowship; it roots a Christian understanding

the relationship between salvation of the individual and the redemption and restoration of creation. "Salvation is the redemption of creation, beginning with the salvation of those who are both creatures and God's vicegerents over creation. If creation is to be saved, that salvation must begin with the salvation of those meant to care for and rule over creation in God's name."[142]

Fundamental to any soteriology is forgiveness for rebellion against the Creator God; the rebellion being manifested in sinful attitudes and behavior. John McIntyre describes a variety of models of soteriology, notions and concepts such as ransom, redemption, salvation, save, savior, sacrifice, propitiation, and ransom.[143] McIntyre deals extensively with the doctrines of salvation, namely what God has done in response to human rebellion.[144] However, it is only in the last chapter of *The Shape of Soteriology* that he deals with the response to the forgiveness offered by God. McIntyre writes, "The single inclusive term for response to the unfolded story of what God has done in Jesus toward the redemption is 'faith.'"[145] He describes the three modes of consciousness involved in believing. The first mode is knowing or cognition. The second is feeling, affection, or emotion. And the final mode is willing, conation, or volition. The process of faith starts with understanding what God has done to forgive. This understanding is usually accompanied by feelings of shame, revulsion, and repentance. And finally, by an act of the will the person accepts what has been offered.[146]

Louis Berkhof in *Systematic Theology* states that there is a logical sequence to how God administers salvation to each individual.[147] *Ordo salutis* (order of salvation) starts with calling, then regeneration, conversion, faith, justification, sanctification, perseverance, and glorification.[148] There are two aspects to conversion – a divine act and a human response. Berkhof writes,

---

of human nature in language about God's relation to his creation; and it serves to underline the saving work of God includes within it a moral and cultural imperative." Webster, "What's Evangelical about Evangelical Soteriology?," 180.

142. Wilson, "Clarifying Vision, Empowering Witness," 188.

143. For a detailed critique of each model, see McIntyre, *Shape of Soteriology*, 29–52.

144. There has been much debate about justification with N. T. Wright and John Piper staking different positions (among many others). See the discussion in Bates, *Salvation by Allegiance Alone*, Kindle Location 239.

145. McIntyre, *Shape of Soteriology*, 121.

146. McIntyre, 121–23.

147. Berkhof, *Systematic Theology*. Though published in 1941, this book is still used extensively in evangelical seminaries.

148. Berkhof, 415–16.

> Active conversion is that act of God whereby He causes the regenerated sinner, in his conscious life, to turn to Him in repentance and faith . . . passive conversion is the resulting conscious act of the regenerate sinner whereby he, through the grace of God, turns to God in repentance and faith.[149]

While this text may indicate the complexity of conversion, there are a number of critiques of Berkhof's formulation of conversion.[150] One critique is that it is a reductionist view of conversion focusing primarily on the cognitive element. Berkhof is in effect stating that faith that saves can only operate when there is knowledge of the content of biblical propositions. He writes, "The knowledge of faith consists in a positive recognition of the truth, in which man accepts as true whatsoever God says in His Word."[151]

Another critique of evangelical soteriology (especially of American evangelicalism) as described by Berkhof is the focus on the individual and a marginalization of the social dimensions of the gospel and of conversion. Bishop Lesslie Newbigin, drawing on his experience as a missionary in an Asian communal society (which was similar to the biblical contexts), writes,

> The hope set before us in the gospel is fundamentally corporate, not individualistic. . . . This purely individualistic conception of the Kingdom robs human history as a whole of its meaning. According to this view, the significance of life in this world is exhaustively defined as the training of individual souls for heaven. Thus, there can be no connected purpose running through history as a whole, but only a series of disconnected purposes for each individual life. History, on this view, has no goal, no *telos*.[152]

This focus on the cognitive, the individual, and a logical systematization of theology in evangelical soteriology has resulted in what sociologist

---

149. Berkhof, 483. Other traditional books on systematic theology also approach conversion as Berkhof has. For example, Wayne Grudem in his widely used textbook *Systematic Theology* also refers to the same aspects of salvation (regeneration, justification, conversion, etc.) as Berkhof has. In chapter 35 Grudem writes about "accepting Christ as Savior" as being the key human response. Grudem, *Systematic Theology*. Another traditional book on soteriology, Kevan, *Salvation*, discusses the issue of "new birth" as the work of God, and there is very little mention of the process of how individuals come to experience this new life. It is assumed that it is by repentance and faith.

150. Markham, *Rewired: Exploring Religious Conversion*, 13–16. See also Kallenberg, "Conversion Converted," 335–64.

151. Berkhof, *Systematic Theology*, 503.

152. Newbigin and Wainwright, *Signs Amid the Rubble*, 24.

James Davison Hunter refers to as the methodization and standardization of spirituality within evangelical tradition. He states that evangelicalism is built on a propensity for the "rationalization of spirituality" in eighteenth and nineteenth century Protestantism.

> What is different about contemporary *American* Evangelicalism is the intensification of this propensity to unprecedented proportion. This intensification came about as an adaptation to modern rationality. Thus, one may note the increasing tendency to translate the specifically religious components of the Evangelical world view, previously understood to be plain, self-evident, and without need of elaboration, into rigorously standardized prescriptions.[153]

These "rigorously standardized prescriptions" are evident in evangelical missional practices such as Campus Crusade (Cru)'s use of "The Four Spiritual Laws," Billy Graham's "Four Steps to Peace with God," and other evangelistic tools such as the "Bridge Illustration" and the "Roman Road."[154] All of them incorporate a standardized process of emphasizing a broken relationship with God and the need to accept the forgiveness that he provides in Christ. This practice culminates in a "sinner's prayer."[155] However this practice does not

---

153. Hunter, *American Evangelicalism*, 74–75, emphasis added. Matthew Bates writes that this rationalization of spirituality is the result of the impact of the Enlightenment on not only the Christian faith, but also on mission. Bates, *Salvation by Allegiance Alone*.

154. The rationale used for standardized presentations of the gospel is that it enables the rapid communication of the gospel to as wide an audience as possible. Hunter writes about the parallel to a market economy.

> In the rationalized economy, mass production allows for widespread distribution and consumption while maintaining a high degree of quality control over the product. Likewise, the reduction of the gospel to its distilled essence and the methodization of the conversion process makes widespread distribution of the gospel possible, while maintaining a cognitive uniformity in substantive quality of the message and an experiential uniformity in functional quality of the process.

Hunter, *American Evangelicalism*, 83–84. Karl Barth was highly critical of D. L. Moody's method of evangelism, namely revivalism. While he was impressed with Moody's revivals and their impact, Barth states, "The Apostles did not ask people whether they would accept or not [the gospel], but told them of reality, not in a sense of false freedom but of true freedom. Concentrate on teaching and preaching the Word of God, and let experience take care of itself." Barth, *Karl Barth's Table Talk*, 38.

155. Billy Graham suggests the following as the "Sinner's Prayer." "Lord Jesus, I need you. Thank you for dying on the cross for my sins. I open the door of my life and receive You as my Savior and Lord. Thank you for forgiving my sins and giving me eternal life. Take control of the throne of my life. Make me the kind of person You want me to be." Graham, *How to Be Born Again*, 287.

consider the influence of context on people's perception and understanding of spiritual issues, or their needs where in their desperation God meets them.

While New Testament scholar Joel Green acknowledges that there is no typical understanding of conversion, he writes that there is an "order of salvation" – namely that God initiates, people hear the message of salvation, and people respond. From Luke's narrative in Acts, Green identifies three generalizations about conversion; 1) baptism in the name of Jesus is a normal response; 2) repentance or turning to God is often mentioned as an appropriate response to God's work of salvation; and 3) the importance of faith in understanding salvation.[156]

Theologians Ivor Davidson and Murray Rae react to a standardized and universal language of redemption. They warn against the assumption of possession or any kind of domestication of a transcendent God by his created beings by dictating that he can only work in certain ways. Conversion remains an intensely personal experience. It is an encounter with the living God, and conversion language may not fit into "a broader moral or existential state of affairs."[157] Davidson and Rae write,

> As confession, soteriology can be nothing less than witness to saving experience, the activity of Christians telling their story about what their God has done for them. Such precisely is the model of Israel's testimony to the one who delivered her through water, desert, fire, and sword, and such is the pattern perpetuated by the Spirit-enabled worshipers of Israel's risen Christ (cf. 1 Cor 12:3): "Who is God?" – The Lord who has redeemed us *thus*.[158]

Gordon Smith writes that there is an emerging understanding among theologians and missiologists that conversion is not only a cognitive process: "People are converted not because they have come to terms with 'spiritual laws' or questions that might be asked 'when they get to heaven,' or even 'evidence

---

156. Green, *Salvation*, 113–15.

157. Davidson and Rae, *God of Salvation*, 7. Below, emphasis original.

> To encounter God's salvation is genuinely to know the one who saves, for his saving work, attested in Scripture, is the reiteration and opening up in creaturely time of his eternal character. . . . The boundaries of speech about reconciliation are marked out by the marvel of its *positum*: "This is the God who is known – by *us*. . . ." Soteriology's particular but spacious remit is to retell the grand sweep of this divine economy as announced in Scripture: to identify the source, occurrence, and consequences of salvation by speaking of the nature of the one who lets us know him as he really is.

158. Davidson and Rae, 7, emphasis original.

that demands a verdict' – but because they experience the transforming grace of God through an encounter with the risen and ascended Christ."[159] In a recent analysis of Billy Graham's preaching, Michael Hamilton writes that though Graham emphasized the importance of making a decision, he understood that people came because they sought help with the problems in their lives. Hamilton states that the purpose of Graham's sermon was to get people to see that they needed help and change.[160] Graham would then awaken a desire to begin a new life in Christ and encourage them to decide.

To explain Graham's understanding of the human motivation to encounter Christ, Hamilton draws on George Whitefield's analysis of what was happening during his and Jonathan Edwards' revival meetings. Whitefield concluded that emotions (what he referred to as "affections") lay at the heart of true religion. More recently, philosopher James K. A. Smith in his book *Desiring the Kingdom* encourages Christian education to move away from a preoccupation with the mind to also include the heart (emotions and desire).[161] John Piper draws on Edwards' writing to state that people do not come to Christ through thoughts or ideas but through their desires – the things that they crave.[162] To him, it seems that people want more than thoughts, ideas, and a message; they desire an authentic encounter with Christ that they can experience (feel), as it addresses their deep needs.

One of the recent contributions to evangelical soteriology, and specifically conversion, is by theologian Matthew Bates.[163] Drawing on writings from antiquity and the Old Testament understanding of gift giving (grace), Bates writes that God's gift is given regardless of our worth. However, the reception of the gift requires – obligates – the receiver to give a gift in return. Bates suggests Scripture teaches that this obligation or gift in return is allegiance to Christ, or discipleship (using evangelical missional terminology). In the Foreword to Bates' *Salvation by Allegiance Alone*, Scott McKnight writes, "Grace required

---

159. Smith, "Conversion and Redemption," 219–20.

160. Hamilton, "The 'Religious Affections' of Billy Graham's Evangelism."

161. Smith, *Desiring the Kingdom.*

162. Piper, *Desiring God.*

163. Bates, *Salvation by Allegiance Alone.* Another very recent publication explores the soteriology emerging from the Majority World (not necessarily evangelical) versus traditional (Western) Christian (Catholic, Orthodox, Lutheran, Calvinist, Anabaptist, Arminian, Wesleyan/ Holiness, and Pentecostal) soteriology: Green, Pardue, and Yeo, *So Great a Salvation.* They identify the different types of soteriology. While interesting, they are not directly relevant to this study as their focus is on soteriology and not on conversion.

a life of gratitude, praise and . . . allegiance to Jesus as king."[164] So in effect, conversion involves a change in allegiance.[165] Bates writes, "With regard to eternal salvation, rather than speaking of belief, trust, or faith in Jesus, we should speak instead of fidelity to Jesus as cosmic Lord or allegiance to Jesus the king."[166]

An Evangelical Consensus on Conversion

While there have been diverse understandings of conversion, conversion as a crisis event has dominated missional practice of fundamentalists and evangelicals since World War II. Gordon Smith writes that for most evangelicals until recently "the language of conversion *was* the language of revivalism; it shaped and, in many ways, determined their approach to worship, evangelism, and spiritual formation."[167] The language of revivalism focused on a punctiliar experience, where the person could point to the specific moment they had prayed the "sinner's prayer" and had received assurance of their salvation.

Evangelicals are reexamining and "reenvisioning the nature of conversion and redemption."[168] One of the follow-up meetings of the Lausanne Congress in 1974 was the International Consultation on Gospel and Culture held in Willowbank, Bermuda, in 1978, which looked at the experience and understanding of conversion across cultures. Right at the outset of the section on conversion and culture, the Willowbank Report states, "Too often, we have thought of conversion as a crisis, instead of as a process as well; or we have viewed conversion as a largely private experience, forgetting its consequent public and social responsibilities."[169] It refers to conversion being trivialized, with no more than a surface change, while Scripture describes the radical nature of conversion, which requires a break from the past, using the language of death and resurrection. The theological foundations are in the resurrection

---

164. Scott McKnight in Bates, *Salvation by Allegiance Alone*, Kindle Location 80.

165. According to Bates, terms such as "faith" and "believe" derived from the Greek word *pistis* have a much broader meaning than just regarding something as true or real. The broader range of meaning involves concepts such as reliability, confidence, assurance, fidelity, faithfulness, commitment, and allegiance. Bates, Kindle Location 263.

166. Bates, Kindle Location 288. In the rest of the book, he argues that the biblical narrative is about the kingdom of God and of Christ as King, rather than of forgiveness of sin and deliverance from this world. For an early critique of Bates' book see Schreiner, "Saved by 'Allegiance' Alone?"

167. Smith, "Conversion and Redemption," 209, emphasis original.

168. Smith, 210.

169. Stott, *Making Christ Known*, 93.

of Christ as the beginning of God's new creation, in which we share through union with Christ.[170]

The influence of participants from the Majority World and religiously pluralistic contexts is evident in the Willowbank Report section on conversion. Rather than describing an event where one repents and accepts Christ as Savior, it states, "We are clear that the fundamental meaning of conversion is a change of allegiance. Other gods and lords – idolatries every one – previously ruled over us. But now Jesus is Lord. The governing principle of the converted life is that it is lived under the lordship of Christ or (for it comes to the same thing) in the kingdom of God."[171] This changed allegiance affects a person's worldview, behavior, and relationships. Lesslie Newbigin, defines conversion primarily as a moral and spiritual change, a turning around and recognition of and participation in "the dawning reality of God's rule."[172]

The Willowbank Report also tackles the controversial issue of power encounters during conversion. The participants from the Majority World firmly acknowledged the reality of evil spirits, while some others wondered whether a belief in spirits is compatible with a modern scientific understanding of the universe. The Report states, "We think it vital in evangelism in all cultures to teach the reality and hostility of demonic powers, and to proclaim that God has exalted Christ as Lord of all." Earlier it states, "It means that he is Lord of the powers, having been exalted by the Father to universal sovereignty, principalities and powers having been made subject to him (1 Peter 3:22)."[173]

Another of the Lausanne Movement's meetings was the Consultation on Conversion and World Evangelization held in Hong Kong in 1988. One of the distinctions that was made was between "insider conversions" and "outsider conversions." Insider conversions involve people who have a substantial set of Christian beliefs. Outsider conversions involve people who have little or no prior Christian knowledge.[174] This is an important distinction, as often the strategies and methods used to evangelize people within "Christian" contexts were being used in religiously pluralistic contexts, or with those who have little or no understanding of Christianity, with limited effect. Outsider conversions are usually a process, as described in the next section.

---

170. Stott, 93–94.

171. Stott, 94.

172. Newbigin, "Conversion," 31.

173. Stott, *Making Christ Known*, 96.

174. Stott, 223. The papers from this consultation were published in Wells, *Turning to God*.

John Stott distinguishes between regeneration, which is the work of God, and conversion, which is human responsibility. He writes, "Regeneration is a new birth, a birth 'from above' (*anothen*), a birth 'of the Spirit.' It is the peculiar work of the Holy Spirit who himself infuses life into the dead. Conversion, on the other hand, is what we do when we repent and believe."[175] He states that regeneration is unconscious, while conversion is normally conscious.[176] Regeneration is an instantaneous and complete work of God, while conversion (repentance and faith) is more of a process rather than an event.[177]

While there is overlap, there is a distinction between the doctrine of salvation and a "theology of conversion." Stott writes that the salvation Christ gives "is freedom from sin in all its ugly manifestation and liberation into a new life of service, until finally we attain 'the glorious liberty of the children of God.'"[178] He refers to Kittel's *Theological Dictionary* which agrees that the words for salvation are primarily negative and emphasize what we are saved from. Stott writes that in Greek literature, salvation is a dynamic act in which the gods or men by force snatch others from danger. However, salvation involves not only being saved *from* but also being saved *for* – adoption and sonship. Stott then states that "salvation" is equivalent to "justification," which is the opposite of condemnation. So salvation, specifically justification is God's act of removing the guilt and penalty of sin and being declared righteous through the atoning sacrifice of Christ.[179] It is a legal process. A theology of conversion, on the other hand, is understanding *how* human beings respond to this work of God, which is influenced by culture, context, history, and personality.

Conversion as an Event or a Process?

Throughout much of church history, conversion has been seen as a process rather than event. Following Christ and becoming part of the kingdom of God required not only justification by God; it had to be manifested in the person's life through repentance, turning away from idols and ideologies, and abandoning old practices and rituals. Conversion included a significant change in behavior and a transformation of belief systems, which happen

---

175. Stott, *Christian Mission in the Modern World*, 169–70.

176. Stott clarifies by stating that many who were brought up in Christian homes may not recall a specific time when they believed. He quotes J. I. Packer who writes that convertedness as a condition matters more than conversion as an experience. Stott, 170.

177. Stott, 171–74.

178. Stott, 151.

179. Stott, 153–54.

only over a period of time. In addition, it was recognized that conversion was not just moral transformation but involved encountering the living God. Scot McKnight writes, "to enter the kingdom means a person surrenders to live under King Jesus."[180] He adds, "to live under Jesus, one must come under Jesus or 'enter' the kingdom, which means there is either a moment when that happens or a series of moments when conversion begins."[181]

The Willowbank Report referring to this issue states,

> Justification and regeneration, the one conveying a new status and the other new life, are works of God and instantaneous, although we are not necessarily aware when they take place. Conversion, on the other hand, is our action (moved by God's grace) of turning to God in penitence and faith. Although it may include a conscious crisis, it is often slow and sometimes laborious.[182]

One of the earliest models of conversion, particularly of those from other religious traditions, which was to influence other missiologists was by Alan Tippett in his 1973 book *Verdict Theology in Missionary Theory*.[183] Based on his missionary experience, Tippett sees conversion as a process with several stages and key events or moments as a person moves from a period of awareness to a point of realization, a period of decision, a point of encounter, and then periods of incorporation into a new community and maturity.[184]

Arthur Glasser, reflecting on missions in the Third World and the mission planted churches, writes that much time has been spent on establishing and maintaining clear boundaries that define who is a member of the church and who is not, which has meant identifying uniform and essential characteristics that are static and do not change. "Right doctrine, right polity plus right action" were measurable.[185] However, what may become lost in this approach is a transformational and contextual encounter with Christ. Missiologist Paul Hiebert, who had extensive experience in India, refers to this approach as a bounded set. He asks not only what knowledge a non-Christian must have to become a Christian, but also whether this knowledge is "perceived in a particular way, from a particular worldview." Foundational to this knowledge

---

180. McKnight, *Kingdom Conspiracy*, 161.

181. McKnight, 160.

182. Stott, *Making Christ Known*, 79.

183. Tippett, *Verdict Theology in Missionary Theory*.

184. For a critique of Tippett's model, see Hibbert, "Negotiating Identity," 59–72.

185. Glasser, "International Perspective," 26.

in a religiously and culturally pluralistic context is the question, what does it mean to be a Christian?[186] The answer to this question will determine how people become Christians and their conversion experience.

Hiebert identifies four categories that define how a potential seeker relates to a community of faith.[187] There are two types of *bounded* sets.

- Bounded sets with *clear boundaries* – These sets clearly define whether a person is part of a community or not. The Christians inside a bounded set (a church or denomination) are homogenous in that they believe the same doctrines and ascribe to the same behavior. Second, bounded sets have clear boundaries – for example church membership – and limit nonmembers from certain types of participation. The core function in bounded sets is evangelism. Conversion involves crossing the boundary into the community of faith. The focus is on maintaining the identity, integrity, and organization of the church.

- Bounded sets with *fuzzy boundaries* – Like in the bounded set with clear boundaries, the beliefs and practices of the church or denomination are clearly defined. However, membership and involvement are of degrees. Some may affirm only some of the beliefs necessary to be a Christian, while others may believe all the truths. There is a gradual movement from the edges to the center as a person gradually acquires the necessary beliefs, but there is no point where a person suddenly becomes a Christian. In missions, there is no stress on the proclamation of the gospel or for people to convert. The focus is on dialogue and encouraging people to find Christ in their own religions.

There are two types of *centered* sets. Hiebert observes that the Hebrew worldview was a centered set, as they knew God "in relational terms as Creator, Judge and Lord." They were in a covenant relationship with God. Christ and Paul in their teachings spoke extensively about one's relationship with God and with others. In contrast, the Greek worldview saw God as supernatural, omnipotent, and omnipresent. So God was distant and faith was defined by creeds.[188]

---

186. Hiebert, *Anthropological Reflections on Missiological Issues*, 109–10.

187. Hiebert, 110–33.

188. Hiebert, 124–25.

- *Well-formed* centered sets – These sets are defined by a center with everything else relating to it. Christians are defined as followers of the Christ of the Bible and not a Christ that is a creation of their mind. They do have a boundary defining who is part of the group and who is not, but the focus is on members moving toward Christ. Conversion therefore involves crossing the boundary and becoming part of the group and turning away from evil and moving toward Christ. There is an acknowledgement that only mental assent of biblical history and truths do not make a person a Christian. Being a Christian involves self-disclosure, listening, and obedience. Christian identity is not based on belonging to a specific group but on following Christ.[189] Members are moving toward Christ but may vary in their distance from him as well as in their knowledge and maturity. In mission, conversion involves turning away from evil and idols and toward righteousness and God (the concept of *shub* discussed earlier). Scholar in Islamic and Christian thought Joseph Cumming writes,

  > Ever since the Wesleyan revival and the Great Awakening of the 18th century, evangelicals have insisted that what matters most to God is not one's identity as "being a Christian," but rather whether one has a life-transforming relationship with Jesus Christ.[190] David Brainerd was expelled from Yale University in 1742 for remarking that a certain faculty member (a loyal "Christian") had "no more grace than this chair," because he did not have a personal relationship with Jesus.[191]

- *Fuzzy* centered sets – Unlike well-formed centered sets, fuzzy centered sets have a defined center but unclear or no boundaries. Membership is a matter of degrees – all the way from full membership to no membership. Conversion is then a process of gradual change and turning, rather than a decision to turn away from something and toward God.

---

189. This view is controversial as some missiologists working with Muslims say that one can stay a cultural Muslim and be a follower of Christ. They cite the example of Messianic Jews who do not identify themselves as Christians.

190. However, fundamentalist groups such as large portions of the Southern Baptists operate on the basis of bounded sets with clearly defined boundaries.

191. Cumming, "Muslim Followers of Jesus?"

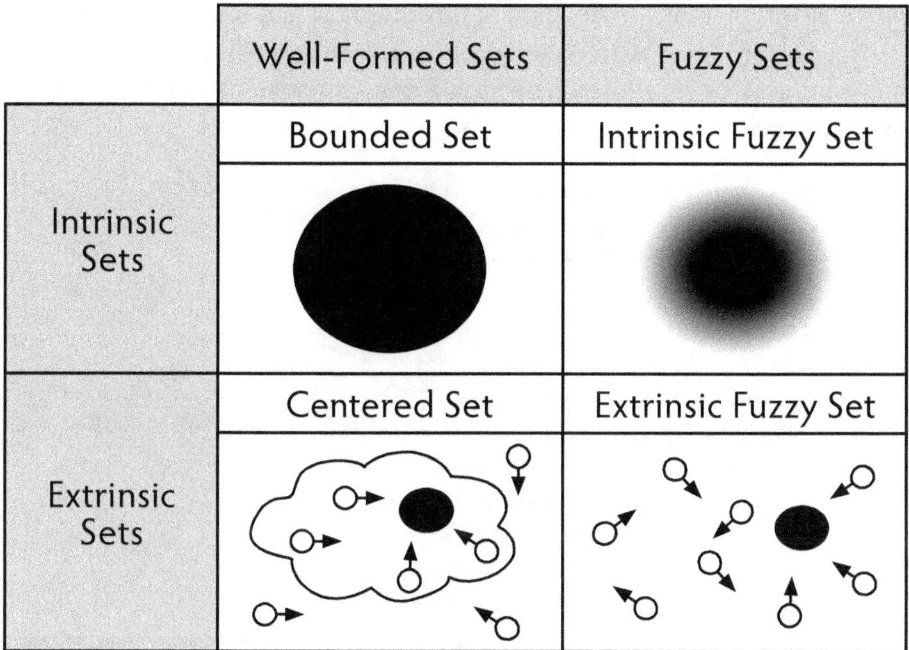

Figure 2.1. Typology of Sets[192]

Hiebert's model provides a framework for understanding when and how conversion is an event or a process. Usually in a context where there is some kind of cultural Christianity and a vaguely Christian worldview that provides some recognition of Jesus Christ, of sin, and of an awareness of the Bible, conversion tends to be an event. These are insider conversions. In non-Christian cultures, conversion tends to be a process because of the changes in worldview that are required to understand the gospel.[193] Theologian Roger Olson writes that "authentic evangelicalism is defined by its centrifugal center of powerful gravity and not by outlying boundaries that serve as walls or fences. The center is Jesus Christ and the gospel. People gathered around the center or moving toward it are authentically evangelical."[194]

There are other models that look at conversion as a process. The Engel's scale developed by behavioral specialist at Eastern University James F. Engel

---

192. Adapted from Hiebert, 112.

193. For a more detailed critique of Hiebert's model, see Yoder, et al., "Understanding Christian Identity," 177–88; and Hiebert's own critique in Hiebert, *Anthropological Reflections on Missiological Issues*, 133–36.

194. Olsen, *Reformed and Always Reforming*, 60.

provides insights into what changes in worldview and understanding need to occur before "new birth" takes place. A person in a Christianized context may start at -7 or -6, while a person in a non-Christian context may start at -8 or even below.

+5 Stewardship

+4 Communion with God

+3 Conceptual and behavioral growth

+2 Incorporation into Body

+1 Post decision evaluation

New birth

-1 Repentance and faith in Christ

-2 Decision to act

-3 Personal problem recognition

-4 Positive attitude towards gospel

-5 Grasp implications of gospel

-6 Awareness of fundamentals of gospel

-7 Initial awareness of gospel

-8 Awareness of Supreme Being, no knowledge of God

Figure 2.2. The Engel Scale[195]

Based on his experience with the Far Eastern Broadcasting Corporation (FEBC), Frank Gray feels that the Engel's scale is a very fixed linear approach and has suggested modifications. In the Gray Matrix, he adds how open or closed people are to encountering God and then plots where they are in relationship to understanding the gospel using a matrix.[196]

---

195. Adapted from Engel and Norton, *What's Gone Wrong with the Harvest?*, 45.

196. Gray, "The Gray Matrix – Tracking Its History (1977–2015) ver1.0" (2015).

The Complete Metric Extended

Continued Growth	6
Aware of Responsibilities	5
Knowledge of God's Kingdom	4
Knowledge of Adoption	3
Experience of God's Love	2
Initial Knowledge of Father God	1

CLOSED   -3   -2   -1 | 1   2   3   OPEN

Aware of Cost	-1
Grasps Implications	-2
Aware of Personal Need	-3
Aware of Basic Gospel	-4
Interested in Jesus	-5
Aware of Jesus	-6
Wonders if God can Be Known	-7
Vague Awareness and Believe in God	-8
God Framework	-9
No God Framework	-10

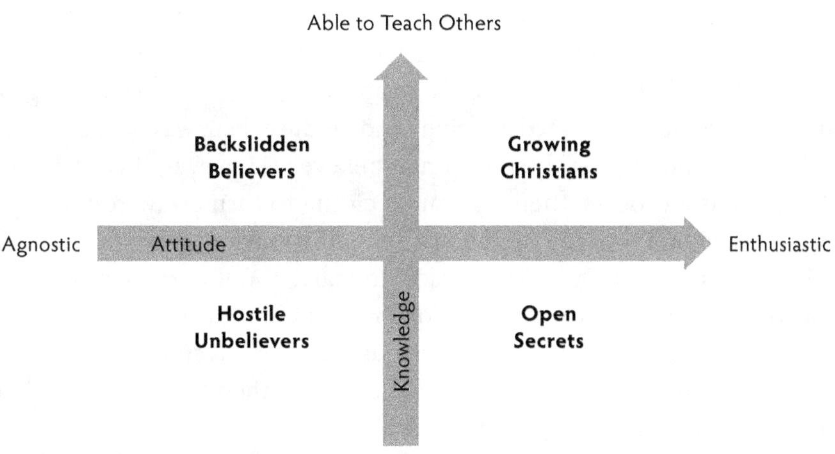

Figure 2.3. The Gray Matrix[197]

---

197. Gray.

Any model, whether it is Hiebert's, Engel's or Gray's, has weaknesses and only partly explains the process and dynamics of conversion. However, each of the models provides insight into how people encounter and understand God as they turn away from the god(s) they worship or the ideologies they follow to worshiping the true God revealed in Jesus Christ. Theologian Orlando Costas summarizes the process as follows:

> For the complexity of conversion does not lie in a fixed number of experiences but in the fact that it is a plunge into an ongoing adventure. Christian conversion is a journey into the mystery of the kingdom of God which leads from one experience to another. Initiation in the journey of the kingdom implies a plunge into an eschatological adventure where one is confronted with ever new decisions, turning points, fulfillments, and promises which will continue until the ultimate fulfillment of the kingdom.[198]

Challenge of Group Conversions – Belonging before Believing

In the history of mission, conversions in communal societies have sometimes involved whole families, tribes, or communities turning away from the gods they worship to acknowledging the living God. The group's desire for radical change is usually communicated by the head of the family or the leader of the community or tribe rather than by each member. The question that has plagued missiologists is whether these can be categorized as conversions.

If conversion is understood only as an event, then none of these group conversions would be accepted as being valid because there was no discernment whether each member of the group had believed. However, if conversion is understood as a process, then a group deciding to turn away from the gods they have worshiped would be a first step in the journey of conversion. This turning would then allow each person to learn about and encounter God revealed in Christ. The precedence for understanding this process is in the practices of the early church and the various stages of catechumens growing in their understanding of their new faith and changing their behavior accordingly until they were formally baptized.

However, there are a number of challenges to utilizing this process to understand group conversions. The example of the early church was how they handled individual seekers and not groups. The process used by the early

---

198. Costas, "Conversion as a Complex Experience," 182.

church has come to be understood as "believing before belonging."[199] While seekers were part of the local church community, they were not allowed to participate in the rituals and sacraments until they were baptized, by which time they knew what to believe in. In group conversions, people were usually baptized once it was confirmed they, as a group, had turned away from their gods and had professed faith in Jesus Christ. There was no accounting for the faith of each individual in the group. It was understood that baptism was the point of conversion, and what came after was teaching and discipling.

On the other hand in the example of the early church, while enquirers and catechumens could not take part in the rituals and sacraments, they were part of the believing community and witnessed and experienced the presence and power of God. Along with the teaching they would have been receiving as catechumens, they would have grown in their faith as they would have experienced the living God. If group conversions are understood as a process, then the initial turning (*shub*) as a group is followed by the continuing process of conversion through teaching and instructing. At various points, as Orlando Costas pointed out, there would be further decisions made and experiences had.

In an empirical study done by Jochen Gebauer at Humboldt-Universität in Berlin and Gregory R. Maio at Cardiff University, they found that a belief in God can be "motivated by the desire to satisfy the need to belong via affiliation with God." The image of a loving and accepting God satisfied the need of some individuals to belong, thus causing them to believe in this God.[200] This understanding of God is not received in a vacuum but through the teaching of the word and through witnessing and experiencing the love and power of God in the midst of a believing community. Seekers need to be part of such a community through which they can perceive God as loving and accepting.

Weyers and Saayman quote church planting consultant Johan Lukasse in identifying how believing and belonging are changing the understanding of the process of conversion. They write that in Victorian times, the church was shaped by a process of *behaving*-belonging-believing. In the modern era, it changed to *believing*-belonging-behaving. In a postmodern age, the attraction is not evangelical beliefs or religious values but an unconditional acceptance into spiritual and faith communities. The process is now *belonging*-behaving-believing.[201]

---

199. Weyers and Saayman, "Belonging before Believing," 1.

200. Gebauer and Maio, "The Need to Belong Can Motivate Belief in God," 23.

201. Weyers and Saayman, "Belonging before Believing," 2–3.

The relationship between belonging and believing would help explain some of the dynamics of group conversions. As the group turns away from their deities, they become part of a believing community or form a believing community. By belonging to such a community, with the proper teaching and experience of the reality of God, each member of the group can then move toward believing. It is assumed that not everyone will end up believing, and the church will be a bounded set with fuzzy boundaries.[202] Weyers and Saayman write, "The subject of conversion can . . . be introduced and forced on individuals too early in the missionary process, not allowing the necessary time to pass in which outsiders can find proof of the power of the gospel in the lives of those claiming to follow Christ, simply through being allowed to belong."[203]

The Willowbank Report challenges the Western perception that conversion is invariably an individual experience. It refers to the covenant theme of the Old Testament and the household baptisms of the New Testament as the basis for us to work toward and expect family and group conversions. The Report states, "Different societies have different procedures for making group decisions, e.g. by consensus, by the head of the family, or by a group of elders. We recognize the corporate dimension of conversion as part of the total process, as well as the necessity for each member of the group ultimately to share in it personally."[204]

---

202. Where group conversions have little impact is where conversion is seen as an event. This event is usually not followed up with the kind of teaching and instruction that will enable members to grow into maturity in Christ.

203. Weyers and Saayman, 5.

204. Stott, *Lausanne Covenant*, 96–97.

3

Contextualization and the Cultures of Poverty

So, whatever it is, contextualization involves mediation, not only of information about God, but the facilitation of a personal encounter with the saving, forgiving, all present, Lord of life, Jesus Christ.[1]

Edward Rommen

The Importance of Context

The previous chapter highlights the fact that the reasons why and how people turn to God revealed in Christ are dependent on their context. As Lewis Rambo points out, conversion is contextual and is influenced by a mix of people, events, ideologies, institutions in the community, expectations, and experiences.[2] Theologian Daniel Migliore writes, "Our response to the questions of who we say Jesus Christ is and how he helps us is shaped in important ways by the particular context in which these questions arise."[3] To understand why the poor turn to Christ, it is important to understand their context and its influence on their spirituality.

Contextualization is now a fundamental part of missional practice. However, contextualizing the message of the gospel to a specific context has been based on a traditional anthropological understanding of culture which focuses on ethnic and religious groups and tribes being unique and homogenous because of their language, worldviews, traditions, rituals, beliefs, and social

---

1. Rommen, *Come and See*, xii–xiii.
2. Rambo, *Understanding Religious Conversion*.
3. Migliore, *Faith Seeking Understanding*, 197.

practices.[4] Because of its anthropological foundations, contextualization has not considered the socioeconomic dimensions of society, and specifically the cultures of poverty with their own worldviews.

Culture is usually defined quite broadly. Mark Cartledge and David Cheetham write, "Culture as a way of life refers to a composite and shared social reality, which gives expression to beliefs and values, attitudes and practices."[5] Paul Hiebert identifies three layers to culture. The surface sensory level is the material culture, patterns of behavior, signs, and rituals. The second layer is the explicit level and consists of belief systems. The deepest layer is the implicit level consisting of worldviews.[6] Hiebert defines worldview as "the most encompassing view of reality we share with other people in a common culture. It is what we think with, not what we think about. It is the mental picture of reality we use to make sense of the world around us."[7]

New Testament scholar Dean Flemming moves beyond culture and writes about *context*. He probably has the most comprehensive definition of context which includes the dimensions of social and economic status and political structures.

> A *context*, then, might be defined by a variety of boundaries: regionality, nationality, culture, language, ethnicity, social and economic status, political structures, education, gender, age, religious or theological tradition, worldview, or values. It is the "life world" of the audience.[8]

Listening to the poor as to what attracts some of them to Christ because of their unique context is positioned within the wider literature of contextualization in Christian missions. This chapter will review the literature on the origins and development of the concept of contextualization and describe how it has been

---

4. Missiologists now make a distinction between contextualization, indigenization, and inculturation. This topic is further discussed in this chapter.

5. "[Culture] is given shape in social institutions in government, education, economics, health care and transportation systems, as well as being mediated by means of signs and symbols associated with food, clothing, architecture and the like." Cartledge and Cheetham, *Intercultural Theology*, 2.

6. Hiebert, "Category Christian in the Mission Task," 153–59.

7. Hiebert, 158.

8. Flemming, *Contextualization in the New Testament*, Kindle Location 123–24, emphasis original.

used in missions.[9] The objective is to understand the influence of context and culture on the spirituality of the poor.

Origins of Contextualization in the World Council of Churches and the Catholic Church

While the term "contextualization" is relatively new in the history of mission, the concept of the gospel in all its fullness being made relevant to a people and a culture is as old as the New Testament. Alan Kreider writes about the early Christians living in the tension between trying to make their faith and the gospel relevant in the society in which they lived (contextualization) and being pilgrims and not allowing the surrounding culture to taint them. As pilgrims, they tried to find alternate lifestyles and ways of behaving, as they did not want to adapt to the society they lived in. Kreider writes, "In the ancient world, when Christians were at their best, they sensed a dynamic interplay between indigenizing and being pilgrims, between affirmation and critique. They lived in the existential tension between being at home and being strangers."[10] In the last two hundred years of Christian missions, terms like adaptation, accommodation, indigenization, inculturation, and to a lesser extent translation have been used at various times to describe how the gospel and the Christian faith could relate to society in specific contexts. While the objectives of each term are similar, there are nuanced differences between them.

The term "contextualization" first appeared in the literature associated with discussions related to the Theological Education Fund (TEF) of the World Council of Churches (WCC) in the early 1970s.[11] The focus of the discussions was enabling Third World theological education to provide "a real encounter between the student and the Gospel in terms of his own forms of thought and

---

9. For an extensive discussion on contextualization in the New Testament, see Flemming. For a very detailed discussion on the history of contextualization starting with the early church fathers and the biblical foundations in the book of Acts, see Prince, *Contextualization of the Gospel*. Terry and Payne in their book on mission strategy make no mention of understanding poverty and the world of the poor as a critical part of mission strategy. Their focus is still on the cultural contexts of the major religions. Terry and Payne, *Developing a Strategy for Missions*. Even in their book *Mission Shift*, Hesselgrave and Stetzer make no mention in any of their discussion of the issues of poverty or the world of the poor.

10. Kreider, *Patient Ferment of the Early Church*, Kindle Location 2885. Andrew Walls describes this polarity with the concepts of "the indigenizing principle" and "the pilgrim principle." Walls, *Missionary Movement in Christian History*, 6–9.

11. Bosch, *Transforming Mission*, 420.

culture, and to a living dialogue between the church and its environment."[12] Some have credited Taiwanese theologian and the head of TEF Shoki Coe (Chang Hui Hwang) for actually coining the term "contextualization" during his presentation at a 1972 WCC consultation.[13] Others state that the term "contextualization" emerged from the Consultation on Dogmatic or Contextual Theology in Bossey, Switzerland, in 1971. Orthodox theologian Nikos A. Nissiotis, the chairman of the consultation, and his colleagues at the WCC elaborated further on what they meant by the term.

> Contextualization has to do with how we assess the peculiarity of Third World contexts. Indigenization tends to be used in the sense of responding to the Gospels in terms of a traditional culture. Contextualization, while not ignoring this, takes into account the process of secularity, technology, and the struggle for human justice. . . . Authentic contextualization is always prophetic, arising always out of a genuine encounter between God's Word and His World, and moves towards the purpose of challenging and changing the situation through rootedness in and commitment to a given historical moment.[14]

This thinking mirrored developments within the Roman Catholic Church. There was a growing awareness in the 1950s in parts of Africa and Asia that the theology inherited from the traditional Western church by the growing local churches did not address the needs of very different cultural contexts. The "Decree on Church Missionary Activity: *Ad Gentes*" that emerged out of Vatican II provided explicit support to the need to adapt theological reflection to local contexts.[15] This support was developed further by the missionary theology of Pope Paul VI in his 1969 address to the bishops of Africa and

---

12. Theological Education Fund, *Ministry in Context*, 13.

13. Wheeler, "Legacy of Shoki Coe," 77–80.

14. Theological Education Fund, *Ministry in Context*, 20.

15. Second Vatican Council, "Decree on the Missionary Activity of the Church: *Ad Gentes*" (1965), Chapter IV.26:

> For anyone who is going to encounter another people should have a great esteem for their patrimony and their language and their customs. . . . All these different kinds of formation should be completed in the lands to which they are sent, so that the missionaries may have a more thorough knowledge of the history, social structures, and customs of the people; that they may have an insight into their moral order and their religious precepts, and into the secret notions which, according to their sacred tradition, they have formed concerning God, the world and man.

then in 1976 in his apostolic exhortation *Evangelii Nuntiandi*.[16] The primary way contextualization was applied was through what Catholic theologian and missiologist Robert Schreiter refers to as the translation model, which "would begin with the church tradition and adapt it to a local cultural setting."[17] By using the translation model, the Catholic Church could address issues like forms of baptism, language of liturgy, style of music in worship, the use of wine in Islamic countries that forbid alcohol, polygamy, celibacy, and the status of women among numerous other issues, not all of which were contextualized.[18]

The Emerging Evangelical Understanding

The discussions in the evangelical world on contextualization were intertwined with the question of the authority and relevance of Scripture in the modern world. Many evangelicals wondered whether contextualization is compatible with a high view of Scripture.[19] The concerns for an uncritical contextualization started surfacing at the 1974 Lausanne Congress of World Evangelization,[20] which then led to the 1978 Consultation on Gospel and Culture in Willowbank, Bermuda, where an effort was made to define contextualization within the framework of evangelical convictions.[21] By the late 1970s, anthropologist James Buswell III warned against discarding words already in use and instead suggested more precision when being context sensitive while using words

---

16. Pope Paul VI, *Evangelii Nuntiand*, 20. See also Schreiter and Schillebeeckx,

> The Gospel, and therefore evangelization, are certainly not identical with culture, and they are independent in regard to all cultures. Nevertheless, the kingdom which the Gospel proclaims is lived by men who are profoundly linked to a culture, and the building up of the kingdom cannot avoid borrowing the elements of human culture or cultures. Though independent of cultures, the Gospel and evangelization are not necessarily incompatible with them; rather they are capable of permeating them all without becoming subject to any one of them. The split between the Gospel and culture is without a doubt the drama of our time, just as it was of other times. Therefore, every effort must be made to ensure a full evangelization of culture, or more correctly of cultures. They have to be regenerated by an encounter with the Gospel. But this encounter will not take place if the Gospel is not proclaimed.

Schreiter and Schillebeeckx, *Constructing Local Theologies*, Kindle Location 169.

17. Schreiter and Schillebeeckx, Kindle Location 305.

18. Schreiter and Schillebeeckx, Kindle Location 186.

19. Fleming, *Contextualization in Theology*; Hesselgrave and Rommen, *Contextualization*, 29–35. This was the period when the "battle for the Bible" was at its height.

20. Moreau, "Contextualization," 321–48.

21. Hesselgrave, *Scripture and Strategy*, 73–113.

such as "indigenization," "inculturation," and "translation theology." While evangelical scholars supported his proposal and other similar ones, there was no agreement on standardization of terms.[22]

Soon, many of the more conservative evangelical scholars adopted the word "contextualization." Rejecting the TEF and WCC definitions, they redefined the word in ways that they felt revealed sensitivity to context while maintaining faithfulness to Scripture.[23] However, the complexity and political sensitivity of the task was reflected by professor of missions Harvie Conn when he criticized Western evangelical theologians and missiologists for limiting the concept of contextualization to only communicating the gospel effectively across *other* cultures. Conn understood the fear of the Western evangelicals to theologize the way ecumenical scholars were doing, as they felt doing so would erode biblical authority. He felt that evangelicals needed to confront their own culture and allow Scripture to judge their own "encultured interpretations and lifestyles." For Conn, contextualization was *conscientization* of the whole people of God regardless of location.[24]

One of the early comprehensive efforts to understand contextualization from within an evangelical theological framework was by anthropologist Charles H. Kraft. He tested his ideas in a series of articles culminating in 1979 with his book *Christianity in Culture: A Study in Dynamic Biblical Theologizing in Cross-Cultural Perspective*.[25] While being rooted in biblical revelation, he viewed local cultures positively and proposed a "dynamic-equivalence transculturation" through which the gospel and biblical truth could be "transculturated" into the hearer's cultural context.[26] Terms that he introduced, such as incarnational ministry, receptor-oriented communication, and dynamic equivalence,[27] have now become commonplace for missiologists.[28] Kraft, who is also a linguist, emphasized the need to

> use receptor-language constructions that function in the receptors' cultural world to convey meanings that are equivalent to the

22. Hesselgrave and Rommen, *Contextualization*, 33.

23. Hesselgrave and Rommen, 33.

24. Hesselgrave and Rommen, 34.

25. Kraft, *Christianity in Culture*.

26. Kraft, 203–27.

27. The dynamic-equivalence Bible translation theory was developed by Eugene Nida. Kraft took the concept beyond its use in Bible translation to being a key concept in contextualization in all aspects of missions.

28. Kraft, xxi.

original meanings in the New Testament Greek-speaking world. Due to the non-equitability of the forms of languages and cultures, these meanings will never exactly duplicate the original meanings in the Greek world. But they should carry as nearly as possible an *equivalent impact* in English.[29]

The dynamic equivalence model was perceived as a threat to the accuracy of the revealed word of God. Kraft's description of the literalists or formal-correspondence model of translation was seen as being highly critical of how evangelicals had carried out theological work and mission with supposedly little understanding of culture. While scholars such a Eugene Nida, J. B. Phillips, and William Smalley (among others) had emphasized the need to use language that is understood by the reader and listener, Kraft pushed further to also incorporate the worldviews and structure of thought of the reader, as well as extending to all aspects of mission – especially evangelism and the establishment of new churches. As Kraft himself acknowledged (in the preface of the twenty-fifth anniversary edition), his book was written at a time before evangelicals were comfortable with the concept of contextualization. It was seen as too radical and as an attack on the authority of the Bible.

Kraft's position evoked strong reactions, with one of the most respected evangelical theologians at the time, Carl Henry, critiquing Kraft's work.[30] This reaction was surprising because Nida, Smalley, William Reyburn, William Wonderly, and Jacob Loewen had published the journal *Practical Anthropology* between 1953 and 1973 which had influenced a whole generation of missiologists and Bible translators (including Kraft) about the importance of "culture and its influence on ourselves, those to whom we go and the way God's truths are presented in the Bible."[31] So the concept among evangelicals of being sensitive to culture was not new with Kraft.

It is in this context that Paul Hiebert in 1987 wrote his article "Critical Contextualization."[32] Hiebert starts by acknowledging the efforts at contextualization by the very early Catholic and Protestant missionaries in

---

29. Kraft, 211, emphasis original.

30. Henry, "Cultural Relativizing of Revelation," 153–64. Others who were very critical of Kraft felt that he had gone too far and that he had become either a theological liberal or "Barthian." Gross, *Is Charles Kraft an Evangelical?*

31. Kraft, *Christianity in Culture*, xxv. Respected Baptist theologian Bernard Ramm, the author of *Protestant Biblical Interpretation: A Textbook of Hermeneutics*, 3rd rev. ed. (Grand Rapids, MI: Baker Book House, 1970), had even written the foreword to the first edition of *Christianity in Culture*.

32. Hiebert, "Critical Contextualization," 104–12.

India as they encountered a very sophisticated Indian culture. However with the rise of colonialism, the "triumph of science," and the theory of cultural evolution, contextualization entered an "era of non-contextualization." Hiebert quotes missiologist John Pobee referring to "the missionary doctrine that [believed] there is nothing in the non-Christian culture on which the Christian missionary can build and, therefore, every aspect of the traditional non-Christian culture had to be destroyed before Christianity could be built up."[33]

Hiebert then makes a case for contextualization based on postcolonialism, postmodern science, and the impacts of phenomenology, structural functionalism, and linguistics on anthropology. His methodology for critical contextualization involves four steps: the exegesis of culture, exegesis of Scripture and the hermeneutical bridge,[34] the need for a corporate critical response, and finally new contextualized rituals. To guard against syncretism, he emphasizes the need to take the Bible seriously and recognize the leading of the Holy Spirit and for the church (not just individuals) to act as a hermeneutical community and for discussion among evangelical theologians across different cultures.

There are a number of reasons why "Critical Contextualization" was more acceptable during the late 1980s than Kraft's publication in 1979.[35] First, Hiebert did not criticize the cross-cultural missional practice of the mission agencies and the missionaries and therefore was not seen as a threat. Hiebert instead focused on "the culture of recent converts, not the cultural baggage of missionaries."[36] Like Kraft, Hiebert provided concrete steps on how to contextualize. But he also provided ways to prevent possible syncretism, while the fear with Kraft's thinking was that "many evangelicals were concerned that calls for contextualization involved a cultural relativism which allowed for and justified syncretism."[37]

---

33. John Pobee quoted in Hiebert, 104.

34. Referring to the hermeneutical bridge, Hiebert writes, "The leader must also have a meta-cultural framework that enables him or her to translate the biblical message into the cognitive, affective, and evaluative dimensions of another culture. This step is crucial, for if the people do not clearly grasp the biblical message as originally intended, they will have a distorted view of the gospel." Hiebert, 109–10.

35. Darrell Whiteman at Asbury Theological Seminary and editor of *Missiology* says that Hiebert's critical contextualization approach has been "employed by students as a theoretical framework in more dissertations than any other." Whiteman, "Anthropological Reflections," 55.

36. Chang, et al., "Paul G. Hiebert and Critical Contextualization," 204. However, Hiebert does point to problems caused by the cultural baggage of missionaries during the non-contextualization era, when there was very little awareness of the need for contextualization.

37. Chang, et al., 204.

There is another major distinction between the works of Kraft and Hiebert. Kraft focused much of his discussion on initial evangelism and the establishment of local churches, where he expressed his concern that the failure of missionaries to contextualize the message by bringing their normative patterns with them hampered or distorted the responses of the cross-cultural listener to the gospel. Hiebert instead assumed the presence of an indigenous church and did not focus on initial evangelism or church planting, and thus did not critique the work of the original missionaries who had established the local church. The missionary in Hiebert's paradigm instead was a dialogue partner with the local church in its efforts at contextualization.[38]

Since the publication of the work of Kraft and Hiebert, a number of other evangelical scholars have developed models and frameworks for missional contextualization.[39] David Hesselgrave and Edward Rommen in *Contextualization: Meanings, Methods, and Models* provide the different perspectives on contextualization, which include the philosophical, theological, anthropological, hermeneutical, and communication perspectives. Building on these, they present a model of contextualization that is "authentic and relevant."[40] Hesselgrave has since detailed his model in *Communicating Christ Cross-Culturally: An Introduction to Missionary Communication.*[41] Scott Moreau provides a very useful framework to categorize evangelical contextualization models. He contrasts it with Robert Schreiter's framework and suggests that evangelical contextualization needs to understand the life-cycle stage of the church; the area being addressed for change, impact or attention; the method; and the different types of initiators of contextualization.[42]

---

38. Chang, et al., 205.

39. The debate in evangelical circles as to whether contextualization is valid or not seems to have ceased, with it now being accepted as a vital part of evangelical missiology and missional practice. The focus now is on how contextualization is done. With the growing understanding of cultural pluralism, most recent literature on contextualization has focused on methods. Even issues like contextual theology, which evangelicals had for a long time dismissed as being part of theological liberalism, is now being explored by some evangelicals as a valid theological expression of local bodies of Christians. Recent books on mission strategies include extensive material on contextualization. See Terry and Payne, *Developing a Strategy for Missions*; Hesselgrave and Stetzer, *Mission Shift*.

40. Hesselgrave and Rommen, *Contextualization*, 127–211. They refer to the need for balance between faithfulness and meaningfulness. The areas that need to be addressed are contextualization and the biblical text, and contextualization and the respondent peoples and cultures – which include addressing their worldviews, cognitive processes, linguistic forms, behavioral patterns, communication media, social structures, and motivational sources.

41. Hesselgrave, *Communicating Christ Cross-Culturally*.

42. Moreau, *Contextualization in World Missions*.

Defining Contextualization

While there is no one agreed definition of contextualization among evangelicals but a series of proposals,[43] Darrell L. Whiteman's definition incorporates most of the key elements:

> Contextualization attempts to communicate the Gospel in word and deed to establish the church in ways that make sense to people within their local cultural context, presenting Christianity in such a way that it meets people's deepest needs and penetrates their worldview, thus allowing them to follow Christ and remain within their culture.[44]

Hesselgrave and Rommen in *Contextualization* provide one of the more widely understood descriptions:

> Christian contextualization can be thought of as the attempt to communicate the *message* of the person, works, Word, and the will of God in a way that is faithful to God's revelation, especially as it is put forth in the teachings of Holy Scripture, and that is meaningful to respondents in their respective cultural and existential contexts. Contextualization can be both verbal and nonverbal and has to do with theologizing; Bible translation, interpretation, and application; incarnational lifestyle; evangelism; Christian instruction; church planting and growth; church organization; worship style – and indeed with all of those activities involved in carrying out the Great Commission.[45]

Hesselgrave and Rommen identify two basic principles that are foundational to contextualization. The first is that the gospel needs to be understood. Second, it needs to be "true to the complete authority and unadulterated message of the Bible while also relating to the linguistic, cultural, and religious background of those listening."[46] In the various definitions, the issue is what is being contextualized. Hesselgrave and Rommen state that it is the message of the person, work, and word of God. While they refer to both

---

43. Hesselgrave and Rommen, *Contextualization*, 35.

44. Whiteman, "Contextualization," 2.

45. Hesselgrave and Rommen, *Contextualization*, 200, emphasis added. While this definition refers to the existential contexts of people, it makes no reference to the social, political, and economic realities beyond the church that influence how people perceive and experience reality.

46. Hesselgrave and Rommen, xi.

verbal and nonverbal communication, the focus of the contextualization is very much on the content and message of the Bible so that it is understood by the hearers in their own culture and context. Whiteman takes a broader approach and refers also to contextualizing the gospel both verbally and by actions. He adds a critical dimension to the objective of contextualization: the way the gospel is communicated must meet people's deepest needs and penetrate their worldviews in order to enable them to follow Christ. What Whiteman emphasizes is the context of the needs and worldviews of people, which in turn influence how they perceive Christ.

Contextualization in Traditional Missional Practice

Traditional missional practice was rooted in the Great Commission stated in Matthew 28:19–20. The Greek word *ethne* in verse 19 was very simply translated as ethnic group or people group, each with a unique culture, and sometimes a unique language and religion.[47] Early Catholic and Protestant missions focused their efforts on contextualizing the gospel to different languages and religions. Addressing poverty and its impact was not considered a part of mission until the 1860 Missionary Conference in Liverpool, when the first medical missionary was commissioned, and after much discussion, education was also acknowledged as an integral part of mission. It was only toward the end of the nineteenth century and with the rise of the social gospel that the reality of the socioeconomic dimensions of society were acknowledged by mission agencies.

David Bosch states that contextualizations of the gospel fall into one of two categories. They either belong to the category of *inculturation*, where the gospel is expressed using different philosophical frameworks and cultural norms, or they are *liberation theologies* that use social analysis of a local context as the starting point for Christian reflection and praxis.[48]

Robert Schreiter writes that there are three approaches to inculturation when developing local theology. The first is the translation model which uses a two-step process seeking to free the Christian message from any previous cultural baggage. Once the revelation is "allowed to stand freely," it can then

---

47. The term *ethne* is discussed in detail later in this chapter.

48. Bosch, *Transforming Mission*, 420–56. Much more current evangelical emphases on integral mission, or whole-life discipleship, take into consideration the ethical qualities of the *evangel*. This emphasis has sprung out of a renewed interest in the implications of the theme of the kingdom of God during the 1980s.

be translated into a new context.[49] The second approach is the adaptation model which takes the local culture more seriously. It trains local leaders in the categories of Western philosophy and theology and then enables them to fit local cultural data into these categories. Thus what emerges is a system of theology with categories, names, and content of a local culture but looks like Western theology.[50] There are variations to this approach. As an example, Schreiter describes Catholic missionary Vincent Donovan's approach among the Masai people in East Africa "of planting the seed of faith and allowing it to interact with the native soil, leading to a new flowering of Christianity, faithful both to the local culture and to the apostolic faith."[51] The third approach is the contextual model which concentrates more directly on the local context in which Christianity takes root and then expresses itself. The difference between the adaptation and contextual models is that in the former, the focus is on adapting the received faith (though there is reference to context), while in the latter, the process of reflection begins with the local cultural context and its needs (as does liberation theology).[52]

Variations of these three approaches are seen throughout the history of missions as missionaries tried to contextualize the gospel and the doctrines of the church into local contexts. However as Schreiter has pointed out, the most common approach in missions has been the translation model.[53] In the era just proceeding the modern Protestant missionary movement, the Franciscan Raymond Lull (Raimundo Lulio, 1232–1315), the first Catholic missionary to the Muslims, understood the importance of context and studied not only Arabic but Muslim theological and philosophical thought as well in order to communicate more effectively.[54] The Jesuits, whose missionary activities became a model for early Protestant missions, understood the tensions between being incarnational versus being a pilgrim.[55] Being incarnational, "the Jesuits studied non-European cultures as part of God's creation, while many other

---

49. Schreiter and Schillebeeckx, *Constructing Local Theologies*, Kindle Location 275–334 .

50. Schreiter and Schillebeeckx, Kindle Location 334–407.

51. Schreiter and Schillebeeckx, Kindle Location 392. See also Vincent Donovan, *Christianity Rediscovered*.

52. Schreiter and Schillebeeckx, Kindle Location 407–92.

53. Schreiter and Schillebeeckx, Kindle Location 275.

54. Zwemer, *Raymund Lull First Missionary to the Moslems*.

55. Missiologist Scott Sunquist (among others) presents these two perspectives in missions. A pilgrim passes through without engaging with the context and the culture. In being incarnational, the missionary engages with the culture to understand how Christ is revealed in a specific context. These perspectives are similar to Andrew Walls' concept of the indigenizing principle and the pilgrim principle. The various ways in which Christ relates to culture is

Europeans of the period tended to denigrate indigenous cultures as evil, inferior, or insignificant."[56] While most Jesuit missionaries contextualized to a certain extent, among the early Jesuits, Roberto de Nobili (1577–1656) followed in Lull's missiological footsteps and adopted local customs in India. Besides mastering local languages and adopting local dress and cultural habits, he adapted or coined local words to communicate biblical truth.[57]

Missionary pioneers such as William Carey and his team, Hudson Taylor, and others understood the importance of contextualization in dress, language, and culture but did not seek to either adopt or adapt local religious and philosophical frameworks to communicate the gospel. Years later, in the early part of the twentieth century, the efforts of E. Stanley Jones in India to use local forms of gatherings to discuss what is truth (the *satsangh*) to communicate who Christ is extended contextualization to not only adapting the message so that it would be understood but to also using a method of communication that was appropriate for a religiously pluralistic society such as India.[58]

However, one of the more radical attempts at contextualization (a variation of the adaptation model) was by British Anglican Bishop John Nicol Farquhar in India who sought to place Christ within Hindu thought and culture. His book in 1915 entitled *The Crown of Hinduism* focused on the theology of "fulfillment," in that Christ not only came to fulfill the Jewish law and the prophets (Matt 5:17) but also all the world's "higher religions." It is in this sense that Christ is the "crown" of Hinduism.[59] Theologian Richard Niebuhr in his taxonomy of how Christ relates to culture identifies one category as Christ who is seen as the pinnacle of human achievement. Niebuhr writes, "In every culture to which the gospel comes there are men who hail Jesus as the Messiah of their society, the fulfiller of its hopes and aspiration."[60]

Another variation of the adaptation model is Don Richardson's missionary work among the Sawi people of Irian Jaya, where he worked on the principle that Christ was already at work in a specific culture, though they may not have perceived or understood the revelation of God properly or thoroughly (Rom 1:19–20). Richardson searched for and found local redemptive analogies to

---

probably best described by Richard Niebuhr's taxonomy of Christ and culture. Niebuhr, *Christ and Culture*.

56. Sunquist, *Understanding Christian Mission*, 47.

57. Rajamanicham, *First Oriental Scholar*.

58. Jones, *Christ of the Indian Road*.

59. Farquhar, *Crown of Hinduism*.

60. Niebuhr, *Christ and Culture*, 83.

explain the redemptive work of Christ using stories, cultural practices, and incidents from within the local indigenous context.[61]

In both of the examples above, the development of a local theology involved finding Christ already at work in the community. However, Robert Schreiter provides a balance between "bringing" Christ to a community through missionary evangelism and discovering how Christ is already at work in the community:

> When described from a Christological point of view . . . the development of local theologies depends as much on finding Christ active in the culture as it is on bringing Christ to the culture. The respect for culture has a Christological basis. It grows out of a belief that the risen Christ's salvific activity in bringing about the kingdom of God is already going on before our arrival. From a missionary perspective, there would be no conversion if the grace of God had not preceded the missionary and opened the hearts of those who heard.[62]

Some Contemporary Issues in Contextualization

Contextualization has moved beyond responding to language, religion, and culture and is beginning to address the relationship between language, religion, and epistemology. It examines the nature of revelation and how that is perceived and understood by people with very different worldviews than a Western one.[63] The challenge of contextualization is in ensuring that the uniqueness of Christ and his work of redemption are not lost in the process of adapting the message to a different culture and worldview.

This issue was highlighted in the controversy of the Bible translation being done into modern Arabic for Muslim audiences by Wycliffe Global Alliance and SIL International. The issue was that Muslims are offended by the use of familial terms when referring to Jesus as the "Son of God" and God as the "Father." So Wycliffe and SIL translators sought to use alternate words that would not emphasize the familial relationships. Unlike Kraft's method of

---

61. Richardson, *Peace Child*.

62. Schreiter and Schillebeeckx, *Constructing Local Theologies*, Kindle Location 758.

63. This method is the newly emerging field of ethno-epistemology.

dynamic equivalence, the issue was not that the Muslims did not understand the concepts but were offended by them.[64]

There has been a similar unresolved debate between indigenous Chinese Christians and some Western missionaries about the names to be used to refer to God in vernacular Bible translations. At issue is whether to adopt the name of a native God (*Shangdi* – the High God) or a generic term (*Shen*) to refer to God in Chinese, or to use the biblical names *Elohim, Adonai, YHWH,* and *Theos* which are foreign to the Chinese culture.[65]

The objective in both cases was to minimize the barriers that hinder people from perceiving and understanding the gospel, while remaining true to the written revelation of God. What translators in both situations were trying to do was what the apostle John had done to contextualize for a Greco-Roman audience the Jewish understanding of God by adopting the Greek concept of *logos.* Underlying both the Arabic and Chinese controversies is the question as to what is meant by the authority of the Bible. Does stating that the Bible is authoritative limit the ongoing contextualization of the revelation of God that was within a specific Jewish and then a Greco-Roman context?

Another of the challenges to inculturation and contextualization is globalization. Thomas Friedman in his book *The World Is Flat: A Brief History of the Twenty-First Century* refers to the standardization of products and services as a result of globalization.[66] Within Christian missions this is seen in gospel presentations such as "The Four Spiritual Laws," the "Bridge Illustration," and the "Roman Road," which can be shared anywhere with anyone regardless

---

64. The report of the World Evangelical Alliance Panel that was appointed to mediate and settle the dispute noted, "The Panel recognizes that there is significant potential for misunderstanding of the words for 'father' and 'son' when applied to God, and that in languages shaped by Islamic cultures, the potential is especially acute and the misunderstandings likely to prove especially harmful to the reader's comprehension of the gospel." To resolve the issue, among a number of other detailed recommendations, the Review Panel,

> recommends that translators consider the addition of qualifying words and/or phrases (explanatory adjectives, relative clauses, prepositional phrases, or similar modifiers) to the directly-translated words for "father" and "son," in order to avoid misunderstanding. For example, as the biblical context allows, the word for "father" might be rendered with the equivalent of "heavenly Father" when referring to God, and the word for "son" might be rendered with the equivalent of "divine Son," "eternal Son," or "heavenly Son" when referring to Jesus. The Panel also encourages translators to use paratextual material to clarify and avoid misunderstanding in these.

WEA Global Review Panel, *Report to World Evangelical Alliance,* 6.

65. Lee, "God's Asian Names."

66. Friedman, *World Is Flat.*

of context or culture. It is also seen in mission strategies such as Evangelism Explosion and in church planting strategies such as Master Plan, "Seven Steps for Church Planting," and those used by Hillsong with the assumption that these tools and strategies are value neutral with regards to culture and context. Lesslie Newbigin warns that there is no pure, unadulterated gospel and pursuing it is an illusion. He writes:

> Neither at the beginning, nor at any other subsequent time, is there or can there be a gospel that is not embodied in a culturally conditioned form of words. The idea that one can or could at any time separate out by some process of distillation a pure gospel unadulterated by any cultural accretion is an illusion. It is, in fact, an abandonment of the gospel, for the gospel is about the word made flesh.[67]

However, there is a growing reaction to globalization and standardized ministry tools and strategies with the reassertion of the uniqueness of local cultures and traditions, of ethnic and religious identities, and nationalism. There is an acknowledgement of the diversity of human values and the importance of the local.[68] This acknowledgement is reflected in the missional community also. The C1–C6 spectrum developed by John Travis (pseudonym) for use in Muslim evangelism[69] identifies six possible types of contexts in a

---

67. Newbigin, *Foolishness to the Greeks*, 4.

68. Ormerod and Clifton, *Globalization and the Mission of the Church*; Held and McGrew, *Globalization / Anti-Globalization*. Karl Vaters, writing in *Christianity Today*, says that due to the increasing complexity of society, the present use of homogenous understanding of society is now changing how we approach different segments of society.

> Sure, people exist in the age range born between 1982 and 2004. But the idea that every generation can be defined by a clear set of distinctives doesn't apply to them the way we've become accustomed to. Baby Boomers were the first generation to be defined as a homogeneous group. . . . The one-size-fits-all, homogeneous generation is over. But it really only existed for 50 years anyway. From about 1945 to 1995. We don't have a name for any generation before the Builders because, without mass media, people were identified ethnically and regionally, not generationally. . . . Millennials are forcing us to minister in a new way. New for us, that is. But it's really the oldest way of all. We can't treat them as a group, or even as subgroups.

Vaters, "Why Millennials Won't Build the Kinds of Churches."

69. Travis, "The C1 to C6 Spectrum" 407–8.

specific geographical area within which the hearer could be living, and any contextualization needs to take these into consideration.[70]

Variations of this spectrum are now being used in evangelism and church planting in other religious contexts. Charles Kraft refers to the work of James Gustafson in Thailand among Buddhists who stay within their social and religious communities while "enabling Christ and the Gospel to be born in the cultures of this world."[71] With echoes of Bishop Farquhar's strategy among Hindus a century earlier, Gustafson writes, "We are currently working on what we call 'New Buddhism.' . . . It is a concept that enables the gospel to both build on and confront Thai Buddhism in a way that enables Christ to be the fulfillment of the 'way' of Thai Buddhism."[72] This concept of insider movements is now an accepted missional strategy, though at times a controversial one, within Islamic,[73] Hindu[74] and Buddhist[75] contexts.

While focus of contemporary contextualization has been on ensuring the relevance of the *message* of the gospel in different cultures, a very different understanding of contextualization is presented by Orthodox priest Edward Rommen. Rommen coauthored *Contextualization: Meaning, Methods, and Model* with David Hesslegrave. In his book *Come and See: An Eastern Orthodox Perspective on Contextualization*, Rommen writes that contextualization is too

---

70. Massey describes the spectrum:

> C1 is a traditional Christian church which either reflects the culture of foreign Christians or that of the minority indigenous national church. . . . C2 is basically the same as C1, except C2 churches use the daily language of the surrounding Muslim population. . . . C3 churches are essentially the same as C2, except C3 makes use of local music styles, dress, art and other indigenous cultural elements. . . . C3 makes a clear distinction between practices that are purely "cultural" and those which are "Islamic". . . . C4 congregations are much like C3 but have also adopted biblically permissible Islamic forms and practices. . . . C5 is much like C4 with the primary difference being self-identity. Whereas C4 believers identify themselves as "followers of *Isa*," C5 believers identify themselves as "Muslim followers of Jesus" – much like Messianic Jews calling themselves "Jewish followers of Jesus". . . . – C6 Secret Believers, may or may not be active members in the religious life of the Muslim community.

Massey, "God's Amazing Diversity in Drawing Muslims to Christ," 7–8.

71. James Gustafson quoted in Kraft, *Christianity in Culture*, xxvi.

72. This situation is an example of C5. James Gustafson quoted in Kraft, xxvi.

73. David Garrison in his survey of Christian missions to Muslims since the seventh century identifies different kinds of contextualized movements of the Spirit of God within the Muslim world over the centuries, which continue until this day. Garrison, *Wind in the House of Islam*.

74. Hoefer, *Churchless Christianity*.

75. Smith, *Strategic Approaches for the Buddhist World*.

focused on information – the message and the content of the gospel, and very little on the person of Christ. "So whatever it is, contextualization involves mediation, not only of information about God, but the facilitation of a personal encounter with the saving, forgiving, all present, Lord of life, Jesus Christ."[76] For Rommen, the gospel is not merely a message but a person.[77] According to Rommen, contextualization from an Eastern Orthodox perspective is the development of an "invitational core context" where a person might experience a personal introduction to Christ.[78] Instead of emphasizing social location, culture, or context, the emphasis is on the context provided by the church. In reviewing *Come and See*, missiologist Steven Bevans at the Catholic Theological Union writes that while the Bible needs to be translated and doctrines explained in ways that people can understand, "Rommen is right in that a lively, faithful, and faith-filled church community is still the best witness to the gospel. No amount of contextualization can substitute for authenticity, fidelity, or holiness."[79]

Rommen's insight is critical, because it opens the possibility of a different epistemology than that used in evangelical missional practice. Rather than conversion only resulting from an intellectual understanding of a gospel presentation, it allows for seekers to "encounter" the living God in Christ in different ways.

The Emergence of Socioeconomic and Political Location in Contextualization

In the last few decades, contextualization has moved beyond language, culture, and religion to also acknowledge the importance of the socioeconomic and political location of the hearer, as well as the impact of historical events at a point in time. While the liberation theologies and theologies associated with the Conciliar Protestant Churches have recognized the importance of socioeconomic and political location and history in mission, evangelicals

---

76. Rommen, *Come and See*, xii–xiii.

77. This idea is reenforced in a recent *Christianity Today* article in which Andrew Wilson brings the focus back on the person of Christ and not on the salvation message when he writes, "Jesus, not salvation, is God's greatest gift to us." Wilson, "Why Jesus, Not Salvation, Is God's Greatest Gift to Us."

78. Rommen, *Come and See*, 196. This method is applied through direct interaction with the Gospel texts by people wholly outside the message, forms, and activities of the church. It is being applied successfully among students in universities in the *Uncovered* series of interactive introductions to the Gospels.

79. Bevans, "Book Review: Come and See," 44.

have been much slower to incorporate these dimensions of social reality into contextualization.[80] Andrew Prince writes that the debate on contextualization among evangelicals is now focused on specific cultures and religions in geographical areas in Asia, Africa, Europe, and Latin America.[81] There is almost no discussion on including the socioeconomic dimensions of society and its implications for contextualization.

Understanding context is critical in how the spiritual truth is communicated. Conversely, context influences how spiritual truth is perceived and understood – whether by theologians or by the poor. The hermeneutics of liberation theology is an example of context influencing how the Bible is read and understood, and as a result how God is perceived. Brazilian theologians Leonardo and Clodovis Boff identify the rise of nationalistic consciousness and significant industrial development that benefited the urban middle class but marginalized large segments of the peasants in the rural areas or in sprawling urban slums as being among the social and political roots out of which liberation theology evolved.[82] This context influences how Scripture is read with the Exodus as the lens through which reality and theology are understood. For them, liberation is God's central desire for the poor and the oppressed.

Besides the emergence of liberation theology in Latin America, the post-World War II era with new political, economic, and social contexts saw former colonized societies and anticolonial Western thinkers try to find their voice and reflect on the relevance of God and biblical revelation in these new contexts. The 1990s marked the beginning of postcolonial theology.[83] They used the insights and tools from postcolonial political theory to state that the understanding of God, Christ, human beings, and the church are integrally linked with the way imperialism dominated indigenous people by creating and maintaining a certain type of society. Interestingly, postcolonial theologies find no place in Bevan's *Models of Contextual Theology* or other similar texts,[84]

---

80. Evangelicals acknowledged the reality of economics and politics as elements that oppress the poor and perpetuate poverty with the "1973 Chicago Declaration of Evangelical Social Concern" led by Ron Sider, Carl Henry, Jim Wallis, Bernard Ramm, Richard Mouw, Samuel Escobar, John Perkins, and others. This acknowledgement led to programs of social justice and poverty alleviation. However, Chicago 1973 was not a document on theological and missiological contextualization, but rather addressed the question of what constitutes mission and social ethics.

81. Prince, *Contextualization of the Gospel*, Kindle Location 1752–57.

82. Boff and Boff, *Introducing Liberation Theology*, 66–69.

83. See Kwan, *Postcolonial Resistence and Asian Theologies* for a detailed overview of the key theologians and the issues they addressed.

84. Kwan, 10.

partly because postcolonial theologians were not always indigenous to the newly liberated countries but also included Western critics of colonialism.[85] However, postcolonial theology is a contextual theology because it emerged from the new political, social, and economic realities of postcolonialism which influence their perception of spiritual truth.

The early twentieth century (post-World War I) also saw the emergence of Asian and African theologians grappling with the relevance of the uniqueness of Christ and the revelation of God in their religiously pluralistic contexts.[86] Most notable among them were M. M. Thomas in India and Japanese theologian Kosuke Koyama working in Thailand. Thomas, writing within the context of the debates in the WCC of how to relate to the major non-Christian religions, stated that God was not reaching from outside a particular society to bring about his purposes, but through history he had been at work in India through the Hindu renaissance (for example, the *Brahmosamaj* movement) and the growth of secularism in India.[87] He referred to the hidden Christ now being revealed through these events in history.[88] Koyama's water buffalo theology is similar to Thomas' theology in that it starts with an awareness of God already at work in history. Koyama did not believe in transplanting one's faith and then adjusting it to the local context, but "in locating the *living seed* of faith" in a local context and then guarding, watering, and nurturing it till it is rooted in the context and culture.[89]

---

85. Some of the key proponents and publications were Catherine Keller, Michael Nausner, and Mayra Riversa who edited *Postcolonial Theologies: Divinity and Empire*. Keller has published extensively in this area. Some of the other proponents include Reiger's *Christ and Empire* and theologians from the Majority World including Africans John Mbiti and Jesse Mugambi, Indian K. C. Abraham, and feminist theologian Kwok Pui-Lan, among others.

86. Among the African theologians, the most prominent is John Mbiti (also a postcolonial theologian).

87. Two of his most important publications (among others) are Thomas, *Acknowledged Christ of the Indian Renaissance*; and Thomas, "India: Towards an Indigenous Christian Theology."

88. Hesselgrave and Rommen, *Contextualization*, 73–79. While Thomas has theologically built on Farquhar's understanding of Christ's revelation within Hinduism, the challenge of Thomas' theology is that many critiques have wondered whether it has crossed the boundary into syncretism.

89. Koyama quoted in Hesselgrave and Rommen, *Contextualization*, 79–85, emphasis original. Koyama states that theology needs to be rooted in Thai history, in Thai cultural thinking, in Thai Buddhist life, and in a Christian lifestyle.

Christopher Wright states that calling such theologies "contextual" reflects certain attitudes of how existing systematic theology is understood.[90] He writes, "This term [contextual theologies] in itself betrayed the arrogant ethnocentricity of the West, for the assumption was that other places are contexts and they do their theology for those contexts; we, of course, have the real thing, the objective, contextless theology."[91]

Argentinian theologian Jose Miguel Bonino states that any theologian belongs to a specific culture, a social class or group, and a tradition, and as a result writes from within that context, influenced by human, social and historical realities.[92] He writes:

> Since theologians are human beings and not God, they must occupy one place in space and time. Theologians – perhaps even more than other thinkers – have claimed a sort of "extra-territoriality," a "location" outside or above the flux and conflicts of history. It is true that a theologian, like anybody else, who practices an intellectual discipline, lives in a special territory, defined by the presuppositions, the methods, the traditions of such discipline. No responsible theologian can vacate such location. But it is "a

---

90. An alternate term that emerged out of Europe and the UK, and that is now increasingly accepted in the US, is "intercultural theology." In the 1970s, Lutheran missiologist and ecumenist Hans Jochen Margull at Hamburg and Walter J. Hollenweger at Birmingham (both from Reformed and Pentecostal traditions) advocated a decolonized theology that would incorporate non-western and non-literary traditions. They were later joined by Roman Catholic missiologist and historian Richard Freidli at Fribourg. (Werner Ustoff, "Cultural Origins of 'Intercultural' Theology," 11–12.) Using the term "intercultural" implied (Ustoff refers to David Bosch) "the mutual process of theological giving and receiving that characterizes the history of Christianity in its post-colonial and polycentric period." Ustoff, "Cultural Origins of 'Intercultural' Theology," 14. In contrast, contextual theologies are unique to specific contexts and do not necessarily relate and interact with other theologies. Ustoff describes the difference. "Intercultural theology was not designed to 'parade the liveliness of non-western Christianity as a model in front of Europe's "dead" Christianity,' but rather was meant to be an agent of change and liberation in Western Christianity by challenging the pseudo-certainty of ossified Church traditions in the West." Ustoff, 21.

91. Wright, *Mission of God*, 42. Wright continues, "This assumption is being rightly challenged, and the West is seen for what it is – a particular context of human culture, not necessarily any better or any worse than any other context for reading the Bible and doing theology."

92. Jose Miguel Bonino, formerly at the Institute of Higher Theological Studies in Buenos Aires, Argentina, and a former president of the World Council of Churches. A Protestant, he was a contemporary of Gustavo Gutiérrez and the other pioneers of liberation theology. It is important to recognize that there were Protestant theologians in Latin America asking similar question about social injustice and poverty. Many of them have been identified in Wagner, *Latin American Theology*.

place within a place" i.e. in the context of a wider reality defined by the historical coordinates.[93]

Only by being aware of their social location can theologians then look at it critically.[94] It would be naïve to believe that anyone could read the Scriptures without the lenses of their own culture, gender, social and economic status, life experiences, ethnicity, season of life, political ideology, and value system. Trinity Lutheran Seminary professor Mark Allan Powell gives an example of life experiences influencing how one reads the Bible. He had his American students read Luke 15:11–31, the parable of the prodigal son, close their Bibles, and then retell the story as faithfully as possible to their student partner. Powell notes that not a single one of his students mentioned the famine in Luke 15:14. Sometime later while teaching in St. Petersburg, Russia, he asked fifty participants to do the same: forty-two of the fifty mentioned the famine.

Why the difference? The Russians remembered or had been told firsthand of the Nazi siege of the city (then known as Leningrad) during World War II when 670,000 died from starvation. Their experience and memory influenced how they read the Bible. Powell notes that for the Russians, the parable was about God rescuing them from a desperate circumstance. While for the American students who had never experienced a famine, the parable was about a disobedient son who repented and returned to his father, who in turn forgave him.[95]

Since the late 1970s, there has been a growing acknowledgement among theologians that context influences how God, Christ, the gospel, and spiritual reality are perceived. Socioeconomic and historical location and the perception of spiritual truth are integrally linked. Daniel Migliore emphasizes the need to be aware of context and values. He writes, "Confession of Jesus Christ takes place in particular historical and cultural contexts."[96] Philosopher Nassim Nicholas Taleb refers to this connection between perception and context as *domain specificity*. It means that a person's reactions, mode of thinking, and

---

93. Bonino, "Doing Theology in the Context of the Struggle of the Poor," 369–70.

94. Bonino, 370.

95. Powell, "Forgotten Famine," 265–74. Tabor Laughlin discusses the difference between Western and Chinese approaches to theology. Western theologians tend to systematize theology while Chinese theologians are not interested in systematic theology that has no contexts but focus on theology that is related to the issues that they face in their local and national contexts. Laughlin, "Western vs. Chinese Theology."

96. Migliore, *Faith Seeking Understanding*, 197.

intuition are dependent on the context in which the matter is presented.[97] Evolutionary psychologists call the context the "domain" of the object or event. Taleb writes, "We react to a piece of information not on its logical merits, but on the basis of which framework surrounds it, and how it registers with our social-emotional system."[98]

So while truth is universal, theology is contextual as it influences how we live out our faith and spirituality in a specific historical and social location.[99] Gustavo Gutiérrez highlights the influence of historical and political context on the leaders of the early church. "People today often talk about contextual theologies but, in point of fact, theology has always been contextual. . . . When Augustine wrote 'The City of God,' he was reflecting on what it meant for him and for his contemporaries to live the gospel within a specific context of serious historical transformations."[100]

Throughout church history, there have been different understandings of how Christ is understood within a specific context and culture, and their understanding is reflected in the various ways a believing community relates to their context. Richard Niebuhr's taxonomy on Christ and culture elaborates on this connection.[101] However, there are significant challenges when theology and context interact.[102] Douglas John Hall points out that a focus on a single dogmatic theology in its

------

97. Alongside all this debate has been the philosophical influence of postmodern perspectives, the belief that all truth claims are no more than individual or group perspectives on the issues in question, which has also been carried over into the exact sciences in discussions about the contextual nature of scientific hypothesis and discovery.

98. Taleb, *Black Swan*, 53.

99. Canadian theologian Douglas John Hall states that the challenge of relating systematic theology to context is in the very nature of what systematic theology is meant to be. He writes:

> Systematic or dogmatic theology has been slow to learn the lessons of contextuality, especially its place-component, and one cannot avoid the conclusion that a (if not the) predominant reason for this lies in the character of the enterprise as such. The very adjectives *systematic* and *dogmatic* . . . betray a predilection to permanency. It so easily happens that a . . . desire to "see the thing whole," to integrate, to describe connections, to honor the unity of the truth, and so on becomes, in its execution, an exercise in finality.

Hall, *Cross in Our Context*, 45.

100. Gutiérrez quoted in Hartnett, "Remembering the Poor," 12.

101. Niebuhr, *Christ and Culture*. Niebuhr's taxonomy positions Christ in relationship to culture: (1) Christ against culture; (2) Christ of culture; (3) Christ above culture; (4) Christ and culture in paradox; and (5) Christ the transformer of culture.

102. The reason theology will always struggle with the world is because there is a moral dimension rooted in a biblical worldview in theology's interaction with culture. The gospel will always confront the evil in culture and society. Paul Hiebert warns that contextualization is not

> reluctance to open itself to the great *variety* of worldly contexts . . . has again and again resisted criticism from the perspectives of those whose worlds were virtually ignored or excluded in the great systems of Christian thought. This is not a mere academic concern, for the excluded ones have not just been individuals, or tiny minorities but whole populations, whole races, whole economic and other groupings.[103]

While there has always been a concern for the poor within the church, the voices and concerns of the poor are among the large group of minorities who do not find a place in dogmatic theology.

The social and contextual "location" of theologians, states Bonino, regardless of whether they are academic theologians or the poor as agents in theology, significantly impacts their thinking and perspectives, and as a result their spiritual priorities. He states that perspective based on "location" will make some things visible while hiding other things from view. Bonino writes:

> Since poverty is the dominating reality in our world, a theologian who looks at the world from the social location of the rich will remain unavoidably blind to reality – she/he will ignore the deepest contradictions and conflicts of our world, the reality of the human condition of the majority of humankind, the depth of suffering and the persistence of hope. How can a theologian be able to articulate the meaning of God's word of grace, of judgment, of hope from such a perspective?[104]

---

an indiscriminate adopting of culture, customs, and values. He stresses the need for critical contextualization.

> The foreignness of the culture we add to the gospel offends and must be eliminated. But the gospel itself offends. It is supposed to offend, and we dare not weaken its offense. The gospel must be contextualized but it must remain prophetic. It must stand in judgment of what is evil in all cultures as well as in all persons.

Hiebert, *Anthropological Reflections on Missiological Issues*, 86.

103. Hall, *Cross in Our Context*, 48. Scottish missiologist Andrew Walls addresses this challenge through what he refers to as the "translation principle," when the gospel, the Good News of Jesus Christ, is communicated in different cultures and places. "Incarnation is translation. When God in Christ became man, divinity was translated into humanity. . . . The first divine act of translation thus gives rise to a constant succession of new translations. Christian diversity is the necessary product of the incarnation." Walls, *Missionary Movement in Christian History*, 27.

104. Bonino, "Doing Theology in the Context of the Struggle of the Poor," 371.

The perspective of theologians based on their social location and context will determine their priority for reflection. Bonino states that no theologian, whether it be Thomas Aquinas or Karl Barth, is able to understand the full depth of human need and express the totality of God's revelation. Their "location" will determine the priority of what is worth thinking about (he uses German philosopher Martin Heidegger's expression *denkwürdige*[105]) and what is secondary, superfluous, and alienating. Bonino writes,

> Thus, perspective does not simply give us a global view of reality but it helps to define an "agenda." The emphasis given by third world theologians to the ministry of Jesus, to the prophetic tradition in Scripture, to the eschatological perspective, to discipleship – over against, for instance, the "subjective" themes characteristic of nineteenth century liberal theology – illustrate this point.[106]

Poverty is an all-consuming life experience for the poor in their daily struggle to survive. It is not something that is shared with other sections of society or even understood by them. Chilean sociologist Samuel Palma Manriquez writes, "To the poor, poverty means more than scarcity of goods or lack of access to basic services; poverty is a way of being in society; it is a biographical experience, a 'life experience.'"[107] The poor have their own priorities for reflection and how they view spiritual reality because of their life experiences arising out of their social and economic location. Their views need to be acknowledged and affirmed by the church as valid spiritual expectations and expressions. However, because of a very narrow definition of context and culture by evangelicals, the world of the poor has not been acknowledged as unique with its own cultures, worldviews, values, and expectations.

Ethne, Homogenous Units, and the Contexts of the Poor as Distinct

Evangelical missional thinking has moved from understanding the Greek word *ethne* in Matthew 28:19 translated as "nations" – political or geographical entities as envisaged in early modern Protestant missions – to meaning ethnic or people groups. This shift then provided the biblical foundation for the growing awareness of the uniqueness of each context and that the gospel and

---

105. *Denkwürdige* literally means "memorable" or "important."
106. Bonino, "Doing Theology in the Context of the Struggle of the Poor," 371.
107. Manriques, "Religion of the People and Evangelism," 36.

spiritual truth need to be communicated in ways that people understand. The concept of *ethne* and the homogenous unit principle (HUP) that developed out of it have probably had the most significant impact on evangelical missional strategy and the recent focus on contextualization than anything else.

The Greek word *ethnos* is used in the New Testament 161 times and is translated as "Gentiles" eighty-four times. Sixty-three times it is translated "nation," six times "people," six times "pagan," and one time each as "country" and "heathen." The Gospel writer Matthew uses the word as "nation" seven times and as "Gentiles" five times.[108] The earliest use of the word is found in the Septuagint in Genesis 18:18 where the phrase "all the nations" is *panta ta ethne*, the same as in Matthew 28:19. Classical scholar H. G. Liddell in *A Lexicon: Abridged from Liddell and Scott's Greek-English Lexicon* states that Plato, Xenophanes, and others used the word to mean a special class of people, a caste, or a tribe.[109] In the New Testament, the *Greek-English Lexicon of the New Testament and Other Early Christian Literature* defines the word as a group of people who are united by culture, common traditions, and kinship.[110] Biblical scholar Gerhard Kittel in the *Theological Dictionary of the New Testament* describes the word *ethnos* to mean "mass" or "host" or "multitude" bound by the same manners, customs, or other distinctive features.[111]

Indian Bible translators have translated the word *ethne* as *jati*, meaning community or caste, because each caste and subcaste is culturally distinct. The lowest castes are identified by their economic role in society and as a result have developed their own cultures. The lowest castes and the outcastes (Dalits) are among the poorest communities in India. The March 1982 Lausanne Strategy Working Group meeting in Chicago defined a people group (derived from an understanding of *ethne*) as "a significantly large grouping of individuals who perceive themselves to have a common affinity for one another because of their shared language, religion, ethnicity, residence, occupation, class or caste, situation, etc., or combinations of these." For evangelistic purposes, it is "the largest group within which the gospel can spread as a church-planting movement without encountering barriers of understanding or acceptance."[112] Jim Haney writes that the meaning of the word *ethnos* is very broad and should

---

108. Bush, "Meaning of Ethne in Matthew 28:19," 31.

109. Liddell quoted in Bush, "Meaning of Ethne in Matthew 28:19," 32.

110. *Greek-English Lexicon of the New Testament and Other Early Christian Literature* quoted in Bush, 34.

111. Gerhard Kittel quoted in Bush, 34.

112. The report of the March 1982 Lausanne Strategy Working Group quoted in Bush, 35.

not be limited by our categories and understanding. With this understanding, he says (along with Donald McGavran) that the castes and subcastes of Hinduism are to be included in the understanding of *ethnos* and people groups.[113] What was not recognized by missiologists is that castes and subcastes are not merely social classifications in society resulting in distinctive cultures, but they also incorporate economic dimensions which identify certain subcastes to specific economic functions. The lower castes and outcastes, as a result, often live in poverty which defines their daily lives as much as their religion, traditions, rituals, and language.

The idea of *ethne* was the basis of McGavran's 1955 book *The Bridges of God*[114] and the concept of the homogenous unit principle (HUP). The origins of HUP can be traced back to McGavran's work in India and his association with J. Waskom Pickett. As a missionary in India, McGavran had been frustrated by the rigidness of the Hindu caste system, and he writes, "Men like to become Christians without crossing racial, linguistic, or class barriers."[115] Along with Pickett and A. L. Warnshuis of the International Missionary Council, McGavran first published *Church Growth and Group Conversions* in 1938.[116] For McGavran, the concept of "all the nations" (*panta ta ethne*) is not just political entities but includes tribes, castes, and languages, and is the biblical foundation for his strategy of using "people groups" for church growth. *HUP was a strategy for evangelism and church planting and was never intended to be a paradigm that could be used in contextualization.*

Chuck Van Engen quotes McGavran in defining HUP.

> . . . a section of society in which all the members have some characteristics in common. Thus a homogeneous unit might be a political unit or subunit, the characteristic in common being that all the members live within certain geographical confines. . . . The homogeneous unit is an elastic concept, its meaning depending on the context in which it is used.[117]

Peter Wagner expands on this definition.

> Such a section of society (HU) can be a culture or language, a tribe or caste, a clan or geographical unit. The members of a

---

113. Haney, "Meaning of Ethnos in Matthew 28:19," 33.
114. McGavran, *Bridges of God.*
115. McGavran, *Understanding Church Growth*, 223.
116. Van Engen, "Is the Church for Everyone?," 11.
117. McGavran quoted in Van Engen, 13.

> homogeneous unit think of themselves as enjoying a common bond of unity, simultaneously feeling different from others. The term is also frequently used as an adjective, such as in homogeneous unit church, meaning a church characterized by having members of just one social group.[118]

The debate around homogenous units is whether God's intention for society is one of unity or plurality.[119] Peter Wagner refers to the tower of Babel and people being scattered across the globe and speaking different languages as evidence of God's objective of diversifying the human race that he had created. Wagner does not see this diversifying as a result of human sin but a fulfillment of God's command in Genesis 1:28 to "Be fruitful and increase in number; fill the earth."[120] McGavran is simply stating the obvious when he writes, "The distinctions of education, wealth, poverty, colour, and occupation will remain but these will be seen to be minor."[121]

There has been considerable support within the missiological community for HUP as a missional strategy.[122] They state that God values cultural and ethnic diversity as evidenced in passages such as John 3:16 (God loves all the world); Genesis 10 (the inclusion of the Table of Nations); 2 Chronicles 6:32–33 (v. 33 "so that all the peoples of the earth may know your name"); Isaiah 56:6–7 and Mark 11:17 (the temple would be a house of prayer for all nations); and Revelation 5:9; 7:9 (every tribe, language, people, and nation).[123] Part of the appeal of HUP is that it describes the reality of a fragmented world today with its diversity of languages, migrant and ethnic groups, cultures, etc. and provides a strategy for contextualization, evangelism, and church planting. McGavran writes,

> The one world we often speak of is made up of numerous ethnic units, suddenly brought close together but not yet fused into one race. Nor are they likely to be so fused in the near future. . . . The

---

118. Wagner, *Our Kind of People*, 64.

119. This section will not discuss in detail the merits or challenges of such issues as the homogenous unit principle and people groups. There is considerable research and publications on these issues.

120. Wagner, *Our Kind of People*, 111.

121. McGavran, *Momentous Decision in Missions Today*, 98.

122. For example, see Wagner, *Church Growth and the Whole Gospel*, 180, where Wagner states that the Southern Baptists (with the largest North American mission agency – International Mission Board) have wholeheartedly embraced HUP.

123. Van Engen, "Is the Church for Everyone?," 2–4.

hard fact is . . . that by far the largest number of *growing* churches are growing *in* some tribe or segment of society.[124]

While there is validity in the concept of homogeneity within specific subcastes in India and tribes and clans in Asia, Africa, and elsewhere, translating the concept into urbanized and particularly Westernized contexts which value individualism has been a challenge. The closest parallels of HUs are migrant and ethnic churches which are based on national or regional language and culture rather than smaller homogenous ethnic units. Chuck Van Engen refers to the cultural blindness of Western culture and churches and the homogeneity of Western white culture(s) and their relations to ethnic and migrant communities when he writes, "Western, WASPS [White Anglo-Saxon Protestant] culture is itself a particular contextualization of the gospel and a specific and particular cultural context for the gospel in relation to multiple cultures and ethnicities in the North American reality."[125] Without this recognition, the concept of the HUs is weakened.

There has been significant criticism of the HUP.[126] Basing their argument on Ephesians 2:11–22 and Galatians 3:28, most critics argue for the unity Christ brings by removing the various barriers and dividing walls of hostility between God and human beings, and between human beings. They see the biblical model as multiethnic and multicultural congregations.[127] Missiologist Orlando Costas writes,

> The fellowship of faith (the church) is . . . a sign of the coming kingdom. If the kingdom of God represents the definitive reconciliation between God and humanity, between individuals, peoples, sexes, generations, and races, and between humanity and the rest of creation – a promise that will be fulfilled in the second coming of Christ – then the community of God's people is an

---

124. McGavran, "Wrong Strategy, the Real Crisis in Mission," 451–61. This quotation is taken from the reprinted version of the article in McGavran, ed., *Crucial Issues in Mission Tomorrow*, 103–6.

125. Van Engen, "Is the Church for Everyone?," 29.

126. Interestingly, since the early debates on the validity of the HUP as a missional strategy, there have been no further nor recent discussions on the topic other than whether insider movements, a specific elaboration of the HUP within the contexts of the major religions, are biblical or not.

127. Some of the most prominent missiologists who have responded critically to the HUP from a variety of perspectives (for and against) are Bosch, "Church Growth Missiology," 13–24; Gibbs, *I Believe in Church Growth*; Glasser, "Church Growth at Fuller," 401–20; Padilla, "The Unity of the Church," 289–302; Fong, "Critique of the Homogeneous Unit Principle."

> overriding necessity, in order that the world might understand
> what the salvation that God offers in the gospel really is.[128]

The only nonbiblical and nontheological critique of the HUP is by sociologist Wayne McClintok, who provides a sociological critique. Being a missionary with Interserve, he starts with a biblical critique. He challenges McGavran's statement in *Bridges of God* that the New Testament churches were monoethnic in character. McClintok refers to a journal article by David Smith stating that from all evidence, the churches that Paul founded included people from diverse backgrounds and all levels of society.[129]

McClintok's first critique is that HUs are defined too loosely as having a common language or culture and shared geographical location, political unit, tribe, caste, or clan. There are no membership criteria, and therefore it is hard to have any objective measure to determine the social boundaries between members and nonmembers. It is left up to the field person to determine these. Second, McClintok states that McGavran's assumptions follow those of the structural-functional school of anthropology, which tends to view the basic units of social organization (village, ethnic group, etc.) as isolated entities, ignoring the complex web of relationships and interactions members of the group have with people outside the unit. The wider social and economic contexts influence the group and how it changes over time. Third, structural-functionalists have a static view of history and don't consider the process of social change. Once a social group has been studied at a point in time, that point then becomes how the group is defined, not accounting for the changes that have occurred since. A fourth critique is the simplistic analysis of class structure. Class structures vary across cultures and are a complex mix of social, political, and economic relationships. So McGavran's call to disciple the masses and promote people movements will require a much more detailed and nuanced analysis of a specific context than what McGavran proposes. Fifth, while he has not defined the boundaries of HUs, McGavran, along with other structural-functionalists, believes that geographical and social isolation is critical in maintaining cultural diversity. These geographical and social boundaries are not static, as people move in and out of them on a regular basis. Such isolation is only possible in remote rural and tribal areas.

---

128. Costas, *Christ Outside the Gate*, 32.

129. McClintok, "Sociological Critque of the Homogenous Unit Principle," 108; Smith, "Church Growth Principles of Donald McGavran," 25–30.

One of the important observations that McClintok makes which has relevance to this book is that the concept of HUs disregards the economic dimensions of social structures. He writes:

> He [McGavran] discusses the elite or power structure and land rights but fails to recognize the important consequences that the organization of the means of production, distribution, and exchange have for both the overall quality of life and the distribution of wealth within a particular society. Access to such vital human needs as food, clothing and shelter are regulated by the manner in which the economic system is organized. A wholistic approach to mission, therefore, should concern itself with the economic dimensions of social structure.[130]

While McGavran's definition of HUs does not acknowledge the economic dimensions of social structures, the Lausanne Theology and Education Group that met in Pasadena in 1977 to discuss HUP in its statement includes economics as one of the bonds that holds certain groups together.[131]

Acknowledging the criticisms of the HUP, Wagner states that it is a *principle and strategy in evangelism* and is not to be understood as being normative for Christian nurture and maturity. "The homogeneous unit principle should be regarded as a penultimate spiritual dynamic. . . . The ultimate is that believers are all one in the Body of Christ, and the more this is manifested in a tangible way, the better."[132] While the cultural and social dimensions of each context have been acknowledged for some time now because of the work of Kraft, Nida, Hiebert, and others, the reality of cultures of poverty is only now gaining traction.

Is There a Culture of Poverty that Requires Contextualization?

The literature on contextualization in Christian mission shows that the social and cultural (including religious) contexts of people influence *how* and *who* they perceive God to be and how they practice their spirituality.[133] So, do

---

130. McClintok, "Sociological Critique of the Homogenous Unit Principle," 116.

131. Quoted in Stott, *Making Christ Known*, 61.

132. Wagner, *Church Growth and the Whole Gospel*, 167–68.

133. Some of the key publications on this topic are Jones, *Christ of the Indian Road*; Farquhar, *Crown of Hinduism*; Niebuhr, *Christ and Culture*; WEA Global Review Panel, *Report to World Evangelical Alliance*; Lee, "God's Asian Names; Kwan, *Postcolonial Resistance and Asian Theologies*; Thomas, *Acknowledged Christ of the Indian Renaissance*; Thomas, "India: Towards an

socioeconomic and political factors in some way also influence people to perceive God in certain ways? More fundamentally, is there a culture of poverty, and how does it impact the lives of the poor?

Anthropologist Oscar Lewis, based on his studies of urban slums in Mexico and Puerto Rico,[134] coined the term "culture of poverty" to describe a set of seventy values, beliefs, and cultural attitudes (some refer to them as traits) across four dimensions: (1) the attitudes, values, and character structure of the individual; (2) the nature of the family; (3) the nature of the slum community; and (4) the community's relation to society.[135] These values, attitudes, and beliefs result from sustained poverty and in turn perpetuate in future generations even if the social and economic structural conditions change. Two specific sets of characteristics Lewis identifies are first that people with a culture of poverty have a strong sense of helplessness, of dependency, of marginality, and of not belonging. Second, they have very little sense of history. Being rooted in their neighborhoods and consumed by issues in their own lives, they have no sense of others in the world experiencing similar problems.[136]

Daniel Patrick Moynihan, in his study of the African-American family in the US in 1965, arrived at similar conclusions that the cumulative effects of slavery and subsequent structural poverty experienced by African Americans resulted in a "tangle of pathologies" which were similar to Lewis' culture of

---

Indigenous Christian Theology"; Iyadurai, *Transformative Religious Experience*; Hilderbrand, "What Led Thai Buddhist Background Believers," 400–415; Bonino, "Doing Theology in the Context of the Struggle of the Poor"; Powell, "Forgotten Famine"; and Richardson, *Peace Child*.

134. Lewis, *Five Families*; Oscar Lewis, *La Vida*.

135. Lewis describes a culture of poverty as having

> a structure, a rationale, and defense mechanisms without which the poor could hardly carry on. In short, it is a way of life, remarkably stable and persistent, passed down from generation to generation along family lines. The culture of poverty has its own modalities and distinctive social and psychological consequences for its members. It is a dynamic factor which affects participation in the large national culture and becomes a subculture of its own.

Lewis, "Culture of Poverty," 150. American educator Ruby K. Payne states that there are differences in the culture, attitudes, behavior, and relationships between the poor, the middle class, and the wealthy, which she identifies in a chart. Payne, *Framework for Understanding Poverty*, 42–43. As with Lewis's concept of a culture of poverty, Payne's framework has been critiqued extensively.

136. Lewis, "Culture of Poverty," 170. Lewis writes, "They are like aliens in their own country, convinced that the existing institutions do not serve their interests and needs. Along with this feeling of powerlessness is a widespread feeling of inferiority, of personal unworthiness."

poverty.[137] However, Lewis differentiates between impoverishment and a culture of poverty. The lower middle class who may experience periodic bouts of poverty may become impoverished but do not have a culture of poverty. Similarly, he describes the Jews who lived in poverty in Eastern Europe as not having a culture of poverty because they had a tradition of literacy, a common heritage, religious beliefs, and had a sense of identification with Jews elsewhere.[138]

While the concept was used extensively by the US government in the 1960s and 1970s in the development of social policy,[139] ever since its publication, the concept of a culture of poverty has been criticized extensively.[140] A widely stated criticism is that it puts the blame for poverty on individuals and families and ignores the socioeconomic and political structural dimensions of poverty. More specifically, research has shown that there is a wide variety of ways people cope with poverty and that there is no one culture of poverty that is homogenous across all contexts globally.[141] Rather than looking for a set of traits and values that are common in all contexts of poverty, there should be comparison and analysis of individual traits and values shared by the poor and the nonpoor.[142]

Other studies have shown that there are theoretical inconsistencies in Lewis' theory in developing a more thorough understanding of the factors that produce and sustain poverty. There is a need especially to analyze in greater detail and accuracy how the poor make sense of and explain their current conditions, options, and decisions.[143] Finally, there is no consensus as to what is meant by culture when discussing a culture of poverty.[144] What all the empirical studies show is that there may be a high degree of cultural homogeneity within small groups of poor in specific contexts, but this homogeneity cannot be

---

137. Daniel Patrick Moynihan, "The Negro Family: The Case For National Action" (Washington DC, Office of Policy Planning and Research, U.S. Department of Labour: 1965). Often referred to as the "Moynihan Report."

138. Lewis, "Culture of Poverty," 170.

139. Chilman writes about the implications of the concept on US public social policy. "From the available evidence, it seems clear that changes in subcultural patterns of a number of very poor people are probably indicated as one of a number of measures designed to facilitate upward mobility for themselves and their children. Unfortunately, planned changes in culture patterns are extremely difficult to effect." Chilman, *Growing Up Poor*, 17.

140. Rodman, "Lower Class Value Stretch," 270–85; Valentine, "Culture of Poverty" 193–225; Roach and Gursslin, "Evaluation of the Concept 'Culture of Poverty,'" 383–92; Leeds, "Concept of the 'Culture of Poverty,'" 226–84.

141. Portes, "Social Capital," 1–24; Ulf Hannerz, *Soulside*; Small, *Villa Victoria*.

142. Valentine, *Culture and Poverty*, 114–15.

143. Valentine.

144. Small, Harding, and Link, "Introduction: Reconsidering Culture and Poverty," 11.

extrapolated to all the poor in any context regardless of race or ethnicity to support a theory of a culture of poverty.[145]

While a homogenous culture of poverty may not exist across all contexts, poverty does have a significant physical, psychological, and sociological impact on most who live in extreme and chronic poverty. Evidence suggests that poverty affects the cognitive functions of poor adults.[146] However, the greatest impact is on children. There is strong evidence that poor nutrition as a result of extreme and chronic poverty affects the physical and cognitive development of infants and young children.[147] The development of children and adolescents growing up in chronic poverty lags behind those from more privileged homes.[148] Empirical evidence also suggests that extreme chronic poverty affects areas of the brain in young children responsible for the working memory, impulse regulation, and visuospatial, language, and cognitive development. This impact is usually the result of factors in their environment such as exposure to toxins, chronic stress, chronic exposure to substandard cognitive skills, and impaired emotional-social relationships.[149] According to research on risk and resilience of children, during the preschool, kindergarten, and primary years of schooling, there is a high correlation between family income and academic success.[150]

A review of the existing social science literature on the psychological impact of poverty reveals that in general, people have negative attitudes, emotions, and stereotypes toward people in poverty and identify them as an out group. This view is seen in language used to describe the poor, resulting in more negative stereotyping, which also affects how the poor perceive themselves and their abilities as somehow diminished human beings.[151] Other research states that those in the lowest socioeconomic category are between two and five times more likely to be diagnosed with a psychiatric disorder than those in the wealthier economic categories. Research also shows that unemployment significantly increases the risk of various psychiatric disorders including phobias, functional psychosis, drug dependence, depressive episodes, generalized anxiety disorder,

145. Coward, Feagin, and Williams, Jr., "Culture of Poverty Debate," 624.

146. Mani, et al., "Poverty Impedes Cognitive Function," 976–80. Also Fell and Hewstone, *Psychological Perspectives on Poverty*, 28–30.

147. Martorell, "Undernutrition during Pregnancy and Early Childhood."

148. Misra and Mohanty, "Consequences of Poverty and Disadvantage," 121–48.

149. Noble, Norman, and Farah, "Neurocognitive Correlates of Socioeconomic Status," 74–78.

150. Van Ijzendoorn, et al., "Assessing Attachment Security," 1188–1213.

151. Fell and Hewstone, *Psychological Perspectives on Poverty*.

and obsessive-compulsive disorder. Also confirmed by research, poverty is strongly correlated with increased incidence of problematic drug and alcohol use and related mortality.[152] In the psychology of scarcity, cognitive resources such as attention and self-control are limited.[153] Further empirical evidence indicates that poverty results in stress and negative emotional states "which in turn may lead to short-sighted and risk-averse decision-making, possibly by limiting attention and favoring habitual behaviors at the expense of goal-directed ones. Together, these relationships may constitute a feedback loop that contributes to the perpetuation of poverty."[154]

The sociological impact of poverty is also considerable. Poverty increases the risk of weakening social relations and decreasing civic and political participation resulting in a "downward spiral of social exclusion" as it shrinks their social networks and access to social capital that could help them find jobs and other socioeconomic support.[155] More families in poverty tend to be "broken" than those who are not poor, with death being the primary cause for involuntary family dissolution. Considerably more poor families tend to be female headed households. The poor live in significantly poorer quality housing, are more likely to be in unskilled jobs, have unemployment in the family, and have serious money problems.[156] Other research provides evidence that about 35 percent of poor families experienced six or more risk factors such as eviction, divorce, or sickness.[157]

What is evident from existing research is that there may not be a homogenous, universal culture of poverty as Oscar Lewis suggested. While there may not be differences in language and religion, poverty has a unique physical, sociological, and psychological impact on the poor in any specific location which shapes their behavior, values, priorities, worldview, and spirituality, thus making the context and culture of the poor in that location different than that of the nonpoor surrounding them.

---

152. Fell and Hewstone.

153. Mullainathan, "Psychology of Poverty," 19–22.

154. Haushofer and Fehr, "On the Psychology of Poverty," 862–67.

155. Mood and Jonsson, "Social Consequences of Poverty," 1–20; Coward, Feagin, and Williams, "Culture of Poverty Debate," 626.

156. Coward, Feagin, and Williams, "Culture of Poverty Debate," 627–30.

157. Graber and Brooks-Gunn, "Models of Development," 18–25.

Context and the Spiritual World of the Poor

An important part of any culture is not only the rituals and celebrations of their religion, but the spiritual world they inhabit which is then reflected in their worldview and spiritual priorities. For the poor, how does poverty intersect with their spirituality?

There is a growing acknowledgement that there is an integral link between poverty and spirituality and this acknowledgement is not linked to a specific religion. Research by a Gallup poll found that religion has a functional role in the lives of those in the poorest countries as it helps them cope with the daily struggles of providing for themselves and their families.[158] Another multicountry study found that personal insecurity evidenced by income inequality was an important determinant of religiosity.[159] An extensive study in North America on socioeconomic status (SES) and beliefs about God in everyday life found that individuals from poorer communities professed higher levels of divine involvement and control in their everyday lives compared with individuals with a higher socioeconomic status.[160]

Poverty is not just a socioeconomic reality and a denial of human rights. With the interconnectedness between poverty and spirituality, there is a growing awareness of the spiritual dimensions of poverty. Just as the individual is foundational in a rights-based approach to poverty,[161] a biblical understanding of poverty is based on the intrinsic worth of individuals because

---

158. Gallup in researching in 114 countries found that 98 percent of the population in ten of the poorest countries in the world with per capita incomes below $5,000 stated that religion was an important part of their lives. This finding is in contrast with those in the richest countries with average per capita incomes higher than $25,000, where 47 percent indicated that religion is important to them. Cited in Steve Crabtree, "Religiosity Highest in World's Poorest Nations."

159. Countries with shorter life expectancy, higher infant mortality, higher rates of violent crime, higher abortion rates, and less peace (all indicators of poverty) had higher than average levels of personal religiosity, which was measured by the frequency of prayer. Rees, "Is Personal Insecurity a Cause," 1–26.

160. Schieman, "Socioeconomic Status and Beliefs," 25–51. While the higher SES individuals "practiced" their religion by being involved in religious activities, those from lower SES were more likely to "believe" in their religion and that God was involved in their lives regardless of whether they were involved in religious activities or not. One interesting insight is that in countries where there is marked inequality, the wealthy are attracted to religion because the religions can justify their "elevated" positions. Tobin Grant at *Christianity Today* quotes Tomas Rees who states that their research "is the first really solid, empirical evidence that the rich use religion as a tool to keep the poor in their place." Grant, "Religion and Inequality Go Hand-in-Hand."

161. Boesen and Martin, *Applying a Rights-Based Approach.*

they are created in the image of God.[162] Wanting to highlight this intrinsic dignity in contexts of oppressive poverty, the All India Congress on Mission and Evangelism in Madras, India, in 1977 stated that evangelicals needed to "define and defend [the image of God in the poor] . . . identify violations of human rights and assist the victims in obtaining their legitimate rights."[163] Poverty disfigures the image of God in human beings and does not allow them to live with dignity. Since human beings bear his image and likeness, God has a stake in how humans are treated.[164] Mother Teresa was often misunderstood when she would state that she saw Christ in the poor. She was able to see through the dirt, filth, brokenness, and poverty of those who had been abandoned the image of God, in spite of it being marred.[165]

The Bible has much to say about the causes of poverty. While there are warnings against laziness leading to poverty and destitution, the main reason for poverty in ancient Israel and in New Testament Palestine was social injustice.[166] There is a distinction between individual sinfulness and the sinfulness and evil of parts of the social order which oppress and marginalize individuals and whole communities. Walter Rauschenbausch writes:

> The individualistic gospel has taught us to see the sinfulness of every human heart and has inspired us with faith in the willingness and power of God to save every soul that comes to him. But it has

---

162. John Stott affirmed the divine worth of each individual in his commentary on the Lausanne Covenant as the basis to address poverty and social injustice. "It is the divine image in man which gives him *an intrinsic dignity* or worth, a worth which belongs to all human beings." Stott, *Lausanne Covenant*, 27, emphasis original.

163. Sugden, *Radical Discipleship*, 186.

164. Laniak, *Finding the Lost Images of God*, 48.

165. "Seeing the face of God in everything, everyone, everywhere, all the time, and seeing His hand in everything. Seeing and adoring the presence of Jesus . . . in the distressing disguise of the poor." Mother Teresa, *In the Heart of the World*, Kindle Location 223. Mother Teresa is supposed to have said every time she pulled a beggar from the gutter that she saw Jesus Christ. She was anchored in Matthew 25:35–40:

> "For I was hungry and you gave me something to eat, I was thirsty and you gave me something to drink, I was a stranger and you invited me in, I needed clothes and you clothed me, I was sick and you looked after me, I was in prison and you came to visit me."
>
> Then the righteous will answer him, "Lord, when did we see you hungry and feed you, or thirsty and give you something to drink? When did we see you a stranger and invite you in, or needing clothes and clothe you? When did we see you sick or in prison and go to visit you?"
>
> The King will reply, "Truly I tell you, whatever you did for one of the least of these brothers and sisters of mine, you did for me."

166. Das, *Compassion and the Mission of God*, 43–86.

not given us an adequate understanding of the sinfulness of the social order and its share in the sins of all individuals within it. It has not evoked faith in the will and power of God to redeem the permanent institutions of human society from their inherited guilt of oppression and extortion. Both our sense of sin and our faith in salvation have fallen short of the realities under its teaching.[167]

Sinfulness of the social order imbedded in institutions – banks, churches, governments, corporations, the military, and others – may in effect represent a far more insidious evil that is more likely to abuse power and is usually more resistant to change.[168] There are social, legal, and economic structures in society that have been corrupted or are unjust and inherently evil. These may be in the form of deeply imbedded social and religious attitudes and practices, or legal and economic systems and institutions that discriminate against the poor, specific groups, and individuals. Racism, apartheid, communalism, nationalism, sexual exploitation, female genital mutilation, political oppression, hyper patriotism, human trafficking, poverty, discrimination, social marginalization, and ethnic cleansing are just some examples of how these socially imbedded attitudes surface in everyday life.

It is important to note that social institutions and systems are not inherently evil. God allows the creation of civil, socioeconomic, and legal institutions and systems for his purposes. These institutions and systems are given by God in order to bless human beings with peace and security and to enable them to prosper – the humanizing purposes of God.[169] However, "an institution becomes demonic when it abandons its divine vocation[170]– that of a ministry of justice or a ministry of social welfare – for the pursuit of its own

---

167. Rauschenbausch, *Theology for the Social Gospel*, 5.

168. Niebuhr, *Moral Man and Immoral Society*.

169. Wink, *Engaging the Powers*, 72. These institutions and systems are what Wink says are described in Colossians 1:16–17 as "thrones or powers or rulers or authorities."

170. Heim describes what this "demonization," the perversion of what is good, looks like:

> Nothing that God has created is protected from this demonization. Everything can be seized by it. Therefore, there is demonic self-adulation of the ego, the image of God; a demonic sexuality of which man [sic.] is no longer the master; the demonism of technology; the demonism of power, the demonic degeneration of nationalism. There is demonism of piety, and prayer itself can get lost in demonic convulsion. . . . The satanic element in the matter lies in this: the demonic power depends entirely on God and what he has created. It possesses nothing that does not come from God. Whatever is demonized and turned against God is always but a distorted image of the glory of God.

Karl Heim quoted in Georg E. Vicedom, *Mission of God*, 19.

idolatrous goals."[171] What God had intended for his purposes becomes warped and corrupted by misuse of power and greed. The "spiritual interiority" of the socioeconomic and political systems and structures are *god-complexes*. These god-complexes keep the poor in captivity and powerless. They are

- Clusters of power (social, economic, bureaucratic, political, and religious) within the domain of poverty relationships that render themselves absolute to keep the poor powerless;
- A function of structures, systems, people, and spiritual interiority within each cluster of power.[172]

Liberation theology has understood salvation as God using human agents in history to address socioeconomic and political injustice. The exploitation and economic and political dependence that the poor in Latin America were forced into caused some Catholics to reflect on the relevance of their faith in such a context. "The theology of liberation developed from this reflection. . . . The word 'liberation' was chosen for two basic reasons: it formed a direct contrast to the concept of dependence, and it had a long historical usage in biblical and church tradition as a synonym for salvation."[173] At the heart of liberation theology is the understanding that addressing poverty is not just about addressing social, political, and economic issues, but that God is working in and through history to bring justice and salvation to the poor (God's preferential option for the poor). "The theology of liberation is a theology of salvation in the concrete, historical, and political conditions of our day."[174] Poverty and injustice are spiritual issues as much as they are economic and political.

Any attempt to address poverty, seek social justice, and transform social systems without also addressing the spiritual nature of the institutions and systems is doomed to failure.[175] In trying to bring about social transformation, not only the practices and policies of the institutions that are not aligned with the values of God need to be changed, but the institutions themselves will also need to be redeemed, and the underlying values and attitudes prevalent in the institutions and systems (the spiritual interiority) will need to be addressed. "The political, economic, and social institutions of our complex society also have to be 'converted.'"[176]

---

171. Wink, *Engaging the Powers*, 72.

172. Christian, *God of the Empty-Handed*, 124–25.

173. Kirk, *Liberation Theology*, 26.

174. Gutiérrez, *Power of the Poor in History*, 63.

175. Wink, *Engaging the Powers*.

176. Nicholls, "Strategy Paper: The Relationship of Proclamation to Service," 3.

4

Is It Possible to Hear the Voices of the Poor?

The poor are the ones that tell us what the world is and what service the church must offer to the world.[1]

Archbishop Oscar Romero

Where Are the Voices of the Poor?

In all the theologizing about poverty and the poor, where are the voices of the poor themselves reading Scripture and describing their experience of God and understanding who he is? Secular community development researchers, as well as theologians and missiologists who have written extensively about poverty, are nonpoor outsiders who look into the world of the poor to describe the realities of poverty as they see and understand it. While there is value in their perspectives, they have not been balanced by what the poor themselves say about their socioeconomic reality and their spiritual lives. Robert Chambers, both an academic and a development practitioner, writes,

> The simple definition of the bad condition – poverty – is made, then, not by the poor, from their experience, but by the well-off, for their convenience. The need planners and academics have for a single scale of numbers narrows, distorts and simplifies their perceptions. Deprivation and poverty come to be defined, not by the changing and varied wants and needs of the poor, but by the static and standardized wants and needs of professionals.[2]

---

1. Romero, *Violence of Love*, 189.
2. Chambers, *Whose Reality Counts?*, 46.

Part of the challenge of listening to the poor is that they don't use the same language as the academic researcher or theologian. The question that academics have is whether the poor in the Majority World, who tend to be semiliterate and without academic training, are able to think abstractly and articulate in some cohesive manner spiritual concepts related to their spirituality and their experience of the divine. The "language" used by the poor and how they conceptualize spiritual reality is influenced by illiteracy or very low levels of literacy.

So, does illiteracy inhibit the ability to think abstractly, a requirement of theology? Professor of literature and languages Donna Dunbar-Odem writes that it used to be assumed that increased literacy was necessary to be able to think abstractly.[3] This assumption has been disproved by American cultural psychologist Sylvia Scribner's field research among the Vai people of West Africa.[4] What is now known is that people in oral cultures (including individuals who are illiterate) think differently. In the early twentieth century, anthropologist Franz Boas maintained that people from orally based cultures think like people from literacy based cultures but use different sets of categories.[5] The difference is as Dunbar-Odem describes, "Oral cultures tend to use concepts in situational, operational frames of reference that are minimally abstract in the sense that they remain close to the living human life world."[6] The implication of Dunbar-Odem's statement is that people who are illiterate can think abstractly but use physical references and objects in their world.

There are Christian traditions of listening to the voices of the poor and of the poor articulating their spiritual reality and yearnings. Liberation theologians (and proponents of the other liberation theologies that followed) identified injustice and oppression as the causes of poverty. They attempted to empower the poor by helping them understand and articulate the realities of poverty and marginalization that they experience, so that the poor could take responsibility for their liberation from the oppression of poverty.

---

3. Dunbar-Odem, *Defying the Odds*, 1.

4. Scribner and Cole, *Psychology of Literacy*.

5. Franz Boas cited in Dunbar-Odem, *Defying the Odds*, 50.

6. Dunbar-Odem, 49. This book will not discuss further the relationship between illiteracy and abstract thinking since there is research and literature on this topic. Considerable literature supports this observation, and the most significant include Luria, *Cognitive Development*; and Vygotsky, *Mind in Society: The Development of Higher Psychological Processes* (Cambridge, MA: Harvard University Press, 1978).

Glimpses of the Poor Theologizing

The poor having a voice is a fundamental part of empowerment in liberation theology. Often the ability of the poor to articulate their reality and experience has to be nurtured. This empowerment is referred to as *conscientization*, which is the process by which a person "[learns] to perceive social, political, and economic contradictions, and to take action against the oppressive elements of reality."[7] Each person, through a process of conscientization, wins the right to "say his own word, to name the world."[8] Richard Shaull writes about the value of conscientization.

> Every human being, no matter how "ignorant" or submerged in the "culture of silence" he may be, is capable of looking critically at his world in a dialogical encounter with others. Provided with the right tools for such encounter, he can gradually perceive his personal and social reality as well as the contradictions in it, become conscious of his own perceptions of that reality, and deal critically with it.[9]

Drawing on liberation theology's method of reflecting on Scripture, Ernesto Cardenal recorded the conversations of Nicaraguan peasants (*campesinos*) based on the day's reading of the gospel during their Sunday gatherings in the Solentiname archipelago and then documented them in *Gospel in Solentiname*. As the peasants struggled to understand what the gospel means, they spoke about their oppression by the rich and powerful capitalists and about their community of the lake and the islands, as well as the fishing, farming, and carpentry – all of which made Jesus real to them because these were his reference points, too. A discussion on Christ's teaching of the kingdom of God being like a mustard seed had an earthy reality because it is rooted in their rural context.

> Marcelino, with his calm voice, said: "I don't know about the mustard seed, but I do know about the *guasima* seed, which is tiny. I'm looking at that *guasima* tree over there. It's very large, and the birds come to it too. I say to myself: that's what we are, this little community, a *guasima* seed. It doesn't seem like there's any

---

7. The term "conscientization" was coined by Freire, *Pedagogy of the Oppressed*, 19. Andrew Kirk refers to this process of education and conscientization as "a subversive tool, which would cause the dominated to demand the removal of their shackles." Kirk, *Liberation Theology*, 25.

8. Shaull, "Foreword," 13.

9. Shaull, 13.

connection between some poor *campesinos* and a just and well-developed society, where there is abundance and everything is shared. . . . I said: The great tree with all its branches and its leaves is already present in the seed, even though in a hidden form. In the same way, the kingdom of heaven, which is a cosmic kingdom, is already present in us, but in a hidden way.[10]

What Cardenal shows is that the rural poor in Nicaragua with whom he worked, by being "agents in theology,"[11] were able to understand and define their world using a biblical and theological lens while being firmly rooted in the physical realities and objects in their environment. These objects and experiences of their physical world became mediators for them to understand spiritual reality. As Cardenal shows, poor do not necessarily find a place for God in their lives, but as they understand that they are part of the larger narrative of God, they experience the presence of God.

Another tradition of the poor and oppressed articulating their spiritual encounter with God is the spirituals of African-American slaves. Even though most were illiterate,[12] they knew the stories of the Bible and saw it as a book about people who were oppressed and slaves just like them.[13] So the Bible became the source for the images they used to process their experience and express themselves in spirituals through the use of "sacred time," when past events (in the Bible) are seen as being in the present time.[14]

The spirituals then were the primary expression of the slave community's spirituality, "the message of the Gospel . . . translated . . . into songs in terms of [the slave's] own experience."[15] In the theologizing of American slaves, the awareness of being trapped in poverty and oppression was only mitigated by a cry to God for deliverance one day. This deliverance was the salvation they yearned for. The slaves were powerless and unable to bring about social change and as a result looked to God to bring in a new social order when this world has ceased to exist. "Most often there is also a lack of a social gospel in terms

---

10. Cardenal, *Gospel in Solentiname*, 169.

11. A term used by Bonino, "Doing Theology in the Context of the Struggle of the Poor."

12. African-American slaves relied on oral tradition to pass on their Bible knowledge and core beliefs. One of these oral traditions was the Negro spiritual.

13. Smith, *Concept of Religion Reflected*, 83.

14. Raboteau, *Slave Religion*, 250. The concept of "sacred time" has a wide meaning which incorporates an understanding that the times for rituals, worship, and renewal have spiritual dimensions and are different than chronological time. See Gary Eberle, *Sacred Time and the Search for Meaning* (Boston, MA: Shambhala, 2003).

15. Raboteau, *Slave Religion*, 243.

of a new world to be created by man here on earth working with the help of God."[16] From their spirituals, it is apparent that many of the slaves did not believe that society and their circumstances could be changed.[17]

The symbols in the spirituals were drawn from the slaves' experiences. "These were the only means for making articulate what he thought and hoped. The deeper meaning of it all was that he should one day be a full and free son of God in the highest sense."[18] Their expressions of despair and faith in God was their religion. It reflected a religion of salvation, of deliverance from evil, and of attaining what they needed with the help of God.[19] "The spirituals are theological expressions, not theological treatises."[20]

There have been attempts within some segments of Western Christianity to try and hear the voices of the poor – though they have been very few. The African-American community during the Civil Rights movement of the 1960s and 1970s has provided some of the most significant insights into their understanding of social injustice and poverty and have their own narrative of living in poverty. In *Let Justice Roll Down* and *A Quiet Revolution*, John Perkins recorded the stories of individuals (their testimonies) in the midst of poverty and extreme injustice as they sought to understand what it means to be a Christian. Perkins writes that the stories the poor among the African Americans tell are not just of desperation, but of trying to find dignity. This they find in the cross of Christ and the resulting ability to forgive.

> Ours is not a story of bitterness – it is a story of love and the triumphs of the God of love. But it is a story carved out of the realities of violence and poverty, ending in not some sugar-coated sense of brotherly love but the deep conviction that only the power of Christ's crucifixion on the cross and the glory of His resurrection can heal the deep racial wounds in both black and white people in America.[21]

---

16. Smith, *Concept of Religion Reflected*, 110.

17. It is important to note that there were between 250 and 313 American slave revolts. The five most famous were the Stono Rebellion of 1739, the New York City Conspiracy of 1741, the Gabriel Conspiracy of 1800, the German Coast Uprising of 1811, and Nat Turner's Rebellion of 1831.

18. Smith, *Concept of Religion Reflected*, 107.

19. Smith.

20. Faithful, "Recovering the Theology of the Negro Spirituals," 4.

21. Perkins, *Let Justice Roll Down*, 1; Perkins, *Quiet Revolution, Materials Today*. Others have also researched and written about poor African Americans in the southern US. Robert Coles (a deeply committed Christian) gave voice to the children of share croppers living in

Another attempt to listen to the voices of the poor was by Tim Limburg as early as 1978, based on his pastoral experience in the economically depressed areas of rural Appalachia in the US. Limburg writes about the impact of sin causing economic differences which created a people who experience life, hope, the future, God, and his world in profoundly different ways.[22] The hurts and challenges of the poor define not only their priorities, but also how they view the world. After listening to the poor, Limburg highlights the difference in priorities.

> Pornography and homosexuality may be important questions for us, but they are of small consequence to the poor. Survival, bread, the hope of ever being other than helpless and poor – such are the gutsy issues the poor bring to us and to which the gospel must speak. Issues of oppression, exploitation, land ownership, and the system, which supports the injustices that make up the world of the poor – these are the issues that cry out for a healing and liberating Word from God.[23]

Limburg goes on to state that the gospel has become acculturated to middle-class Christianity (at least in North America) and does not speak to the needs of the poor. He writes, "the message we bring from our world to theirs is often only another accusation and reminder of their inadequacy and failure."[24] The assumption in most ministries to the poor is that, "The word that is preached goes out on the premise that the gospel is the unchanging message of God and applies equally to all."[25] Yet what Limburg was hearing from the poor was that the good news from God had to relate to their daily struggles, and these were not the same as those of North American middle-class Christianity.

The poor are able to articulate and theologize about their experience of God, though as noted earlier, they may not be able to produce written theological treatises. As Dunbar-Odem pointed out, people in oral cultures tend to use situations, experiences, and physical reference points and objects in their environment that are part of their life and world, and out of these

---

poverty. Coles, *Children of Crisis Volume I.*

22. Limburg, "Gospel to the Poor," 22.

23. Limburg, 23.

24. Limburg, 23.

25. Limburg, 23.

concrete realities they are able to develop abstract concepts.[26] Nicaraguan *campesinos* used their physical world as a reference point for understanding spiritual truth. The African-American slaves and those involved in the Civil Rights movement developed their understanding of God and his purposes through the lens of their experiences and suffering. The Appalachian poor had very different priorities because of their challenging socioeconomic context, and these priorities influenced how they approached the word of God.

The poor can theologize. However, when listening to the poor articulate their conversion experiences and their spirituality, there needs to be minimal external mediation. They need to be able to tell their stories the way they want to without the listener telling them what words to use or trying to fit the story into frameworks and categories of spirituality that the nonpoor understand.

The Challenge of Listening to the Poor

How can the voices of the poor be heard without filtering them through the worldviews, language, and conceptual frameworks of the nonpoor?

Liberation theologians developed the process of conscientization which provided a methodology for the poor to analyze the dynamics of their world and then be able to articulate them.[27] It is a guided process facilitated by an outsider, the liberation theologian, who has a commitment to live (pilgrimage) among the poor. "Its theologians are not arm chair intellectuals, but rather 'organic intellectuals' (in organic communion with the people) and 'militant theologians,' working with the pilgrim people of God and engaged in their pastoral duties."[28] The process includes three main stages (mediations) which are (1) a socio-analytical (or historico-analytical) mediation; (2) a hermeneutical mediation; and (3) a practical mediation.[29] The first mediation is the process of *conscientization*, where through a guided process the poor become aware of their social, historical, and political reality.

---

26. Dunbar-Odem, *Defying the Odds*, 49.

27. Conscientization is the process of developing a critical awareness of one's social reality through reflection and action, which is then the beginning of the process of changing the reality. Paulo Freire states that everyone acquires social myths that tend to dominate their thinking and worldview. So, learning is a critical process which depends upon uncovering real problems and actual needs. Freire stresses the need for the poor to liberate themselves from their "dominated-conditioned" mentality and their passive despair. Friere, *Pedagogy of the Oppressed*.

28. Boff and Boff, *Introducing Liberation Theology*, 19.

29. Boff and Boff, 24.

The objective of the whole process is praxis (practical mediation) and not merely theologizing or sociological research. Gutiérrez states that it is not enough for people to come together in dialogue in order to gain knowledge of their social reality. They must act together upon their environment in order to critically reflect upon their reality and so transform it through further action.[30] The dialogical process needed to arrive at praxis requires the liberation theologian in the community to provide the paradigms and questions through which reality is interpreted. Unlike academic research, the objective is not to merely record and interpret the perceptions of the poor but to move toward praxis.

The dialogical process that results in a deeper understanding of our context is dependent on what happens at an "intellectual" level "on which we inquire, come to understand, express what we have understood, [and] work out the presupposition and implication of our expression."[31] However, to be able to do all of this, we have to address the question of "standpoint," which is the frame of reference of the enquirer.[32] This framework then provides "the 'epistemological lens' through which the phenomenon [what is observed in the context] passes before it is seen. It is thus seen, on this deeper level, in terms of the categories of understanding which make up a particular framework of reference."[33]

The "cultural texts" (or major perspectives) that are used for mediation include the psycho-medical, the anthropological, the socioeconomic, the philosophical, and the theological. The choice of "texts" or mediation is a theological decision, and theologians from a particular faith community may choose any of the above sets of cultural texts to articulate what they see and experience as part of a faith community. If they do not use the mediators

---

30. Hartnett, "Remembering the Poor," 11–14.

31. B. J. F. Lonergan quoted by Bate, "Method in Contextual Missiology," 164. The original source is B. J. F. Lonergan, *Method in Theology* (London: Darton, Longman & Todd, 1971), 9.

32. Bate, "Method in Contextual Missiology," 164. Jose Miguel Bonino states that any theologian belongs to a specific culture, a social class or group, and a tradition, and as a result writes from within that context, influenced by human, social, and historical realities.

> Since theologians are human beings and not God, they must occupy one place in space and time. Theologians – perhaps even more than other thinkers – have claimed a sort of "extra-territoriality", a "location" outside or above the flux and conflicts of history. It is true that a theologian, like anybody else, who practices an intellectual discipline, lives in a special territory, defined by the presuppositions, the methods, the traditions of such discipline. No responsible theologian can vacate such location. But it is "a place within a place", i.e. in the context of a wider reality defined by the historical coordinates.

Bonino, "Doing Theology in the Context of the Struggle of the Poor," 369–70.

33. Bate, "Method in Contextual Missiology," 164.

to understand the context, their work would not be "reflective Contextual Theology (rather . . . ideological theology where the ideology is assumed, not questioned and is the only lens used)."[34] The liberation theologians living among the poor primarily use the socioeconomic cultural text along with a theological text.[35] The question that is unanswered is would the poor without an external facilitator (a liberation theologian) use the same cultural texts or have the same perspective of their context?[36] Andrew Kirk adds a note of caution for outsiders as they observe oppression and suffering. "It is particularly dangerous when the claim [as to how God views the poor] is made on behalf of the poor by those who can always walk away from their contact with poverty."[37]

Liberation theology is both integrated and integrating.[38] At the very start it is important to allow the phenomenon to manifest itself in as many different ways as possible. There are three ways of looking:

- What the community sees.
- What those involved in the phenomenon see.
- What those who have looked at the phenomenon at some depth see.[39]

Christians from the base communities recall their experiences, and theologians contribute their insights "deepening the meaning of the events under discussion

---

34. Bate, 164–65.

35. The Boff brothers refer to these texts as "Gospel and life." Boff and Boff, *Introducing Liberation Theology*, 13. The question that has often been raised is whether there is a specific socioeconomic and political lens that liberation theologians use. Peter Wagner identifies the influence of Marxism. He writes, "It is a risk to pin the label 'Marxist' on any of the representatives of the new radical left. But it would be safe to say that a Marxist-oriented ideology has at least as much influence on some of them as the Bible." Wagner, *Latin American Theology*, 59.

36. The question is who is the primary observer – the theologian or the community? Could the community go through a process of conscientization without an external facilitator? Bate states:

> The phenomenon is mediated by the frame of reference or epistemological categories of the observer who is psychologist, anthropologist, philosopher, sociologist, theologian (or a combination of more than one of these). These are culture texts for the observer since through them he receives true messages through symbols he [sic.] can identify and codes he knows. What is seen and what is reported is done so in terms of the particular frame of reference concerned.

Bate, "Method in Contextual Missiology," 165.

37. Kirk, *What Is Mission?*, Kindle Location 1324.

38. Boff and Boff, *Introducing Liberation Theology*, 15. There are three levels of liberation theology – professional, pastoral, and popular.

39. Bate, "Method in Contextual Missiology," 160.

and drawing conclusions from them."[40] In addition, other professionals such as sociologists, economists, teachers, and technicians provide further input. Such integration would provide a comprehensive understanding of poverty in a specific context and could be effective in addressing poverty and injustice. But does this methodology reflect the voices of the poor, or are they lost in the process of integration?[41]

Robert Coles conducted social research in the late 1960s and early 1970s that enabled poor children to "speak" and describe their realities. He studied the lives of children, mostly in poor and deprived communities in the US, and documented them in his five-volume *Children of Crisis*.[42] Coles developed a methodology that came to be referred to as "documentary child psychiatry."[43]

Coles' methodology uses a minimally mediated process without guiding questions directing the whole process. He and his coworkers would ask key questions, and then they would allow the children to draw pictures and speak about their lives. He significantly reduced the amount of mediation required and describes what happened. "They sometimes spoke loud and clear what crossed their minds, or they used crayons or pencils or paintbrushes to show through artistic representation what they saw, experienced, wanted to convey through portraits of themselves, of others, or through rendering of particular faces, buildings, scenes."[44] The children described their reality of being poor in the rural American south, Appalachia, inner-city ghettos, and as the children of migrant workers and marginalized groups such as Eskimos, Chicanos, and Native Americans. Coles' research is one of the earliest documentations

---

40. Boff and Boff, *Introducing Liberation Theology*, 15.

41. This discussion is not on liberation theology but on its methods to enable the poor to have a voice. Liberation theology continues to grow and develop. This development is seen in not only the new liberation theologies such as Dalit, Palestinian, and Black liberation theologies, among others, but it has had to also come to grips with its experience in the Nicaraguan revolution. However, the methodology of conscientization and working among the poor remains unchanged. For insights into where liberation theology is today, see Groody, ed., *Option for the Poor in Christian Theology*. See also Noble, *Keeping the Windows Open*.

42. Coles, *Children of Crisis*. Only the last volume focused on children of the wealthy, as Coles referred to them – the privileged ones.

43. Coles was deeply influenced by neo-Freudian psychoanalyst Erik Erikson who had been involved in longitudinal studies of children which informed his theories of human personality. Erikson's best-known book is *Childhood and Society*. What is unique in Coles's methodology is his interdisciplinary approach to incorporate the techniques from psychoanalysis into social research.

44. Coles, *Children of Crisis*, xiii.

in the social sciences[45] of how the poor experience and understand their everyday reality.

As noted earlier, Robert Chambers pointed out that the theories and insights that explain poverty are usually paradigms that have been developed by outsiders, the nonpoor, to understand the world of the poor rather than the poor explaining their reality. In the early 1970s, Chambers, working with rural communities in East Africa and South Asia, developed an approach to community assessment – participatory rural appraisal (PRA) – that enabled the poor to directly look at their reality without an externally mediated process.[46]

There have been numerous studies since that have used variations of PRA to enable the poor to describe their reality for the benefit of outsiders. The largest of these studies was conducted on behalf of the World Bank by Deepa Narayan and team and reported in *Voices of the Poor: Can Anyone Hear Us?* (Chambers was a consultant to the process.) The team gathered the views, aspirations, and experiences of sixty thousand individuals in sixty countries.[47] They directly quoted the poor but fit the responses into predetermined categories. It is important to note that the team wanted the people's own words and concepts of well-being and ill-being, their priorities, and their experiences of institutions and attitudes toward them.[48] In studying poverty in Lebanon, I used a similar methodology of enabling the poor to describe their context and reality. *Profiles of Poverty: The Human Face of Poverty in Lebanon* was published in 2011.[49] More recently, the Feinstein International Center at Tufts University published *Narratives of Famine: Somalia 2011* which presents "with relatively little accompanying analysis, extended first-person narratives of this experience from the perspectives of those that lived through it. This is an attempt to

---

45. Non-anthropological.

46. Participatory rural appraisal (PRA, now also known as participatory poverty assessment – PPA) is a set of at least forty tools that enables the poor themselves to analyze and describe their world. Narayanasamy, *Participatory Rural Appraisal*.

47. Narayan-Parker, Patel, and Narayan, *Voices of the Poor*.

48. Interestingly, there was some significant criticism for enabling the poor to speak and then documenting what they said. Robert Chamber explains. "The WDR [World Donor Report 2000] was 'a stunning publicity stunt for the World Bank' (Cornwall and Fujita, 2007). We 'ventriloquized the poor'. 'The poor' were domesticated into a category identified and characterized as needing help. The quotations in the WDR were 'illustrations and flourishes', embellishments, disembodied voices without context." Chambers, "Voices of the Poor and Beyond," 9.

49. Das and Davidson, *Profiles of Poverty*.

bring out a Somali 'voice' where the distance between local populations and humanitarian actors is increasing."[50]

The influence of liberation theology and its method of giving a voice to the poor was acknowledged at the 1982 Bangalore meeting of the International Association of Mission Studies (IAMS) where an effort was made in the study of mission to distinguish between the perspective of an "insider" and that of an "outsider." These different perspectives were highlighted in the *Workshop Report*, which states, "As we put ourselves in the shoes of those in poor countries, we can readily see the significance of giving people a sense of their basic identity. From an outside perspective, the needs of the external context, for instance from the viewpoint of North America, require a stress on material poverty."[51] Missiologists affiliated with the World Council of Churches acknowledged that the poor may have a different perspective of spiritual reality and that their spiritual priorities may be different than what the nonpoor think are the needs of the poor.

The meeting attendees acknowledged the powerlessness of the poor in the Majority World, and the implication was that the poor, because of illiteracy, often do not have the means or platform through which they can articulate their perceptions and needs,[52] compared to the nonpoor who are able to document their observations, which then become the only accepted version of reality. Such a mismatch in capacity, means, and ability undermines and undervalues the perceptions of the poor because it results in asserting that the only valid explanations of the world of the poor and their experience can be made by trained outside observers who can document and analyze their findings. The result is that the outside observers try to fit the experience of the poor into their own worldviews and theoretical paradigms to explain the actions and behavior of the poor, as noted by Chambers earlier.[53]

The attendees of the 1982 International Association of Mission Studies (IAMS) meeting also began to be aware of the language used by outsiders to define the reality of the poor. They realized that words and language impose external conceptual and theological frameworks to explain to outsiders what they see. Gutiérrez writes about the need to find appropriate language to speak about God in the midst of poverty, suffering, and deprivation.

---

50. Majid, Adan, Abdirahman, Kim, Maxwell, *Narratives of Famine*, 5.

51. "Workshop II Evangelism and the Poor," 350.

52. Often this lack of a platform is because of illiteracy and being marginalized from the mainstreams of society resulting in the powerlessness. Chambers identifies powerlessness as both a symptom and cause of poverty. Chambers, *Rural Development*, passim.

53. "See also "Workshop II Evangelism and the Poor," 352.

> From the viewpoint of theological reflection, the challenge . . .
> is to find a language about God that grows out of the situation
> created by the unjust poverty in which the broad masses live
> (despised races, exploited social classes, marginalized cultures,
> discrimination against women). . . . A prophetic and a mystical
> language are being born in this soil of exploitation and hope.[54]

What liberation theology and the research methods of Robert Coles and Robert Chambers (PRA) acknowledge is that the contexts of the poor in each location are unique and that only the poor in a particular context can articulate and describe their reality from within their specific contexts. It is also apparent that the language and paradigms that outsiders use to describe the realities of the poor are different from those used by the poor themselves.

A number of implications arise from the challenges of trying to listen to the poor. First, using open-ended questions enables the poor to speak rather than merely answer specific guiding questions. Second, a certain level of mediation is required, especially when using translators. The type of mediation required is that of facilitation to encourage the poor to speak rather than to guide the conversation. However for the voices of the poor to be heard, mediation needs to be kept to a minimum. Third, every effort must be made to enable the poor being interviewed to use their "language" and expressions to describe their reality and experiences. These need to be accepted as valid expressions of their experiences, theology, and spirituality. Those interviewing and listening need to avoid the temptation to take what they are hearing and fit it into their conceptual frameworks.

However, it is important to realize that it would be unrealistic for observers (researchers) not to have any paradigms or cultural texts through which they interpret what they see, and for there to be no mediation at all. Stuart Bate summarizes this point.

> We all mediate phenomena. The fullness of phenomena is never
> available to us and all that we observe is mediated. The importance
> of contextual theologies and the study of the so-called *paradigm
> shift* in epistemology is the attempt to highlight the reality of
> this process and thus to move away from the absolutisation of
> intellectual positions.[55]

---

54. Gutiérrez, *We Drink from Our Own Wells*, 197.

55. Bate, "Method in Contextual Missiology," 165.

5

Voices of the Poor:
Syrian Refugees

The nearness of God is perhaps no more acutely felt than during
an experience of physical displacement, and this nearness is always
a migration on God's part, for God ultimately identifies with
human suffering. . . . God's companionship in suffering signifies
that humanity is deeply cherished by God.[1]

Jenny McGill, missiological researcher

Fidelity to listening and hearing what is being said requires that the context
of speakers be understood. Speakers do not speak in a vacuum but use
words and imagery that have been shaped by their life experiences, culture,
religion, and worldview. These may be different than those who hear the stories.
New Testament scholars Sylvia Keesmaat and Brian Walsh write, "Social,
geographical, and economic locations (often linked to ethnic identity) shape
how we think and how we imagine the world."[2]

The World of Syrian Refugees in Lebanon

Being on the physical crossroads of the Middle East, Lebanon has survived
a turbulent history, most recently a civil war between 1975 and 1990. The
country's population of four million is augmented by at least half a million
refugees from Palestine and Iraq. Since 2011 and the beginning of the Syrian
conflict, at least 1.03 million Syrian refugees have been registered with the UN
in 247,736 households (HH), and thousands of others have not registered. This

---

1. McGill, *Religious Identity and Cultural Negotiation*, 204–5.
2. Keesmaat and Walsh, *Romans Disarmed*, 37.

means that over 20 percent of Lebanon's population is made up of refugees who are supported by the state and the international community.

There are no refugee camps in Lebanon for Syrian refugees,[3] and they are scattered across Lebanon in informal settlements, unfinished buildings, rented spaces, and any place they can find. The UN's 2015 survey assessing the vulnerability of Syrian refugees in Lebanon showed that 19 percent of the refugee households (HH) were headed by women. At least 16 percent of the refugee housing surveyed was deemed as substandard or dangerous. Rent was reported as one of the major expenditures of a HH.[4] For 41 percent of Syrians in Lebanon, affordable shelter was not adequate, and adequate shelter was simply not affordable, particularly over the long term.

Poor quality shelter, overcrowding, and limited access to water, sanitation, and urban services are the norms for the vast majority of vulnerable refugees throughout the country.[5] Thirty-nine percent of the HH report that they have no access to safe drinking water and have to buy bottled water, increasing the strain on their meager finances. About 10 percent do not have access to proper sanitation facilities.[6]

Being refugees who fled their homes with only a few possessions, most now have even less. While the majority of the refugees had been given kitchen and eating utensils and water containers, only 10 percent had enough beds and 15 percent enough tables and chairs. Many families, especially in eastern Lebanon, did not have enough mattresses, winter clothing, or even a gas stove. Fifty-two percent of the children (about two hundred and fifty thousand) were not in any kind of school because the Lebanese government schools were full to capacity in spite of having added a second shift. Very few nonprofits can afford to set up schools for refugee children. Free primary health care was available only to 12 percent of the HH. Besides rent and food, health care was the other major expenditure for a HH. Thirty-seven percent of the children were reported to have been sick during the two weeks preceding the survey done by Lebanese Society for Education and Social Development (LSESD). Only

---

3. The Lebanese authorities say this situation is the result of their experience with the Palestinian refugees who were housed in formal camps and never left. The camps also became semi-autonomous and house militias and other radical elements. The Lebanese don't want the same happening with the Syrian refugees.

4. UNHCR, UNICEF, and WFP, *Vulnerability Assessment of Syrian Refugees in Lebanon 2015.*

5. Quoted in Lebanese Society for Educational and Social Development (LSESD), "LSESD Food Aid Response," 3–4.

6. UNHCR, UNICEF, and WFP, *Vulnerability Assessment of Syrian Refugees in Lebanon 2015.*

half of the children had been immunized, and 78 percent reported concerns for their personal security.[7]

Because foreigners are not allowed to work legally in the country, most refugees (including Syrians) were working illegally, creating resentment among the Lebanese poor, from whom the jobs were being taken. Nonagricultural casual labor was the primary source of illegal employment. Because of these insecurities, families were giving their daughters to be married at very young ages to older men who were willing to pay. Prostitution was growing as a means for women and young girls to provide for their families.[8]

Most HH (54 percent) were reliant on loans and on food packages or food vouchers provided by the UN and international NGOs. One out of three members of a HH reported that they had eaten either only one meal or none the previous day, and 27 percent of the HH reported that they were unable to cook at least one meal a day either because of the lack of food or the lack of fuel. The quality of food consumed by refugees was deteriorating, with the increasing risk of micronutrient deficiencies and the resulting long-term impacts. Eighty-nine percent of the HH had experienced a lack of food or a lack of money to buy food during the thirty days prior to the survey. Their main coping strategies were to take loans (driving them further into debt), eating less so that the children could eat enough, eating fewer meals, and reducing portion sizes. Most had sold the few assets they had (jewelry, household items, equipment, etc.). Other coping strategies included withdrawing children from school and sending them to work. Sixty-five percent of Syrian refugee HH were classified as mildly food insecure. With the present economic crisis in Lebanon, this insecurity has deteriorated even further. As families have even fewer assets to support themselves, their food insecurity will only get worse.[9]

What the data on the condition of Syrian refugees in Lebanon shows is that they were experiencing event-based poverty. Most of the refugees were not poor in Syria but were either middle class or lower middle class. By becoming refugees, they had become destitute. They had lost most of their assets, were unable to support themselves with regular work, and did not have access to health care. More than half of the children were not in school and were at risk health-wise. Families did not have adequate food and were beginning

---

7. Lebanese Society for Educational and Social Development (LSESD), "LSESD Food Aid Response."

8. Anderson, "Syria's Refugee Children Have Lost All Hope."

9. Lebanese Society for Educational and Social Development (LSESD), "LSESD Food Aid Response."

to experience long-term health impacts due to nutritional deficiencies. Their housing was temporary and expensive (for their budget) as they were at the mercy of landlords who could evict them any time. The displaced Syrians in Lebanon were marginalized, voiceless and powerless as refugees. Besides the event-based poverty and destitution they experience, all had witnessed the horrors of the brutal conflict in Syria and carried physical or psychological scars. This is the context of their stories.

Stories of Syrian Refugees Finding Christ
"I was dead, but now I'm alive"

> Saad[10] is a forty-two-year-old married man with four children. He is from Afreen in Syria. In Syria, he worked as a wall painter and decorator. Whenever he can find work, he practices his trade in Lebanon. His wife does not work outside the home. Formerly Muslim, he and his entire family – wife and four children – are now followers of Christ.

I was seeking the truth about the heavenly books. When I came to Lebanon, I was introduced to a Christian center that provides aid to refugees. I received a food package and decided to take a Bible that was available. I attended the meetings at the center. One day I was in bed with an infected leg and could not move. I opened the Bible and started reading the book of John about Lazarus. A brother from Switzerland came to visit me and saw me in tears. He asked what was wrong, and I told him about my reading and that I don't know why I'm crying because I'm so happy. I was touched. Since then, I've been growing in my knowledge of Christ.

I was dead, but now I'm alive. I could never go back to my old religion. What is it that attracts me to Christ? His whole personality, his deity, and humility. He is my Savior and Lord. I now trust in his providence, salvation, and leadership. Life's difficulties (material) will be resolved in due time.

---

10. The names in the stories narrated are not the actual names of those interviewed because of the sensitive nature of Christian conversions in Hindu and Muslim communities.

The true path to God

> Walid is a thirty-four-year-old married man with two children. He is from Aleppo and has been in Lebanon for three years. He worked as an electrician in Syria and is now working as an electrical technician with a construction company. His wife does not work outside the home. He, along with his wife and two children, are followers of Christ.

My family and I were fanatic Muslims, especially my wife. We came to the [church] center and found good relationships and acceptance. I received a Bible and started reading it. My wife was being led to the discipleship courses and was not happy about it. She was afraid of "changing religions" and sliding back from Islam. I saw the difference in society between Christians and Muslims. Along with my Bible reading and after my wife accepted Christ, I decided to learn more about salvation. A servant of the Lord came to teach us, and we prayed with him asking Jesus into our lives. Our children are attending Christian activities and Sunday school, learning a lot. I asked about baptism, and my wife and I are baptized.

I left Islam because of the hatred and violence it was teaching me. We had to think thoroughly about how my wife and I would deal with the community we are in, not hiding our faith, but not raising persecution and offense from our neighbors and families. Nothing would stop us [from worshiping Christ] after knowing Christ.

When I think about following Christ and worshiping him, it means the right way and the true path to God.

God in the midst of the fire

> Nabil is a thirty-seven-year-old married man with three children. He is from Homs in Syria and has been in Lebanon for three years. In Syria, he worked as a clothing designer, and now he works in stitching and hanging curtains. His wife works in a dress store. Formerly Muslim, he, his wife, and three children are now all followers of Christ.

My wife and children went to the [church] center for sustenance [to get food aid that was being provided]. We were happy about the worship, and it broke down almost all Islamic barriers. I was, at the time, fed up in my heart because of my violent religion and was seeking Christianity. We were introduced to a

Christian pastor who wanted to visit our house. He came and talked with us about salvation in Christ. I recall one time I asked about being baptized, but he rejected the idea and asked why I wanted that. I told him I was convinced that Jesus is alive! He saved my daughter from a fire in the house while she was sleeping; the curtains were falling on her with the flames. I watched this happen and was amazed by the peace my daughter had and her faith in Christ. She told me she prayed before going to sleep and Jesus was with her. The second thing I can't forget is that not even one hair on my daughter's head burned. The pastor then led me through the plan of salvation. My wife and I, our two children, and my brother were saved. We are discipled and were later baptized.

During our discipling sessions, we were confronted with the truth of following Jesus alone. Facing the little we knew about our former religion and the hatred it bears toward Christianity, we all took a stand against the false prophets. My entire family.

We were threatened. My brother-in-law was sent from Syria to kill my wife. I kept her away for a couple of weeks and confronted him with the pastor. He agreed to either stay in Lebanon and quit his mission to hurt my wife or return to Syria and be killed because he didn't do what he was sent to do. He chose to remain in Lebanon and moved to the south.

Not even death would divide me and my family from our Lord and Savior. Following Christ for me means joy, peace, assurance, new life full of hope, and perseverance with continuous growth in faith. I can do everything in Christ who strengthens me. I am attracted to his authority and love. He is my Lord, leader, and captain. As a result, there is a great change in the family. A new purpose in life. More discipline and perpetual hope.

"Nothing has changed, but I feel his presence"

> Amira is a thirty-six-year-old married woman with three children. Her father lives with them, since her husband is back in Syria because he was denied entry into Lebanon. She has been in Lebanon for three years. She is working as a teacher in a school for refugee children. She is the only follower of Christ in her Muslim family.

We lived in Lebanon for about two and a half years and returned to Syria to have my third child. Coming back to Lebanon, my husband was denied entry back into Lebanon. I returned with my three children by myself. It was tough. Friends said I should reach out to the center/church for help because I was having a hard time without my husband and providing for my family. I needed help, so I went. It was there that I kept hearing more and more about Jesus. Not only were my physical needs being met, so were my spiritual needs. The Lord used those times to speak to my heart and draw me to him. I now have an amazing community of brothers and sisters walking alongside me!

I saw so much love and life in Christians, but with Islam it is full of fear. I was always taught to fear Allah. I lived in constant fear of Allah. He was the one that punishes us, kills us; our ability to choose is taken away. There is a lot missing in Islam. God is the opposite of all of this. We don't have to be afraid of God. He created us to worship and to be with him.

By worshiping Christ, there have been no real bad consequences yet. My family does not know that I am a believer. If my father, who lives with me, found out, he might disown me. He is a strong practicing Muslim man. But I would never go back to Islam.

For me to worship Christ means loving him with all my heart and resting in him, sharing and being a witness to those around me, knowing God will open doors even unexpectedly, and trusting him to lead me in the right direction. What attracts me to Christ is that he is merciful and love – all the characteristics the Bible teaches about God. He is relational, and I feel his presence inside of me.

My physical circumstances haven't changed, but the way I handle them has. I am no longer worried about tomorrow. Before I was always so nervous and would take it out on my kids. Now I am full of his peace. I used to think God was against me, but now I know he is working for me. I feel his presence at work in our family. I am a new creation.

"I can finally rest: I have peace"

> Fatima is a thirty-year-old married woman with six children. She is from Idlib in Syria and has been in Lebanon for four years. In Syria, they were farmers, and she helped on the farm. Her husband now works in construction, when he can find work. She is primarily a housewife and occasionally works as a cleaner part-time. They occasionally have other members of the family come and stay with them. She and her husband are followers of Christ.

My husband started going to church and heard the message many times through friends at church. He saw answers to prayer for his father in prison in Syria. My husband believed and was baptized. I experienced a lot of trials from that, which eventually led to my believing. I had heard the message from friends at church and my husband. As I kept hearing teaching from the Bible, I felt stirred and a sense of peace from it. I had always felt overwhelmed by evil.

All my friends told me to divorce my husband after he believed and was publicly baptized. I have not told my family about my decision; they are still in Syria. My family doesn't know, and they will kill me if they knew.

To follow Christ means to always be able to pray and have peace no matter what the circumstances or outcome. When I worship by hearing his word, I feel calm and able to have relief from the stresses of life. Peace, prayer, and knowing that no evil is stronger than him.

I used to feel overwhelmed by evil and fear. I can finally rest. I have peace. I don't try to fix everything or stay up at night worrying (about family in Syria and needs), but I pray and I put my head down to sleep. And throughout the day I pray and feel his presence and peace.

"I saw the Lord standing right in front of me"

> Sara is a thirty-five-year-old married woman with two children. They are from Aleppo and have been in Lebanon for three years. In Syria and now in Lebanon, she has been a housewife, and her husband now works as a sign artist whenever he can find work. Formerly Muslim, she, along with her husband and children, are now followers of Christ.

Sixteen years ago, I had a dream, and the Lord revealed himself to me. After this dream, I still did not give my life to the Lord. My husband was a believer, and for seven years he was angry and frustrated that I still read and followed the Qur'an. One day he was so mad, he sent me out of the house to the garden. I sat in the garden yelling, "Lord, if you are who you say you are, I need to see you!" It was at that moment all the hairs on my arms stood up, and I felt this peace every time I took a breath. It was like nothing I had ever felt before. I looked up and saw the Lord standing right in front of me. I pinched myself thinking it was a dream, but it wasn't. It was right then my heart changed, and I knew Jesus was the only way. God revealed himself to me in ways I couldn't deny that he is the Messiah. He consistently pursued me.

Many people in Syria don't know I am a believer; otherwise they would kill me. But I would never go back to how my life was before Christ. For me to worship Christ means making him the most important thing in your life. Reading the Bible daily and learning more about Christ and who he is. I know how much he loves me. The way he pursued me even in my dreams. His light and the way I feel his presence.

What dissatisfied me about my old faith was the fear and violence. But Jesus saved me. I am amazed how he reveals himself to us. Because of him I have a new purpose.

My family life has completely changed. My marriage is much happier because we have Jesus bringing us together. I have a peace like I have never experienced before. I don't worry about my future.

"Jesus is not like anyone else"

> Rima is a thirty-six-year-old married woman with five daughters. She is from Afreen in Syria and has been in Lebanon for four years. She was a housewife in Syria and now works sewing and making crafts to earn some money. Her husband works painting walls, whenever he can find work. She is the only follower of Christ in her Muslim family.

I became a follower of Christ through the discipleship class at church, knowing the Bible, experiencing miracles, and transformation. All prophets came and lived and sinned and died and stayed dead. The rules of my old religion were all in favor of the Muslim leaders and not in favor of the people. The sheikhs preached but didn't live good lives. They spoke badly about women. Only Jesus, in his birth, his death for taking the sins of the world, his resurrection – he is not like anyone else.

I have experienced some persecution and pressure from my relatives. They argue with me about teaching my kids about Jesus. Even pressure from the husband. But they are not stopping me. I don't carry their gossip anymore on my shoulders. Maybe in the past I would be weaker and maybe hide my faith a little bit. But not anymore. I know there is a price because of my faith, and I hope I don't go through this. Jesus gives us strength.

Jesus is number one. He is above all. We follow him in all his teachings and his ways. Be like him. To be clothed with Christ. I am attracted to Christ because of his love. He loved us first. He is kind-hearted – peacemaking. He is attractive in his gentleness. He has all the good qualities. He is my father; a shoulder to cry on; a close friend. You can tell him anything.

I feel joy and peace in my life in spite of all the difficulties. I used to get depressed quickly before. Now I have more hope. I also have more wisdom.

He opens new doors for me. He has made me stronger as a person. He got a lot of the weakness out of my heart.

"I now forgive and love others easily"

> Maha is a thirty-six-year-old married woman with two sons. She is from Aleppo in Syria and has been in Lebanon for four years. In Syria and now in Lebanon she has been a housewife and mother. Her husband paints walls when he can find work. Formerly Muslims, she and her husband are now followers of Christ.

I came to church here in Lebanon – met Jesus and came to faith. We thought that it was by works that we are saved. We understood that it is through Jesus only, and it's a gift. So, we came to him.

My relatives attacked me verbally for going to church. They cannot stop me from going to church. I didn't benefit anything or get anything from Islam that would cause me to go back to it. Everything was obligatory. I was scared of hell. A lot of pressure.

We hear his words and do it. We tell others about him. He is the only right way. He is the right path. He came to earth, and he is the only one who died for us on the cross. He alone can give eternal life. He is God, and he answers our prayers. He is my father, my Savior, my intercession. I used to have a lot of hatred and not forgive easily. I now forgive and love others easily.

"I had a dream of Jesus"

> Iman is a forty-five-year-old married woman with four children. She is from Afreen near Aleppo in Syria and has been in Lebanon for five years. In Syria she was a schoolteacher, and now in Lebanon she is involved in ministry at the church and gets paid something. Her husband is not able to find much work and does tiling when he can. Her sister-in-law and her three children live with them in their temporary shelter. Besides herself, a son, a daughter, and her sister-in-law are followers of Christ, while the rest of the family are still Muslim. A second son is on the way.

I had a dream of Jesus when I was in Syria. I searched for a Bible, tried to find a church but couldn't. Then the war happened, and we came to Lebanon. I immediately found a church. It was like a miracle.

I found a lot of contradictions between the Bible and the Qur'an. God opened my eyes. I always asked him to show me the right way, and he always led me to Jesus. We used to be so scared of dying and facing a judgmental God. My husband always attacks me and mocks me. He stopped me from going to church. But it is impossible for me to go back to Islam. That is one thing that would never happen. God felt so far. There was a lot of fear. I fasted just out of fear. Nothing of the rules convinced me.

To worship Christ means to have a relationship with him; to live like Jesus. What would he have done in my place? Everything about him is attractive. As soon as I read the Bible, I had peace about him. His love is attractive. He is my father, my mother, my everything.

My financial situation has gotten worse. But I have changed. I have joy and peace in my life. Without Jesus in my life, I would have left my husband and kids. Everyone is shocked at my peace.

"When I heard the first worship song"

> Reen is a thirty-one-year-old married woman with two children. She is from Aleppo and has been in Lebanon for three years. In Syria, she worked as a tailor part-time since her husband was a tailor. She now works in the Sunday school ministries of the church. Her husband works as a tailor. Besides her, her husband, her mother, and some of her sisters are now followers of Christ.

I came to church to receive help after becoming refugees in Lebanon. When I heard the first worship song, I cried and wanted to know God more . . . and gave my life to him.

There was nothing realistic in Islam. We had a misunderstanding of the character of God. Anyways, I was not very Muslim to begin with. I was never convinced of it. In Islam you can have multiple wives. Women have to marry to be covered [protected]. It is spread through the sword. And after knowing much more, I can never go back. God really changed me.

In the beginning, my husband was against me and was afraid he'd lose me. But he came to faith. Some in my society also still attack me and mock my faith.

When we follow Christ, we are like him. We make peace. We don't judge. We understand God more and what he did for us. He loves all no matter what. He is merciful and compassionate. He is my peace – my hope – my life. In spite of my financial pressure, I have peace. Our family changed. I raise my kids on God's word now. We have more love for one another.

The Lord tries us

> Ameena is a thirty-four-year-old married woman with six
> children. She is from Homs in Syria and has been in Lebanon for
> five years. In Syria, she was a housewife, and now she works in
> the church. Her husband works as a building attendant (*natoor*).
> She and her children are now all followers of Christ. Her husband
> is still a Muslim.

I first came to the church for assistance since our situation as refugees was very hard. We were completely exhausted. My mother was with me in those days, God have mercy on her [she has since died],[11] and she would pick food up off the ground and the children would eat that. The situation was very bad. In the beginning when I first came to the church, they said, "We will see if we can help you." Brother N said that if you want to come and listen to the word, you are welcome. If you don't want to come, we will still help you.

When Pastor J started teaching me, I didn't know who the Christ was. We had talked about the Christ, but I did not know who he was. In Syria when the Christians talked about the Christ in our village, we laughed. When they said, "Our Lord lives in heaven and on the earth," we would laugh. We didn't know who the Christ was. It was here that I learned who the Christ is. It was necessary that I go through this to know who the Christ is. I thank God now that all of my life has changed.

After all these trials – the Lord tries us but doesn't beat us; the trials were very hard on us – my mother was very tired and ill. We tried to get help from the UN. They would help, but part of the expense was on us. I was praying. There were brothers here praying in the church, praying for me. I heard the story of Lazarus and how the Lord raised him from the dead. I knew that if Jesus is the Christ and he is God, then he can heal my mother. We thought of how many months things were bad and wondered if this was God's will.

Before we used to always say, "This is God's will." Why did God create us; did he create us for misery and suffering? The Lord began to work in me. When I came to church and listened to Pastor J, I learned. I began to see a clear picture of right and wrong. God doesn't want to torment me. The Lord is always with us. He listens to us. He tests us. I praise God. The ways of Christianity are simple; the truth is the gospel.

I am still a secret believer. My husband knows. He just doesn't want me to talk a lot. I'm a believer, but I am not baptized. Jesus said we should be baptized

---

11. The way her mother is referred to is a phrase used for those who have died.

to fulfill all righteousness but not to be saved. I want to be baptized when my husband is ready. I am trying with him. My family knows I come to church, and I have work here at the church. If they knew everything, I would have problems of course. I could never go back to my old religion. Everything is not right. I still wear the hijab; I am not free from it because of my husband and family.

The Lord gave me peace. He blessed me and my children. Everything changed. I walk one path now. A person cannot walk two paths. He is the only Savior, and I have eternal life. He is the only Savior in my life. He is our father. He is God.

Everything changed in my life. When I believed in Christ, I came to know that he is the only Savior. Now I am always praying for God to change things. Without prayer, nothing will change.

"I had more life in those two years than in twenty-five years as a Muslim"

> Bassma is a twenty-seven-year-old married woman with two children. She has been in Lebanon for two years and is from Aleppo in Syria. In Syria and in Lebanon she has been a housewife. Her husband works as a day laborer. She is the only follower of Christ in her family, though she says her husband prays.

I came to the church and heard the lessons. I believed but I have not been baptized. I like to come to church and listen. It has changed me. I believe in Christ. I have to stay faithful because of my children. I was a Muslim for twenty-five years. I came to the church and became a Christian. I have more life in these two years than in twenty-five years as a Muslim.

There's a big difference between Islam and Christianity. Christ gave me more faith. Now everything is different. In Christianity there is more love because of Christ. His religion is greater than our religion. His mercy is greater than Islam. His mercy is in our hearts. Mercy for children, mercy for others. Islam is a different thing. Jesus had a lot of faith, strong faith. There's no faith like this in Islam. I am growing in faith, and my children are growing in faith. My family and husband are against this religion.

Christ is my Lord. He is carrying me and my children. I can't carry them. He gave me strong faith. In Islam, we had no faith like this. There was nothing like this in the heart. Like I said, he gave me faith. There's no one like Christ. He listens to me and shows me things. I don't get anything from the UN. I have nothing but what God gives me. The church helps me.

Tomorrow is a sweeter day

> Ghada is a twenty-nine-year-old married woman with four children. She is from Syria and has been in Lebanon for five years, moving back and forth between Lebanon and Syria. She had been working as a migrant worker before the conflict. Once the conflict started, she became a refugee and stayed in Lebanon. She and her children are followers of Christ, though she says her husband prays.

I was living in Syria, and before I came here, I didn't know anything about Christ. Everyone kept his religion to himself, and we never talked about it, ever. I came to the church for help. I heard there was an evangelical church giving food portions. I came on Sunday at prayer time to get it, and the pastor invited me to stay and pray. I came again to hear more. I learned something about myself and my heart, and it made me very happy. I decided that I would pray; I didn't know what to pray. I didn't know if I was going the right direction or the wrong direction, but I chose to go the right direction. I decided to follow Christ for the love, for peace, for brotherhood. It was the love, the idea that you should love your enemy, that was very important. We don't have that kind of love. He is the true Savior, and I have peace.

I have had a lot of problems since I left my religion. My husband's family knows I am going to church and what I am doing with the kids. I have Christian books. They [my family] give me a lot of trouble; it is scary. Everything in Islam is forbidden, restricted, or shameful. It's about what you eat. It's all about the sword. It's all fear. We have an image of God in Islam that he always wants to punish us and is looking for whatever is not good. We're always afraid; it's always about fear. But it's done. I have made a decision, and I will never go back.

Worshiping Christ has changed me. I'm a daughter of Christ. Jesus thinks of me. His truth has changed me. My kids do what I ask from the oldest to youngest. They encourage me to pray. Christ is love. He is everything good. He helps me. He took me out of darkness and brought me into light. He is my way, my truth, and my life. He won't ever leave me. A lot of things changed. The difference is that now I have something good to look for tomorrow. Tomorrow is a sweeter day.

"I left Islam because of the war"

> Bushra is a twenty-nine-year-old married woman with four children. She is from Syria and has been in Lebanon for two years,

> though her husband worked in Lebanon as a migrant worker before
> the war. In Syria, she was a housewife, and now she works in the
> church. Her husband works in a bakery. She is the only follower of
> Christ in the family, though she says her husband prays.

I became a believer a year and a half ago. I was living in the house of my family before my husband and I came to this [the present residence]. During the war, my children were living with different families because of the rockets and air strikes. It was religion that was causing all of this fighting year after year. We spent a lot of time moving around to all my husband's family. My husband was in Lebanon, and we came here. Later we came to the church here. There were lessons and teaching that we attended. We had been searching but did not find anything. We had been with the Ahmadiyyah [a revivalist sect within Islam]. We arrived at the church and heard the word. We had not heard anything like it. We stayed involved with the lessons about Christ and his love and peace. We had not heard anything like this about God. I am now not living in fear. My Lord is the Savior. He will never leave me and my children. If later someone in my family comes here and sees my life, maybe they will change. The Lord changes people.

The first reason I left Islam was the war. It was religious. It was jihad. It's a religion of the sword. Christianity is a religion of love and peace. I want to live a life of love, peace, and faith – me, my children, and my family. I don't love Islam because it is really against women. Women are always the ones suffering. No, I would never go back.

Following Christ means knowing his love. Peace. His truth has changed me. Our lives changed. Our hearts were always heavy. Now I rejoice. In our religion, there were always demands on you of what to do and what not to do. Now peace and joy are part of the faith. Jesus is my joy and peace. What was black is now made white.

God's identity is love

> Samir is a forty-seven-year-old married man with seven children.
> He is from Damascus and has been in Lebanon for just over three
> years. In Syria, he worked as a carpenter and now works in a
> church's aid center helping with the distribution programs to
> the refugees. His wife is a housewife and stays at home. Only
> he and his wife are followers of Christ. The rest of the family are
> still Muslim.

When we first came to Lebanon, we settled in a Sunni [Muslim] refugee settlement. We needed food aid, so we came to the church. Brother N and Brother J were preaching in the church. Brother N told me how Christ is a Savior for all people. We were from a Muslim background; we had God and his prophet Mohammad. We told Brother N, "You're doing a wrong thing; you are going to hell." He asked why he is going to hell, and we said, "You are preaching about the Trinity. This is associating someone with God. This is apostasy. But, you're a good man."

Brother N said, "We only have one God." He explained the Trinity to me.

I said, "Ok, you only have one God; this is not associating someone with God."

He said, "No, we will never practice polytheism. Our God is one God." My wife and I listened to this. She has taught Islam in Syria; she was in a movement. She had twelve to fifteen people that she was guiding in Islamic evangelism.

We had some books we were reading. One said one thing, and another said another thing. I asked her why we were reading them when we would not learn anything. We got a Holy Bible and began reading in the Old Testament. We read Genesis, about Noah, Moses, Deuteronomy, the law of Moses, but we did not change anything in our lives about living by Islamic law. We figured the New Testament was like the Old, and there was a relationship between them and that there wasn't any new revelation from God, just the same law, like Mohammad.

We kept coming [to the church]. My wife still wore the hijab [scarf covering the head]. They said she could choose to wear the hijab or not, as she wished. It was not a problem. Later in Matthew in the Bible, we studied the testimony of Jesus about the Father and Son and Holy Spirit. It was a hard testimony to accept. But we realized that the identity of God is everywhere. It is in the creation and is talked about by the prophets. But the idea that God would live among us in a body was hard. But in the Gospel of Matthew, we saw in his birth by the virgin Mary that he is God.

In the Bible, we see that God's identity is love. In the Qur'an, there is no name for God that is love. He loves us. This is the true God. This is the living God.

We thought a lot about the law. We thought a lot about the law of Moses because we have the law in Islam. A truth came to me that something is lacking.

The revelation of Jesus is that he is God. This isn't just something that is preached. This is found in all the Old Testament and the Law and the Prophets. The Lord Jesus is God become flesh because of love. This was not because we deserved it, or we had something to offer. We have nothing. Even if I lived on hundred years or two hundred years, God would not save me because I followed the law. He came because of his mercy.

I was praying every day, "God, I want to serve you." We have prayers in Islam, and I ended every prayer with that. My heart was changing. You know in Islam, we follow the law of "eye for eye and tooth for tooth." Christ taught love. He didn't teach to settle every sin by the law. Something big was happening inside me, in my heart. The devil could not do whatever he wanted. I was thinking about repentance and life with God. It was God that entered into me; it was not from me. The devil is our enemy. My enemy is not this person or that person. The devil is the enemy. All of his thoughts are evil. He wants to take us to hell by any means.

To follow Christ is to have life with God – I am an ambassador for God. I am a messenger to my children. I'm also a messenger to myself. Every day I ask God, "What do you require of me today? Not what I want, or what someone else wants, but what You want."

I know Christ is God made flesh. I am a believer because he saved me. He is not just another prophet; he is God. When you look at what the teachers of the law did, they are the same as what the Islamic State [a terrorist group] does today. If anyone believes that Jesus is God, they will cut off his head.

Our life with Jesus is good. We had problems in the camp. My kids had problems. We believed in Jesus three months while we were in the camp. People from the church visited us. Rumors started and people asked if apostates were coming to visit us, and I said, "No, they are my guests, nothing more." A lady helped with rent and got my wife a job as a teacher. Brother N came without knowing this and asked me about work. After a while, we are a big family, we came to the church to live. God has never left us; I give him thanks and glory.

When I was baptized, I saw in the Old Testament and New Testament, I saw in Abraham a story. He believed in the promise of God.

I left Islam because everything is about killing. There is one part of Islam that is about peace and calm and love. There is another part that is about killing, like in the law. This doesn't bring me close to God. I want God in the end. I don't want my children brought into the teachings of Islam. Jesus said if you look at a woman with lust, you commit adultery with her in your heart. There is a pure way of looking at my daughters or my sisters. In the Gospels, it is not about killing. Jesus gave. It was in love. Jesus is the Savior of my life; he is the one who loves me and gives me love.

I am facing a lot of consequences because I left Islam and believed in Christ. I can't visit my family. They wrote me a message saying they will not see my children or me. They said you are people who are lacking and do not have a family. I said, "No, we are good people who believe in God."

They said, "No, you are people who believe in polytheism, apostates who read a forbidden book." I told them to look in their book, and it will direct them to the Bible. They said they will kill me if I return. Here in Lebanon, I have a right to believe what I want. It would be hard to go back to Syria. God is faithful, and he will take care of me.

It is impossible that I will go back to Islam. I can never deny Christ. If I went back to Islam, I would be lying to myself. How can I do this as a father? Nothing can take me back. I am going toward Jesus. I am a servant of him. I am a son. I am wearing a white robe that he gave me. I am saved. I want to learn everything in the Bible about him. I was in Islam, and it didn't teach me anything. Jesus taught me about love.

What dissatisfied me about Islam is the killing. Verses from the Qur'an are about the sword. The mothers of the Shia[12] are crying. The mothers of the Sunni are crying. No one can comfort them. It reminds me of the story of the death of Lazarus. When Jesus saw Mary and the others crying, he was moved with compassion. The testimony of Islam is not from God. There are a lot of things. *Shari'a* [Islamic law] is not from God. The rules about women are not from God. Do I want this for my daughter? God is holy. The *Shari'a* is not from God. Killing and death is from the devil.

Christ for me is my mother and father. He is my life. He is with me every day. He brings me peace and comfort. He is life. I changed as a person. I had lived in fear. My personality was fearful. I was full of hate. Maybe I would have been a killer. Maybe I would have killed my brother or neighbor. Today I cannot think about anyone, even for one minute, and say I am going to kill you. Jesus doesn't teach us to think about killing; he teaches us to think about love.

"I had a dream, and in it was a white light and a voice in the light"

> Abla is a thirty-four-year-old married woman with seven children. She is from Damascus and has been in Lebanon for three and a half years. She was a stay-at-home mother in Syria and is now teaching Arabic in one of the refugee schools run by the church. Her husband also works at the church. She and her children are followers of Christ.

The first thing I want you to know is that I was a teacher of *Shari'a* law. I gave lessons to my neighbors. I had a group of ladies that I taught in my home about

---

12. The Shias and Sunnis are two of the major sects of Islam.

Shari'a law and the life of Mohammed. I taught about the foundations of Islam. I always was taught, and I taught, that there are three heavenly books, Qur'an, Torah, and the Gospel (*Injil*). When I came here, I came to get assistance from the church. I took a Gospel. I wanted to see what was written in the Gospel. I read the Gospel of Matthew. I read about love. I read about peace. I read about forgiving others. This book encouraged me.

I was overcome by love and forgiveness. Islam is always about "don't do this" and "don't wear that." But the Bible is not like that. The Bible requires of me love and forgiveness. Islam always came with a sword; everything goes back to the sword.

After I read all of the Gospel, I thought about converting, but I said, "No, I already have a book, the Qur'an." So, I went on like that for about a year, but coming to the church, and reading a collection of books, including the New Testament and the whole Bible. I read a lot of books.

I began to read the Bible from the beginning. I read the story of Abraham. I read about Moses – how he taught the word of God, how he brought the Torah, and there was wisdom, wisdom, wisdom. I read all of the stories from beginning to end. The Qur'an doesn't have these stories. It takes from here and from there, from ignorance. The sheikhs started to think I was an apostate because I talked about it. But God said to me, "Don't be afraid." God is living; Jesus is the living God.

I started crying one Friday, and I went to Brother J. I had been in the camp for one year. I was not getting anything – no rent assistance or anything, but I was just coming to the church. I listened to the sermon, took the Bible; I studied it, and I came back. The Lord gave me truth through my reading and listening.

The truths I got through reading the stories, through commentaries on the Gospel of John, through studying doctrines of Christ. I read and read, lots of books. I came on Friday to the church for a sermon. I couldn't come on Sunday morning. The owner of the camp was a Salafi sheikh. When I went out on Sunday, he would question me about where I was going outside the camp. He forbade going to church, and if he knew I was going to church, he would throw us out of the camp. I did not have any work or anything. I didn't have any assistance with expenses or rent.

The Lord was testing me in everything and showing me things even when I could not come and go. I would come back to the camp after the sermon, and for a couple of months I cried a lot. But the Qur'an did not give me any answers.

I knew that Christ was Word and Spirit because it's written in the Qur'an that Christ is the Word of God and the Spirit of God. I cried sometimes, and I prayed for an answer. In Islam, there isn't prayer like that, but in Christianity I can tell God, "You are the only one who can give me the answers."

I had a dream, and in that dream, there was a white light and voice in that light. That voice said, "Jesus is God; he is light and the creator."

I was alone on this way. I didn't have a house. My husband didn't have work. I have seven children and a tough situation. The obstacles are many. I wanted to die.

But I kept coming to church. I decided on a new life. My children became new. My life is new. My husband noticed a difference in everything. He said you are going to the church and learning these things. The children are learning these things. Your life is changed. You are leaving your religion. Why are you doing this? I told him I was sleeping, but now I am awake and have come alive. The Bible is full of stories of miracles. He is a living God.

The Gospel of Christ, the four Gospels, in it there is stainlessness. What do I mean by stainlessness? It is all love, pure love. Islam has love and killing. There are verses that talk about love. There are many more that talk about killing. The sheikhs have different opinions on these verses; some of them take just a few verses that talk about love. How can you talk here about love, and then about the sword? The sheikhs try to teach about love while others are loudly yelling, "Kill him!" This is what my husband saw. Christ from the beginning to the end is all about love.

Think about the story of the woman who was brought to Jesus to be killed. She was caught in adultery. There is nothing but death for her in Islam. This is why I chose to follow Christ.

The consequences I am facing are not in my own life; quite the opposite because God has blessed me in everything. But it is in my family relations. My mother, my brothers, all of my family have joined together to reject me. Islam is about condemnation. There is no forgiveness. Condemnation and extremist opinions. My family, my brothers, my mother, they want to kill me. My brother is trying to get me to Syria. What do you think he wants to do? Nobody is allowed to change his religion and live. This is how *Shari'a* is in the Syrian law. But I cannot go back. No, can I go back to poison?

Jesus is love. I am humbled by it. To worship Christ means to live a loving, humble life. What attracts me to Christ is love. The most important proclamation of Jesus is love. He is light; he is salvation. He is everything in my life.

I was baptized and became a Christian. All of us were living in darkness. I am able to speak about Jesus with a new spirit. I can ask anything. If I ask anything according to his will, he will give it to me.

"Something has cleaned me on the inside"

> Bassma is a thirty-year-old married woman with five children. She is from Damascus and has been in Lebanon for two and a half years. She was a housewife in Syria and now tutors refugee children in a city program. Her husband works in a coffee shop. She, her husband, and children are now all followers of Christ.

I fled here from Syria because of the war. I heard about the evangelical church, that they were giving help. I went to the church to get assistance. I didn't have a car, so I walked the first time and got a carton of food portion. When they heard how hard it was for me to come to church with the kids, they offered me transportation. So, they brought us to church each week. They taught us and trained us. My children were involved in programs here, and I liked it. I heard that God would save us and forgive us in Christ. I cried and cried, and I felt something washing me clean on the inside. I went forward, and when I went forward, my husband asked me if I wanted to be a church member, and I said, "I don't know, but something has cleaned me on the inside."

I chose to follow Christ because he is God. He came as a Savior and paid the price for the sin of the world. Why? So that I can be saved. What attracts me to Christ is that he gives us peace. He is truth, freedom. He has freed me from oppression; what more do I want than this?

Islam is about division. My friend from a long time is always asking me why I have done this to my children. The Sunni are killing the Shia, and the Shia are killing the Sunni. I rejoice in the day I came to Christ. I haven't faced any consequences for my new faith. Would I go back to Islam? No.

Christ is father, husband, brother, son – everything in my life. When I first came to faith and my husband asked me why, I said, "He is truth and life; that is everything." Everything changed of course. I can face the world with peace. People ask how God allows bad in the world, but it is the opposite. He made man and the world good.

Thank God for the wreck

> Tariq is a twenty-six-year-old single man. He is from Damascus and had been a migrant worker in Lebanon before the war. When the conflict started, he became a refugee. In Syria, he worked as a house painter. At the time when he shared his story, he had no work. He had been a follower of Christ for four months.

There are a number of trials. The first trial was . . . there were a lot of things I saw that were not right about Islam. A lot of verses and sayings in Islam were dark. I quit believing in Islam for about a year before I became a believer in Christ.

During this year I had left Islam, there were so many things I saw that were dark about Islam. I saw that they were wrong. I quit doing the practices of Islam. I was living in an apartment beside a church, where we had lived for four years. I did not know anything about the gospel, had never seen a Bible, and knew nothing about Christianity. I did see them coming and worshiping in the church. I did ask one to bring me a Bible. I read about the life of the Lord Jesus – his words, his miracles.

Everything in Islam is about apostasy and forbidden things. In Islam, everything you do is forbidden. You have to pray and fast, and when you read the Qur'an, even those who were fasting were not assured. I was not satisfied. It's lies, lots of untruth. They are about killing, sacrifice without love.

I read in the Bible basic principles. Jesus was born supernaturally from the virgin Mary, that he is God, the Word of God. I read about the miracle of Jesus where he fed thousands with bread and fish. I thought Jesus could have fed them or left them hungry. He took them in his hands, so he could do something. He fed them. He invited them and prayed for them.

When people are invited in Islam, they are invited by the sword. Originally, they had to convert or pay money. They would tell non-Muslims to convert or die. So many people thought, "Shall I convert or pay a tax until I die?" They did not convert to Islam but paid the tax.

I still don't know enough about Christ. I am ignorant of Christ. But I do know a simple thing that God is love, and the miracles of Christ are worth more than years of studying Islam.

The second reason was something that happened in Zahle [the town in the Bekaa Valley in Lebanon where he lived]. I was in a motorcycle accident. My cousin and I were going to a monastery to visit a monk named Joseph. We were going to visit him to learn more about Jesus. We had a Bible he had given us. It was a very windy road, and we made it to the top and found out he was out for the day. So, we went downhill, and there was one area where there was just open valley on one side and cars on the others. We had to skid off the road and into an area of two houses, and everything was dirty. The motorcycle was broken, and we were covered with dirt and injured. But I saw the Bible and it was clean. God watched out for that Bible. We went home, and I opened the Bible and read. My dad said we had the wreck because I left Islam. I said, "Thank God for the wreck, then."

But I have now followed Christ is the way of truth and light. I learned that Jesus is the only Savior. There's no Savior like him.

Since I have followed Christ, I have had problems from everyone. I lost my job; I lost my family. But no. I would never go back to Islam. I worship Christ because he is Savior. God is love. Jesus loved us and was crucified and died for our sins on our behalf. He is the Son of God. He is Lord.

Spiritually, I am not talking about material things; there is a big change. The person who was living in Islam lived like this [hands over eyes]. I was living in darkness. Now I am born again spiritually.

"I had a dream: Jesus healed me"

> Nadia is a thirty-five-year-old married woman with four children. She is from Aleppo and has been in Lebanon for four years. She was a seamstress in Syria and now has no work outside the home and is a housewife. Her husband does valet parking. She is the only follower of Christ in her family.

When I came here at first, God began working miracles which brought me to faith. I had problems with my stomach, very bad problems. All of the brothers [in the church] prayed for me. I had a dream where the Lord Jesus came and put his hand on me. I told my husband that I wanted to go to the doctor. I think that Jesus has healed me. So, I went to the doctor, and he said you are completely healed.

The second miracle is that I believed and was saved. He is Savior and saved us from our sin and delivers us from everything. My life was very hard. But then I came here and found hope, and God was glorified. Now I can live in peace.

There were a lot of things working together to change my life. I have not faced any consequences for following Christ. But I would never go back to my old religion. For women, in Islam everything is forbidden; she can't do anything. It's not like that as a Christian. There are a lot of things. Freedom. A woman can have an opinion.

"God healed me"

> Ahmed is a twenty-six-year-old married man with two children. He is from Idlib in northwest Syria and has been in Lebanon for three and a half years, having left his country a couple of years after

> the conflict in Syria started. Along with his wife and two children, he shares his temporary shelter with his brother and sister. In Syria he worked as a carpenter and enjoyed a comfortable life. As a refugee in Lebanon, he works as a mason, if he can find work. His wife does not work outside the home. He is the only follower of Christ in his otherwise Muslim family. As a Syrian refugee, he has no access to health care, and even if he did, he has no money to pay for it.

When I was in Syria, I had friends who were Christians. I wanted to get closer to Christians and to learn about the Christian religion. But in Syria the situation did not allow me to do this until I came here to Lebanon. When we arrived here and registered as refugees, there was freedom for me to get to know Christians. I met you all, and I wanted to get closer to Christ and to know about the life of Christ. I knew from the Qur'an, that Christ was crucified and will return again for eternal life. And here I began to have a great desire to get closer to Christ and to learn everything about Christ; how he gave himself for our sins. So, it was good, and we arrived here in Mansourieh. We met people from an evangelical church, and I began to get closer to Christ.

The thing that most allowed me to get close to Christ was when I was sick, he healed me. It was prayer that allowed me to have more faith. When I was sick and my back was hurting, and I couldn't sit or even go to work, the Lord helped me. We were in your home and you were praying for us. You prayed for me, the group was praying for me. All of us were as servants of the Lord, and believers in the Lord, and you began to pray for me. When you touched me and prayed for me, I felt that God was touching me with his hand. I felt at rest. I began to have more faith to get closer to Christ, to learn more things, to become like those people who had prayed for me, to be able to pray for others and ask on behalf of others, because Christ truly responds to every prayer for healing. And I am one of those people who have experienced that Christ really heals all people. Not that someone came and told me that Christ heals; it happened with me – Christ healed me. My back was hurting, and I had a ruptured disc.

I am one of those people who has had dreams of Christ more than once.

When I go out to other churches, no one sees me [meaning from his community], and I go with my whole spirit, and I feel that my heart is completely with the Lord. And he healed me; he is the one who saved me. I have more faith, and I love him, and I love the Christian religion, and may Jesus the Lord be with me.

My faith in Christ is big, and I have come to know him more and attend lessons, and I am always in the presence of the Lord because really the Lord is the one who healed me. If not, then I am nothing now. My life was lost when I was sick.

Everybody started to say to me, "What, you left the religion of Islam and went to worship the religion of Christ? What has Christ done for you?" I told them Christ didn't do anything for you, but he did something for me in my life. When I was sick, he was the one who healed me. When I was in need, no one came and helped me. If Christ had not healed me so that I could work, I would have been nothing. Say what you want, but Christ healed me and came to me in a dream. Now I have an enormous faith. Any person who is sick, he should approach the presence of God and allow people to pray for him, for he will surely be healed, and the Lord will be with him, if the prayer is from his heart, from within him, not from the decisions of those outside of him. I accepted Christ into my heart inside of me. I have come to have a lot, a lot of faith.

I come home late – eleven or twelve at night, but I sleep peacefully. I wake up the next morning for my work, and I feel that at work the Lord is speaking to me. I feel that he is with me. He is telling me, "Work, Ahmed." He tells me, "Work, and I am close to you; do not be afraid. Do not fear from anyone."

We are all servants of the Lord, of course. To worship Christ is in the way that he walked, in the way that he taught his disciples who were with him, that we are his servants, just as his disciples were. Servants as his disciples were, meaning I speak about what happened with me in my life, share about it, share the good news, how Christ gave me rest, how Christ was crucified for us, redeemed us, Christ – how he rose – to tell about these things. Just as we learn when we study the *Injil* [the Gospels] that Christ offered his entire life for us. There is no one else like him who can save us.

What attracts me to Christ is his love for us. Love. And he guides us in the way that is correct, not in the way of sin. He is our Lord, and he is the one who redeemed us – he is our Redeemer and our Savior, and our life without Christ is nothing.

After I met Christ, I became much stronger, after the prayers when I was sick and Christ healed me and he told me, "I will be with you this year." In the dream, I saw him. "You will have a different and beautiful year, and it will be new for you, and I will be very close to you." First thing, I feel that I am not the old Ahmed that I was. I have become a new Ahmed, and I have been born again. He gave me the strength. *Hamdillah* [Praise God], I am working. True, there are some pressures on me, and I am somewhat in debt, but *hamdillah*,

I am working, and I am paying off my debts a bit. I have my family here, and I am trying, just as I have come to love Christ, that they would also get closer to Christ, that they would love Christ. Because really, with the pain that I was in, he was the only Savior. No one came to me and said, "I will save you from what you're in." No one said, "I will come and save you." No one but Christ touched me with his touch, as when I was sick, was unable to work, and my life was falling and going backward [getting worse]. And in that time Christ came and gave me strength, and I am now working. I feel that I am very close to him, and I have a strong drive to move forward, to get closer to him. May I be at his side to be one of his disciples.

"God gave me a son"

> Jamal is a twenty-four-year-old married man with one son, and his wife is expecting their second child. He is from Hassakeh in Syria. He had been a migrant worker in Lebanon for twelve years, moving back and forth from his home in Syria. It is not unusual for poor Syrian teenagers to be day laborers during harvest season in Lebanon. After the start of the war in Syria, he moved with his family permanently to Lebanon as a refugee so that he would not be recruited by the Syrian army. When in Syria, he worked in a restaurant, and now in Lebanon works as a carpenter, when he can find work. His wife is a stay-at-home mother, though she has a certificate in the aesthetic arts. Jamal and his wife were both Muslims and are now followers of Christ. They had been declared by their doctor to be unable to conceive, despite several medical procedures.

I discovered faith through experience – because of my son. Me and her [his wife], we didn't have faith, and we were attending the meetings [Discovery Bible Study]. We were a bit afraid. But when Joseph came, it comforted me a bit. He said, "Let's pray," and he gave me the strength. He was a support for me – and I prayed. When I discovered this thing, my faith grew a lot, and every day I am experiencing this thing until now. [Joseph who recorded their story said, "One night, we prayed for them in the name of Jesus. Exactly a month later he announced that his wife was one month pregnant. Even the doctor declared it to be a complete miracle. His wife is now pregnant with their second child.] And my life changed a lot, a lot. My life became beautiful and sweet.

And I have a great desire to spread my faith. But I am afraid for my parents. Daesh [ISIS] is there where they live, and I am afraid because of the society. Here, inside Lebanon, it's impossible to proclaim that I am following Christ – maybe only in front of my friends who are with us. In front of my cousins, I can't. I fear for my parents, maybe they could be killed by Daesh. Or maybe my cousins themselves would take revenge on my family. So, I am praying to the Lord that there will come a future where I can, in another country, proclaim my love for Christ. But I am convinced that love in the heart is better than outward love that is a lie.

I chose to follow Christ because of what I am seeing, because up till now I have not seen anything in following Christ that says "kill" or anything like that. Always it talks about love and peace, and love the other, even love the people who are themselves Muslims, love all people. He came for all people.

It was a struggle for me. "Why? Why do I want to do this? Why?" But there was something pulling me forward to worship Christ; there was something inside me that was pulling me. But at the same time, I kept nagging myself, "No, this doesn't happen. To leave [Islam] etc." But there were many things that proved to me that if I deny, I will be denied later.

I used to be a Muslim on the outside; the important thing is that my heart is with Christ, not that my heart is with Islam, and my outward appearance is with Christ. Because all of my days are with Christ.

The meaning of worshiping Christ is that in my worship to Jesus I am carrying some, not much, a simple part of what he tasted of pain for all of us, not for any single person, for all of us, for the whole world. I feel that this gives me hope that there is someone on the Last Day who will defend me.

What attracts me to Christ is that he is present at all times. Once we invite him and ask him to be in our hearts, he is present.

Christ means to me salvation. Salvation. In general, he means salvation. He means peace. It means that the future, *inshallah* [God willing], will be without war, without destruction because Christ doesn't want that. He came to this earth for peace, not for killing and war. If he had come for war and killing, he would not have been crucified.

Many things changed in my life when I started worshiping Christ. For example, I began to respect my wife more. Truly. There are many things, I began to anticipate hurt – people hurting me. Because I have decided to walk in this path, hating someone else or hurting them has become forbidden for me. I became better in many ways – there are many things, in my life, in my ways, in my work. A lot.

6

Voices of the Poor: Indian Slum Dwellers

Hope finds in Christ not only a consolation in suffering, but also the protest of the divine against suffering.[1]

Jürgen Moltmann

Sociologist Arthur Frank says, "Human life depends on the stories we tell: the sense of self that those stories impart, the relationships constructed around shared stories, and the sense of purpose that stories both purpose and foreclose."[2] Stories influence and shape human behavior. Stories are not always myths and legends, but personal stories also capture human experiences in ways that have meaning and significance, thus defining the experience.

The stories that the poor slum dwellers in India tell are about events and encounters that have changed their lives and have defined their spirituality and daily lives. Their stories tell of a God who heard them in their distress and answered them. They came to know him as *Immanuel* – a God who is real and present.

The World of the Indian Slum Dweller

Urban slums are a growing reality in India. Sixty-three percent of the 4,041 towns in India have slums, with 17.4 percent (78.9 million) households nationally being slum households.[3] The National Sample Survey Office (NSSO) of India defines slums as follows: "A slum is a compact settlement of at least 20

---

1. Moltmann, *Theology of Hope*, 21.
2. Frank, *Letting Stories Breathe*, 3.
3. Society for Participatory Research in Asia, *Bengaluru Study Report 2014*, 5.

households with a collection of poorly built tenements, mostly of temporary nature, crowded together usually with inadequate sanitary and drinking water facilities in unhygienic conditions."[4]

The common features of urban poverty are proliferation of slums, increasing casualization of labor, fast growth of the informal sector (business and commerce), increasing stress on civic amenities and support services, and increasing education deprivation and health contingencies.[5] Poverty in slums is relative as it is defined not just by normative (national and international) standards, but also in relative contrast to the communities that surround it and the city within which it is located.

The city of Bangalore has officially 8.52 million people and is the third most populous city in India: 1.4 million (17 percent) live in slums.[6] There are 597 slum settlements in the city itself. The slums are located in the least desirable areas such as low-lying areas that are susceptible to inundation, quarry pits, water tank (large ponds) beds, along railway lines, near cemeteries, or near slaughter houses. A government report states that one third of the slums in the city are located in environmentally sensitive and filthy areas where water stagnation breeds mosquitoes and other health hazards.[7]

In the slums of Bangalore, 51.95 percent of the dwellings have only one room, and over 42 percent are in a dilapidated condition and barely livable. In their homes, 76.8 percent have a water source; 16.8 percent have a water source in a nearby area; and 6.4 percent of the households have to travel quite some distance to get water. Of the shelters, 28 percent are either semipermanent or temporary[8] while others have reported that 90 percent of the dwellings are semipermanent or temporary, depending on the location of the slum.[9]

The gender ratio in the city is 916 females to 1,000 males. This is due to the high migration rate of adult males from the rural areas looking for work. Of families in the slums in Bangalore, 13 percent have migrated from

---

4. NSSO quoted in Rafiq, "Need Assessment: Slum Homes."

5. Society for Participatory Research in Asia, *Bengaluru Study Report 2014*, 5.

6. Urban experts in India feel that the government figures are a "gross underestimation" and that between 25–35 percent of the city's population live in slums. Society for Participatory Research in Asia, 8.

7. Centre for Education and Documentation (CED), *Vulnerability Assessment of Urban Marginalised Communities*, 3.

8. Society for Participatory Research in Asia, *Bengaluru Study Report 2014*, 6–7.

9. Centre for Education and Documentation (CED), *Vulnerability Assessment of Urban Marginalised Communities*, 3. There are no standard definitions to categorize shelters in slums in India.

other states in India, 58 percent have migrated from other parts of the state, and 29 percent are locals. The slum dwellers are divided between the "new poor" who have migrated within the last ten years and live in informal settlements and the "old poor" who have been there a long time and live in better established communities.

Of the slum dwellers, 48.73 percent are either illiterate or have very low levels of literacy; 76.47 percent are unskilled workers, and 85.93 percent work as casual laborers.[10] The lowest paying occupations are *coolie* labor (day laborer), self-employed, flower sellers, and domestic servants, and constitute 62 percent. There are also high incidences of child labor in the slum settlements (between 30–34 percent). Extreme poverty is at high levels, overall 56 percent, and particularly in two of the slums studied by Ramachandran and Subramanian, where the poverty ratio was 67 percent and 80 percent,[11] compared to 29 percent in other urban areas of the state.[12] Of a family's income, 52.89 percent is spent on food, compared to 38.26 percent among the rest of the urban population. Considering the low wages, this is an extremely high percentage and leaves very little for other necessary expenses. More than 50 percent are excluded from the financial system, having no bank accounts, and credit facilities and bank loans are negligible: 47 percent have borrowed from informal sources.[13]

Besides the economic impact of poverty, there are significant social, physical, and psychological impacts. One study by Travasso, Rajaraman, and Heymann found that women in the slums of Bangalore experience extreme depression, including ideas of suicide and attempted suicide. The women who have an alcoholic and/or abusive husband experience marital violence, who are raising children with special needs, or who lack adequate support for child care appear to be more susceptible to severe and prolonged periods of depression and suicide attempts.[14] Noncommunicable diseases such as hypertension and diabetes mellitus are increasingly affecting adults in urban slums. The number of low birth weight babies born to the poor, meaning that the expectant mothers did not receive proper and adequate nutrition, is between 30–40 percent. The child mortality rates are 5 percent for children

10. Society for Participatory Research in Asia, *Bengaluru Study Report 2014*, 13–14.

11. Ramachandran and Subramanian, "Slum Household Characteristics in Bangalore."

12. Shetty, "City Studies on Nutrition: Bangalore, India," 54–58.

13. Society for Participatory Research in Asia, *Bengaluru Study Report 2014*, 12–15.

14. Travasso, Rajaraman, and Heymann, "Qualitative Study of Factors Affecting Mental Health," 4.

under age one and 3 percent for preschool children.[15] Another study done by a national NGO found that 30 percent of the children in Bangalore slums were underweight with 52 percent stunted, meaning malnourished over long periods of time, and 19 percent were suffering from serious malnutrition.[16]

The research data on the poor living in the slums of Bangalore confirms that poverty has significant physical, social, and psychological impacts due to the physical contexts of the slums and the challenges of struggling to barely earn a living.[17] Poverty in the Bangalore slums is chronic or generational, with most families and individuals moving from the rural areas because of their inability to support themselves and survive. For some in their first decade in the slums, their poverty may be transitory as they may move above the poverty line for a while before slipping back. Those in slums not supported by the municipality are the most vulnerable as they receive fewer services and have access to few facilities. While they may be able to vote in elections, with regards to their daily survival, they are marginalized from the mainstreams of society, isolated, voiceless, and have very few assets.

Those whose stories are recorded here lived in four of the poorest slums in Bangalore. While all were poor, seventeen out of the twenty lived in extreme poverty, dependent on daily wages. Most of them had low levels of literacy or were illiterate.

Stories of Indian Slum Dwellers Finding Christ
"Only Jesus can change my life and my family life"

> Danu is a twenty-year-old married woman with no children. She migrated from Tamil Nadu, a neighboring state, eight years ago. She works as a day laborer (*coolie*), and her husband is in jail. She used to worship the Hindu goddess Lakshmi.[18] She is the only follower of Christ in her family.

I am very good in doing *pujas* [ritual worship of an idol or deity]; as a family we adopted all Hindu customs. COME [an indigenous mission organization]

---

15. Shetty, "City Studies on Nutrition: Bangalore, India."

16. Fernandes, "Over 30% of Children in Bangalore Slums Are Underweight."

17. One of the best descriptions that gives a sense of the destitution and desperation of poverty in India is Kamala Markandaya's novel *Nectar in a Sieve*.

18. Lakshmi is the Hindu goddess of prosperity who leads human beings to achieve the eight types of goals that they have in life – spiritual enlightenment, food, knowledge, resources, progeny, abundance, patience, and success.

missionaries were visiting our house weekly. I was not interested [to listen] about Jesus. Previously, at one time I fell in love with a person and ran away from my family and got married. Within a week, police arrested him and took him to jail. I was discouraged when this happened, and I wanted [to] hang myself. But the COME missionaries shared about Jesus. They explained that Jesus will change your life and family life. I realized at that moment only Jesus can change my family. And I finally accepted Jesus as my personal Savior.

I stopped worshiping Lakshmi and chose to worship Christ because my husband went to jail. [She felt no one had helped her during that time.] I have faced some pressure from my parents and relatives. But I would never go back to my former religion, because Christ has given life to me. He is almighty God, gives life, and provides. For me, Christ is the eternal God, and the true God. I am attracted to Christ because of God's word, songs, stories. My life has changed as a result. I stopped doing witchcraft, eating tobacco, pan parag [an addictive mix of spices], and things like that.

"He is a peace-giver, Almighty God, he forgives my sins"

> Neha, is a thirty-one-year-old married woman with two children. She is from Nagshettikopa, Bhopsundra, another part of Bangalore, and moved ten years ago. She used to be a housewife and now works as a street sweeper for the municipality. Her husband is also a day laborer working for the municipality. She is the only one in her family who is a follower of Christ.

I am Hindu and come from a very poor family. As a family, we used to do all kinds of *pujas* and maintained all ritual festivals. I was very passionate in wanting to do *pujas*. I hated Jesus, thinking that he was a foreign God. I never, never wanted to go anywhere to hear about him. Whenever Pastor V used to come to my home to visit, I used to get angry at him and chased [him out] many times. But he would keep on telling me about Jesus. One day he conducted a prayer meeting in my relative's house. I forced myself to sit through the meeting. He shared from James 1:13–14 – that from our desires we commit sin [and these were] put on God. These verses touched me, and I thought that only Jesus can wash my sins, forgive, and will give eternal life. So after listening to him, God spoke to me, and I cried bitterly and accepted him as my personal Savior, Jesus Christ.

There is no peace, no forgiveness in Hinduism. We were always quarreling about spending money. We had no peace, and we had financial problems. My husband told me to leave. He wears Ayyappa's *malas* [a flower garland for the god Ayyappa[19] as a sign of devotion to the deity], and he tried to burn me. I will never go back to my old religion.

I worship Christ because he is a peace-giver, almighty God; he forgives my sins. I'm attracted to Christ because of God's message, his lifestyle, that he gave his life for me. Jesus is almighty God, the only One God, the true God, and the eternal God.

My life has changed now. There is no fighting or jealousy, and I don't do witchcraft.

"Jesus healed me"

> Ammu is an eighteen-year-old single girl. She is from Nagshettikopa, another part of Bangalore, and moved twelve years ago. She is a student in school. She used to worship the goddess Lakshmi and the god Krishna.[20] She, her parents, and her sisters are all now followers of Christ.

When I was studying in the seventh standard, I suffered from psoriasis. My father told me to leave the house because of my sickness; my whole body and face was covered with pimples/psoriasis. In that moment Pastor V from COME ministries came to my house and shared that Jesus can heal your disease. I believed in Christ and prayed continually for two weeks without any medication. Jesus healed me completely. Then I accepted Christ as my personal Savior. I am so happy because my face became like a baby face. I love God Jesus.

I stopped worshiping Krishna and Lakshmi because of my sickness [psoriasis]. I did not get well after doing a lot of *puja* and taking medication. But Jesus healed me without any medication other than by the anointing with oil which was prayed over by Pastor V. I will never go back to my old religion. Jesus is the only healer in this life. He is almighty God, healer, true God. What attracts me to Jesus is the miracles done by Christ, God's message, and that he is a loving God.

---

19. Ayyappa is a Hindu deity revered in South India for being able to defeat evil. He is also revered by Muslims for having defeated a Muslim brigand.

20. Krishna is a major deity in Hinduism. A supreme god in his own right, he is known for compassion, tenderness, and love.

My life changed after I started worshiping Jesus. He healed me from my sickness. We stopped quarreling and fighting; we stopped doing *pujas*, and I'm not angry anymore.

"God gave me a baby"

> Aradhana is a twenty-eight-year-old married woman with two children. She is from Chinthamani, a town in eastern Karnataka, and left ten years ago. She used to worship the god Narashima.[21] She used to be a housewife and is now a street sweeper with the municipality. Her husband is a driver. She and her children are followers of Christ.

As a family, we worshiped and were dependent only on our god and goddess. I wanted to get married with a good handsome person. Keeping that in mind, I was doing even more *pujas*. I got married with a Hindu man, who turned out to be a drunk. After my marriage, we had a child. We were planning for a second child but that failed. We did many *pujas*, which in the end were useless. We were very sad as a family. But one day Pastor V from COME ministries visited our home and prayed and explained about the life of Jesus. I was in deep depression at that time because of not having another child. I took the decision . . . that if God Jesus gives me a child, surely, I will accept him as my personal Savior. By the grace of God Jesus, I got a baby, and I accepted Jesus as my personal Savior. He is the only One God.

Because I could not have a second child, there was no peace in my life. So, I decided to follow Jesus, who gave me a child and peace in my life. We stopped doing witchcraft, chewing tobacco, and we stopped quarreling. I have not faced any negative consequences for my decision to worship Jesus. I would never go back to my old religion. Not only did I not have a second child, but before I accepted Jesus there was no peace, and we were constantly quarreling. For me Jesus is provider, almighty God, and the eternal and true God. I am attracted to God's message, to spiritual songs, and to the lifestyle of Jesus.

"Jesus is the only One God in this universe"

> Bharti is a twenty-four-year-old married woman with one child. She is from Andhra Pradesh, a neighboring state, and left nine

---

21. Narashima is a Hindu deity who is part lion and part man to destroy evil and end religious persecution and calamity on earth.

> years ago. She used to be a student and is now a housewife. Her husband works in real estate. She used to worship the god Narashima. She is the only follower of Christ in her family.

I was worshiping Narashima. While I was studying in school, a man (now my husband) was trying to force me to marry him. I was not interested in marrying him. One day he forced me to meet his family members. I thought I would talk to his parents and get rid of him. But he cheated me and locked me in a room, slept with me and married me. I did not have any way to escape from him, and I got pregnant and had a baby. I was discouraged. One day Pastor V came to my home and shared about the love of Christ and that he can forgive your sins. From that day onwards, my husband started to come home and stayed with me and accepted me as his wife. Then I realized that Jesus is the only One God in this universe, and I accepted him as my personal Savior, Jesus Christ.

I stopped worshiping Narashima after my husband cheated me. He also drinks alcohol, and I had no peace. My life was spoiled. When I started worshiping Christ, my husband started beating me and sent me out from our home. I would never go back to my old religion because Jesus rescued me from the clutches of Satan. My life has changed now. I left doing witchcraft, eating tobacco, fighting. Christ is life-giver, almighty God, eternal God, and a real God. I am attracted to God's word, stories, songs.

"Jesus came to me and gave me life"

> Heema is a twenty-eight-year-old married woman with three children. She is from Raichur, in north Karnataka, and left six years ago. She used to be a housewife, but now works as a day laborer (*coolie*). Her husband is a driver. She used to worship the goddess Yellamma.[22] Besides her, other members of her family also follow Christ.

We were struggling a lot as a family. After my marriage, my husband and I came to Bangalore, and stay in a small hut. We had no peace and a lot of financial problems. We struggled for daily food. The COME missionary pastor visited our home four years back and shared the good news of Jesus. Every week he would visit and pray for us. Jesus came to me and gave life [to] me, died for me . . . I accepted Christ.

---

22. Yellamma is the patron goddess of the southern states of India and is revered as the "Mother of the Universe."

I have not faced any pressure from my family for worshiping Jesus. I would never go back to worshiping Yellamma. I had no peace. We were always quarreling, and we had financial problems. Jesus is almighty God, eternal God, the true God. I like listening to God's messages and singing songs. My life has changed. Now I don't eat *paan parag*; I have stopped quarreling and doing witchcraft.

"Jesus healed me"

> Anand is a thirty-eight-year-old married man with four children. He is from Raichur and left two years ago. He used to work as an agricultural laborer but now works as a day laborer (*coolie*). His wife works as an agricultural laborer. He used to worship the goddess Yellamma. He and his wife are followers of Christ.

I was suffering from TB (tuberculosis).[23] I could not get well even after doing *pujas* and visiting many Hindu temples. There was no peace in the family. Someone came to my house and shared about Jesus and told me that Jesus can heal you. So, I listened and began to believe in him. Within a few months, I got healing from him. Seeing this miracle, I accepted Christ as my personal Savior, Jesus Christ.

I like hearing God's word and singing songs. For me Jesus is the healing God, life-giver, the real God. I can never go back to my old religion. It could not heal me from my sickness. My life has changed. There is no quarreling, eating tobacco, or drinking alcohol.

"God provided me with a baby boy"

> Bala is a twenty-seven-year-old married woman with one child. She is from Raichur and left five years ago. She used to work in agriculture, and now she and her husband are day laborers (*coolies*). She used to worship the goddess Yellamma. Both she and her husband are followers of Christ.

For seven years I did not have a child. I used to go to many temples to do *pujas*, and attend many festivals to get a child. But everything was in vain. There was no peace in the family, always quarreling, with debts and financial problems. By

---

23. Tuberculosis (TB) is known in India today as the disease of the poor because of the unhygienic conditions they live in.

the grace of God, we met COME missionary Brother V. He shared about Jesus and prayed often. I put my faith in Christ and attended the prayer meetings regularly. God provided me wonderfully with a baby boy, and I accepted Christ as my personal Savior.

In spite of doing a lot of rituals of Hinduism, I did not get a child. So, I decided to worship Christ. He gave me a baby boy. In the beginning my husband would quarrel with me for attending the prayer meeting and accuse me that I had stopped doing *pujas* to idols. I will never go back to my old religion. I will live for God and die for God because he is almighty God, only One God. When I think of Jesus, he is the real God, almighty God, father, friend, anointed, and Savior. I think of Jesus's lifestyle, God's message, and I want to know the truth. I'm attracted to Jesus because he gives deliverance, peace, and happiness in his name. I like hearing God's message and singing spiritual songs. Our life has changed. Problems are getting solved; there is now no fighting or quarreling in the family, and no witchcraft.

"God delivered me from an evil spirit"

> Bharti is a twenty-five-year-old married woman but with no children. She is from Raichur and left four years ago. She used to work in agriculture but now works as a house servant. Her husband is a driver. She and her husband are both followers of Christ.

I was in the clutches of an evil spirit. While growing up I had problems. I then got married and did not have a child. We moved to Bangalore. There, a Brother V from COME ministries came to our house with his team and told us about Christ and prayed for me. He would visit our house often, and one day even kept a fasting prayer in my home. That time I got delivered from the evil spirit. Then after a few days I began to follow Christ, and put my faith in him. I accepted him as my personal Savior, Jesus Christ.

I decided to worship Christ after being delivered from evil spirits and knowing the truth that Jesus is God. Since then there is peace in my life as well as in my family. After accepting Jesus as my personal Savior, my husband left the family and was drinking alcohol even more. My mother-in-law and brother-in-law told us to leave the house. I had problems with my relatives. I married again. I would never go back to my old religion. For me Christ is peace from God, deliverance from evil, forgiveness from my sins, blessings. He is almighty God, Creator, the anointed one. I like hearing God's message, singing songs, hearing about Christian lives, and God's miracles. My life has changed. I am no longer doing witchcraft by doing mantras, or quarreling, or lying. I have given up bad habits like eating *supari*.[24]

"God healed my father"

> Anand is a twenty-three-year-old single man. He is from Raichur and left five years ago. He used to be a student and is now a supervisor. He used to worship the goddess Yellamma. He is the only follower of Christ in his family.

I was a good person in my hometown. Even in school I did not have any [bad] habits in my life, but I used to worship a Hindu goddess. When my father became ill, we went to doctors and visited many temples, and spent a lot of money. But he was not cured and almost died. In that point, I heard that Jesus can heal my father and went for prayer. They prayed for my father. From the next moment, my father got new life and lived. Seeing this miracle in my father's life, I accepted Christ and believed that he is the only One God.

Because of my father's illness (he was supposed to die) and that Jesus gave life to my father, I stopped worshiping Yellamma. I have not yet faced any consequences because of that. I would never go back to my old religion. Why do I have to go back since Jesus healed my father and gave him life. He is the only One God in this universe. He is almighty God, life-giver, miracle God, raising dead people, healing God. I like to hear God's word. He died for me. He gave his life for me.

Since following Christ, we have been able to purchase land and constructed a house. We have good health and finances. Got my father's life back. Good job for me.

"Jesus is the only one who can give me life and peace"

> Lakshmi is a thirty-three-year-old widow with three children. She is from Raichur and left two years ago. She used to work in agriculture and is now a day laborer (*coolie*). She used to worship the goddess Yellamma. She and her children are followers of Christ.

---

24. Betel nut, an ingredient in *supari* that has a psychoactive effect and is cancer causing.

I am a very hard woman, always fighting with my husband. He then committed suicide. I was so sad and did *pujas* because of his death. I was searching for peace, love in life. But I was also trying to commit suicide. But a COME missionary came and shared God's word and counseled me. And I believed that Jesus is the only one who can give me life and peace. Even my children accepted Christ. So, I began to attend prayers, and God spoke to me – "I have died for you and came to give life to you." By listening to this word, I accepted Christ as my personal Savior.

I stopped worshiping Yellamma because of my husband's quarreling and his death. I have not faced any problems because of my faith in Jesus. I would never go back to my old religion because Jesus gave me life. He is the only One God, almighty God, life-giver, eternal God, giving eternal life and deliverer.

A lot has changed in my life. I did not commit suicide; controlled my quarreling; not angry or doing *pujas*.

"Jesus changed my husband"

> Danna is a twenty-eight-year-old married woman with four children. She is from Bellary district and moved three years ago. She used to be a housewife, but now she and her husband work as day laborers (*coolies*). She used to worship the goddess Yellamma. Other members of the family are also followers of Christ.

I used to worship a Hindu goddess. I got married. The person I married was a heavy drinker. I was doing a lot of *pujas* to change his life, and also witchcraft so that he would change. But nothing happened. I moved to Bangalore with my husband, and I met COME missionary Brother V. He shared about Jesus and told us to attend church. I began to attend church. Within a few months my husband stopped drinking alcohol. Then I believed in Jesus and accepted him as my personal Savior. Now we have peace in the family. I stopped worshiping Yellamma because of my husband's alcohol problem. We used to quarrel and had problems with finances. Accepting Christ has changed my family situation.

I have experienced community opposition and mocking. But I would never go back because Jesus is the only One God in this universe. He is almighty God, a real God, miracle God. A healing God and forgiving God. Jesus gave his life for me. He is forgiver of sin and provides our daily needs. I have stopped eating *supari* and tobacco, and quarreling. I had some health problems (bleeding), and now I have been healed.

"He is the one who is going to come back"

> Ravi is a thirty-three-year-old married man with four children. His is from Hoskote and left three years ago. He used to be a driver, but now he and his wife work as day laborers (*coolies*). He used to worship the goddess Yellamma. Besides himself, other members in his family are also followers of Christ.

I was a heavy drinker and worshiped Hindu goddesses, quarreling at home. What I was earning I used to spend drinking alcohol. I lost everything. I came to Bangalore by selling my motorbike for Rs.500 [about $7] and landed at Ranchanahalli [one of the slums in Bangalore]. Pastor V shared the gospel of Christ, and I agreed with what he was saying and began to attend church. I left drinking alcohol and accepted Jesus Christ as my personal Savior.

I stopped worshiping the goddesses because I had failures in my life and did not have peace in my family. After worshiping the Hindu goddesses, I was tense and drinking alcohol, no peace in mind and the family, and we had problems with finances – starving for daily food. There was no peace – we were always fighting. Soon after receiving Christ in my life – my neighbors began to oppose me and started to mock me. Even my relatives. In the midst of all the circumstances, I stood for Christ and worshiped him alone. He is the only One God. Almighty God. Truth is in him. He is peace-giver. I would never go back. Why do I have to go – after knowing reality and truth – God is Jesus Christ. He is the one who is going to come back. He is deliverer and the true God.

I am attracted to God's word because it helps me to be closer with Christ. I like spiritual songs as well. I have stopped drinking alcohol, eating tobacco, quarreling, cheating, and beating my wife.

"He gave his life for me"

> Raj is a thirty-two-year-old married man with no children. He is from Raichur and left four years ago. He used to work in agriculture and is now a driver. His wife works as a day laborer (*coolie*). He used to worship the goddess Yellamma. He and his wife are followers of Christ.

I am from a Hindu background. I wanted to become most popular in doing *pujas* and was drinking alcohol due to not having a child. I was discouraged in my marriage. I had visited various temples and gone to doctors, and we still did not have a child. We had financial problems, and I had no peace of mind;

we were quarreling. In that situation, COME missionary Brother V shared the good news of God when he visited my home regularly. I listened to what he said about Jesus, why he came to earth, that he forgives my sin, and that he gave his life for my sin. And I cried before the Lord and accepted him as my personal Savior and left drinking alcohol and smoking.

My family members have opposed me saying, why are you leaving our god and accepting a foreign god? I would never go back because Jesus is the only One God. He is the only one almighty God. The true God. Peace-giver. I love hearing God's word and singing spiritual songs. I have stopped doing witchcraft, drinking alcohol, smoking, and eating tobacco.

"My husband got healed"

> Annama is a twenty-eight-year-old married woman with four children. She is from Raichur and left two years ago. She worked in agriculture, and now both she and her husband work as day laborers (*coolies*). She and her husband are followers of Christ.

I have accepted Christ as my personal Savior after my husband got healed from TB (tuberculosis). I was dissatisfied by my old faith because my husband could not be healed. I would never go back to my old religion. Christ is almighty God, the real God. I have now stopped eating *supari* and chewing tobacco. There is peace in the family now. I like listening to God's word.

Jesus is Peace-Giver, Almighty God, the Real God, the Eternal God

> Sati is a thirty-eight-year-old married woman with two children. She is from Tamil Nadu and left twenty-five years ago. She used to be a housewife and is now involved in a small business. Her husband does private work. Other members of her family also follow Christ.

I had grown up in a rowdy area. I acted rowdy, beating people, doing all bad habits and married to two husbands. I was doing business by giving money for interest. Being rowdy became my daily habit. I did not fear anything. I had no peace, and I was always quarreling. One day missionaries from COME ministries visited my home and shared about Jesus. They started visiting my home regularly. One day God talked to me through God's word, and I cried before the Lord and accepted him as my personal Savior.

I would never go back to my old religion. My life has changed – I stopped being rowdy, doing witchcraft, and eating tobacco. I am attracted to God's word. Jesus is peace-giver, almighty God, the real God, the eternal God.

"Jesus gave us jobs"

> Puja is a twenty-seven-year-old married woman with two children. She is from Tamil Nadu and left fifteen years ago. She used to be a housewife, but now she and her husband are day laborers (*coolies*). She and her husband are followers of Christ.

I am from a Hindu family, a very religious family, and I adopted all Hindu customs. I was facing a lot of problems in the family. My husband and I lost our jobs for no reason. We were struggling for even daily food. Last year in 2015, COME missionaries distributed Christmas cake. I started attending the prayer meeting from that day onwards. COME missionaries would visit our home, and we asked them to pray to get jobs. Always they were telling me to go to church. One day I prayed to Jesus and accepted Christ as my personal Savior and prayed to get a job. By a miracle, Jesus gave us jobs and changed our lives and gave peace in our family. Now we are blessed by him and living peacefully.

I would never go back to my old religion. We lost everything, even our jobs. There was no peace in the family, and we had financial problems. We love God's message and the songs. Our lives have changed. I stopped doing witchcraft, quarreling, and eating *supari*. Jesus is almighty God, the eternal God. He is the only One God. Peace-giver.

"Jesus healed my husband"

> Poonam is a twenty-three-year-old married woman with two children. She is from Gulburga and left ten years ago. She used to be a day laborer (*coolie*) and now is a housewife. Her husband works as a day laborer (*coolie*). She used to worship the god Anjnaya.[25] She is the only follower of Christ in her family.

I am from a Hindu background from Gulbarga, and I fell in love and married a Marathiperson.[26] I worshiped Anjnaya – that he can help my family and

---

25. Anjnaya Swamy is also known as Hanuman, the god of strength and victory and the supreme destroyer of evil.

26. From the state of Maharashtra. Her marriage is with someone outside her community.

provide everything for us. My husband began to drink alcohol every day. Our family situation worsened. One day my husband fell sick from dengue fever. Someone told me to call the COME missionaries to pray. They prayed and shared about Christ. My husband was supposed to die because of extremely low blood platelet count. Even the doctor said that he would not recover. But the servants of God, they prayed continually. My husband recovered from dengue fever. By seeing this miracle, I accepted Christ as my personal Savior.

I will never go back because Jesus healed my husband, and I gave my life to him. I stopped worshiping Anjnaya because of my husband drinking alcohol and because of his sickness. Jesus is the healer. He sustains. He is almighty God. He is the real God, life-giver. I like to pray, sing songs, and hear God's word. My life has changed. I have stopped doing witchcraft, eating *pan parag* and tobacco, and quarreling.

"I lost my job and everything"

> Ramu is a thirty-eight-year-old married man with two children. He is from Tamil Nadu and left fifteen years ago. He and his wife work as day laborers (*coolies*). He and his wife are both followers of Christ.

I am from a Hindu fanatical group and from a poor family. As a family, we were doing all kinds of *pujas*. Even after doing all the *pujas*, we lost everything that we had in the family, even our jobs. We had no peace in the family. The COME missionaries would come to my house regularly and would share about Jesus and pray for my job. One day they told me to believe in Jesus – he will give you a job and change the family situation. Soon after they shared, I cried before the Lord, and I accepted him as my personal Savior.

I like hearing God's message, the Jesus story, and the songs. Jesus is almighty God, peace-giver, the eternal God, the true God, and he provides. I would never go back to my old religion. We had financial problems, no peace in the family, and I lost my job and everything. My life has changed now. I have stopped drinking, eating tobacco and other bad habits, and doing witchcraft.

"Jesus gave me life"

> Madhu is a seventeen-year-old single woman. She is from Gulbarga and left eight years ago. She is a student and also works

part-time as a house servant. She used to worship the goddess Yellamma. She and her sisters are followers of Christ.

I am seventeen years old. I come from a Hindu family. I lost my parents at a young age. I had lost hope in the goddess. Then I decided that there was no god in this universe. We moved our home to Bangalore. Now I am staying with my grandmother in this area. Pastor V called me to a prayer meeting for girls and shared the good news of God. And I accepted Christ as my personal Savior.

I stopped worshiping Yellamma after I lost my parents. I can never go back to worshiping the goddess because Jesus gave me life. He is almighty God and provides. He is the eternal God. I have since stopped my bad habits and fighting. I like the stories in the Bible and the Sunday school songs.

7

Understanding Conversion to Christ among the Poor

> Rumors that God was present in Christian gatherings may have also attracted outsiders to investigate Christianity.[1]
>
> *Alan Kreider on the pre-Christendom early church*

This book is about conversion and the poor in their contexts. The conversion stories of the poor recorded here point to the deep yearnings of people trapped in the throes of poverty for a God who is real. Having heard the voices of some of the poor telling their stories of conversion from the deities and gods they worshiped to the living God revealed in Christ, the question is where do these stories and experiences reside within missiological thinking and practice?

Understanding the Stories That Have Been Told

While the stories stand on their own integrity and indicate life-changing impact on the poor, how are the nonpoor, the outsiders, to understand what they have heard?

In a phenomenological[2] approach to understanding how some of the poor become followers of Christ, the aim is to hear and record, as accurately as possible, the phenomenon being narrated through the stories told, without any predetermined framework. The phenomenologist is concerned with understanding the psychological and social phenomena from the perspectives of the people involved – those experiencing the phenomenon.[3] Missiologist

---

1. Kreider, *Patient Ferment of the Early Church*, 109.
2. Groenewald, "Phenomenological Research Design Illustrated," 3.
3. Groenewald.

David Garrison writes that such an approach "temporarily suspends evaluative judgments until the phenomenon [being studied] has been accurately described. Once it has been described, the phenomenon can be interpreted, assessed and evaluated in the light of the observer's standards and values."[4] Such a descriptive approach is used when there is a need "to appraise terrain in a new continent that we have previously not seen and thus are likely to misunderstand."[5] However it is important to note that phenomenologists are not detached, unbiased observers. "Phenomenologists, in contrast to positivists, believe that the researcher cannot be detached from his/her own presuppositions and that the researcher should not pretend otherwise."[6]

Argentinian theologian Jose Miguel Bonino writes that any theologian belongs to a specific culture, social class, economic status, geographical location, and tradition and writes from within that context.[7] I am very aware that I am outsider, a nonpoor who is listening to the poor living within their own contextual realities and challenges. While deeply rooted in historical Christianity, theologically I am part of the evangelical tradition, having grown up in a traditional evangelical home. However, I do not fit neatly into any of the different types of evangelicals that Gabriel Fackre describes.[8] While very much a neo-evangelical, there are strong charismatic and radical evangelical influences on my spirituality, ministry, and work. I have worked ecumenically fairly extensively, and in my writings I have drawn from across a wide range of Christian traditions. Because I straddle many cultural worlds, I am provided with insights and empathy. But I am aware that I look at the world from a position of privilege. All of these factors influence my perceptions and analysis.

In order to interpret and assess the stories through the lens of missiological history and practice and practical theology, five questions will be explored:

- Are the stories those of genuine spiritual conversion to Christ?
- How did the poor who told their stories become followers of Christ?

---

4. Garrison, *Wind in the House of Islam*, 33.

5. Scott Moreau quoted in Garrison, *Wind in the House of Islam*, 33.

6. Groenewald, "Phenomenological Research Design Illustrated," 7.

7. Bonino, "Doing Theology in the Context of the Struggle of the Poor," 369–70.

8. Gabriel Fackre identifies five very broad classifications of evangelical: (1) fundamentalist, which stresses biblical inerrancy in defense of doctrine; (2) old or traditional, which stresses conversion and personal holiness reminiscent of old German pietism; (3) new or neo-, which stresses social relevance but not at the expense of personal faith, compassion, and intellectual development; (4) charismatic and Pentecostal which focus on signs and wonders, the power of the Holy Spirit, and experience; and (5) justice and peace, also known as radical evangelicals. Gabriel Fackre quoted in Tizon, *Transformation after Lausanne*, 3.

- Why did they choose to follow Christ?
- What were their perceptions of who Christ is and what it means to follow him?
- Were there differences in perceptions of Christ between the two groups – the Hindu and Muslim followers of Christ?

It is important to be reminded that the stories will be analyzed using the lenses of the history of Christian conversion and the literature and practice of contextualization. So reference will be made to material presented in chapters 2 and 3.

The key to understanding the responses of the poor to the above questions is to interpret their responses in the contexts of the poverty in which they live and their life experiences. These determine their worldview and their spiritual priorities, and ultimately how and why they chose to become followers of Christ.

Genuineness of the Conversions

The question of the genuineness of conversion is important because it changes how the local church or the community of Christ-followers relates to the individual. In the early church, the genuineness of a conversion which was attested by instruction, observation, and baptism allowed the convert to participate in Christian worship and the sacrament of communion, and be introduced to the mysteries of their new faith by the power of the Holy Spirit. In the past few centuries, a liturgical act such as baptism or confirmation or an intentional action such as reciting the "Sinner's Prayer" or going forward in an evangelistic meeting have been evidence of conversion.

Right at the onset it was important to determine that those who told their stories had in fact turned from worshiping their traditional deities to becoming followers of Christ. This genuineness was critical to establish since many of the points in the discussion that follows refer to the questions of when and how conversion took place with the assumption that conversion did in fact take place.

The genuineness of their encounter with Christ was attested by their change in allegiance from the deities they had worshiped to Christ and Christ alone. This change was confirmed by changes in behavior, attitudes, and relationships and by the evidence of spiritual life reflected by a desire to read the Bible, listen to biblical teaching, pray, and worship, all directly of which are attributable to their new-found faith. Local Christian leaders and mission workers in each location also used the above criteria to attest to the genuineness of the faith of new converts. Though the converts did not have a complete understanding of God's plan of salvation, they knew that because of Jesus, God is real. In most cases that was enough to change their allegiance from their traditional deities to Christ. John Stott writes that the result of evangelism is conversion, which he emphasized is "a radical change in lifestyle with new relationships with Christ, the church, and the world."[9]

This radical change in lifestyle was evidenced in a number of ways. One Syrian refugee said,

> I changed as a person. I had lived in fear. My personality was fearful. I was full of hate. Maybe I would have been a killer. Maybe I would have killed my brother or neighbor. Today I cannot think about anyone, even for one minute, and say I am going to kill you. Jesus doesn't teach us to think about killing; he teaches us to think about love.

Another Syrian refugee told her story. "My family life has completely changed. My marriage is much happier because we have Jesus bringing us together. I have a peace like I have never experienced before. I don't worry about my future." Speaking further about her faith she said, "God revealed himself to me in ways I couldn't deny that he was the Messiah. He consistently pursued me. . . . Making Christ the most important thing in your life. Reading the Bible daily and learning more about Christ and who he is."

A slum dweller in India said,

> I am from a Hindu family, a very religious family, and I adopted all Hindu customs. I was facing a lot of problems in the family. My husband and I lost our jobs for no reason. We were struggling for even daily food. . . . I started attending the prayer meeting from that day onwards. COME missionaries would visit our home, and we asked them to pray to get jobs. Always they were telling to me to go to church. One day I prayed to Jesus and accepted Christ as my personal savior and prayed to get a job. By a miracle, Jesus gave us jobs and changed our lives and gave peace in our family. Now we are blessed by him and living peacefully.

Her spiritual allegiance changed. The God she worshiped is not an idol but "almighty God, Eternal God . . . peace-giver." As part of her changed allegiance,

---

9. Stott, *Down to Earth: Studies in Christianity and Culture*, 23.

she had turned away from witchcraft, addictive substances, and conflict in the family. Her testimony is not just about getting jobs but about a new relationship with Christ and a new way of living and worshiping.

The refugees and slum dwellers spoke about how their lives had changed as a result of their decision to follow Christ. Though some Syrian refugees shared how hard life continued to be for them as refugees, many spoke about the joy, peace, and hope they had in the midst of the civil war and their very difficult circumstances. Even though materially little had changed, God had answered prayer for their needs and provided for them. Some spoke about not worrying any more about the future. Others shared about how their attitudes had changed, and some spoke of how they had moved from the "darkness" of their traditional religion. For 61.9 percent of the refugees, following Christ meant living out their new identity as a servant, son, or daughter of God. This meant serving him, having a devotional life, loving him, obeying him, and being a witness.

For the slum dwellers in India, their decision to change their allegiance and to convert to Christ resulted in immediate behavior changes. Many spoke about being freed from addiction to chewing tobacco and alcohol. Some were physically healed or had seen family members healed through their new-found faith in Christ. Others spoke about how they stopped practicing witchcraft as a means of having some control over their lives and trying to have their needs met. All of them stopped worshiping idols once they had encountered Christ. The changes were not only immediate, but also had a long-term impact. One person spoke of how his changed life and broken addictions had enabled his family to save money and be able to buy a small piece of land.

Further evidence was sought for the genuineness of their conversion by assessing whether their faith had been tested. A little less than half (42.8 percent of the refugees and 45 percent of the slum dwellers) said that they had faced mild to severe persecution and harassment because of their spiritual allegiance. In spite of this trouble, all the participants in both locations could not imagine going back to their traditional deity and worshiping the way they used to because their conversion experience had been so profound.

This emphasis on changed lives as evidence of conversion and not just mental assent to the fact that Jesus Christ is God and forgives sin is important because Hindus can believe many of the truths about Jesus Christ and remain a Hindu in their faith and religious affiliation. They reject the exclusive claims of Christ and include him in the pantheon of gods they worship. Muslims will also state that they believe in Christ, but only as a prophet because he is mentioned as such in the Qur'an. They reject the deity and sonship of Christ. Such partial beliefs about Christ sometimes cause confusion among the outsiders who may be involved in conversations with Hindus and Muslims. So, while having correct beliefs about Christ are vitally important in the process of conversion and subsequent spiritual growth, the main evidence of conversion is a radical change in allegiance in whom they worshiped, resulting in changed lives.

These criteria for conversion are in sharp contrast to the traditional evangelical understanding (with roots in the Puritans and Jonathan Edwards) that states that conversion happens when a person acknowledges Jesus Christ as Redeemer and Savior, as the one who forgives their sin and saves them, and they are thus "born again." Their understanding is based on commonly used key verses as proof texts on conversion such as John 3:3, 16–18, Acts 16:30–31, and Revelation 3:20.[10] A verse often used is Romans 10:9, "If you declare with your mouth 'Jesus is Lord,' and believe in your heart that God raised him from the dead, you will be saved." So an act of faith in a moment of time attested by a verbal confession, as well as the content of a person's belief, are the indicators of conversion. This understanding assumes that conversion is a punctiliar event.

This study does not negate the need for an act of faith and the fact that there is a moment in time when the Spirit of God breathes new life into the individual. There is a need to distinguish between regeneration, which is God's work, and conversion, which is the human response.[11] According to Stott, regeneration is unconscious, while conversion is normally conscious. Regeneration is an instantaneous and complete work of God, while conversion – repentance, a turning away from, and faith – is a process rather than an event.[12]

The reality of conversion being attested by a changed life and a transformed spiritual allegiance while the individual grows in understanding of who Christ is has deep historical roots in the practice of the early church. In the early church, conversion consisted of four stages during which catechumens would learn the basic truths of the Christian faith – especially Christ as Lord and Redeemer. Throughout the process, the quality of their life and spirituality

---

10. John 3:3, 16–18: "Jesus replied, 'Very truly I tell you, no one can see the kingdom of God unless they are born again. . . . For God so loved the world that he gave his one and only Son, that whoever believes in him shall not perish but have eternal life. For God did not send his Son into the world to condemn the world, but to save the world through him. Whoever believes in him is not condemned, but whoever does not believe stands condemned already because they have not believed in the name of God's one and only Son.'" Acts 16:30–31: "'Sirs, what must I do to be saved?' They replied, 'Believe in the Lord Jesus, and you will be saved – you and your household.'" Rev 3:20: "Here I am! I stand at the door and knock. If anyone hears my voice and opens the door, I will come in and eat with that person, and they with me."

11. Stott, *Christian Mission in the Modern World*, 169–70.

12. Stott, 171–74.

were observed for evidence of genuine conversion.[13] It was assumed that conversion would only have occurred if what the catechumen believed resulted in a changed life. As noted earlier, this process of conversion changed with the advent of Christendom and Byzantium, where a person could claim to be a Christian without having been a catechumen, being baptized, or showing any evidence of a changed life, as long as the person did not worship idols.

What is evident from the stories of the refugees and slum dwellers is that intellectual beliefs and the experienced reality of God were integrally linked. Either one or some combination of both can lead to changed lives. Much of modern evangelism is based on specific models of counseling therapy[14] which place emphasis on facts and beliefs as foundational for behavior change. These stories instead show that an initial supernatural experience can also lead a person to faith in Christ even before the person fully understands the issues of sin and salvation. This initial experience is then reinforced and confirmed by facts and beliefs. An initial experience, an encounter with Christ, resulting in changed lives and changed spiritual allegiance is attested by David Garrison in his review of mission among Muslims, as well as by the research of Iyadurai among Hindus and Hildebrand among Buddhists.[15]

---

13. Key verses that illustrate this understanding are from the teachings of the apostle Paul about how the reconciling grace of God results in changed lives. Rom 12:2: "Do not conform to the pattern of this world, but be transformed by the renewing of your mind. Then you will be able to test and approve what God's will is – his good, pleasing and perfect will." 2 Cor 5:17: "Therefore, if anyone is in Christ, the new creation has come: The old has gone, the new is here!" Eph 4:22–24: "You were taught, with regard to your former way of life, to put off your old self, which is being corrupted by its deceitful desires; to be made new in the attitude of your minds; and to put on the new self, created to be like God in true righteousness and holiness." Col 1:21–22: "Once you were alienated from God and were enemies in your minds because of your evil behavior. But now he has reconciled you by Christ's physical body through death to present you holy in his sight, without blemish and free from accusation."

14. Rational emotive therapy (RET) developed by Albert Ellis is a school of cognitive behavior therapy. It believes that thought patterns (including beliefs) influence a person's emotions and behavior. There are evangelical Christian models of this therapy, particularly in the work of Larry Crabb described in his book *Basic Principles of Biblical Counseling* (Grand Rapids, MI: Zondervan, 1975). This therapy is also seen in the model that Campus Crusade (Cru) used to use – facts lead to faith which then influence feelings. However, John Piper writing in *Desiring God* states that people do not come to Christ because of ideas, intellectual propositions, and thoughts, but because of desire, that which people crave. For Piper, evangelism is not meant to persuade people to "make a decision for Christ" but should lead them to desire Christ. Piper, *Desiring God.*

15. Garrison, *Wind in the House of Islam*, 235; Iyadurai, *Transformative Religious Experience*; Hilderbrand, "What Led Thai Buddhist Background Believers," 400–415.

How Did They Become Followers of Christ?

When analyzing the stories of the poor, there were two observations about how they became followers of Christ. The first is that in all the stories, conversion was a process punctuated by encounters, experiences, and decisions at various points and accompanied by a growing understanding of who Christ is and what he has done for them. The second observation is that in a significant number of stories, the poor had had a supernatural encounter with Christ that was decisive in their abandoning their traditional faith and becoming followers of Christ.

The reality and challenges of poverty resulting in specific personal or family crises made them deeply aware that their traditional faith and the gods they worshiped did not provide the help and support they needed to cope. This realization then opened them to the possibility that God revealed in Christ is compassionate and is present with them in their circumstances. They experienced this reality of Christ either through the love and compassion of Christians during their time of need, through reading the Bible or hearing it preached, at prayer meetings or church services, through supernatural encounters (dreams, visions, and miracles), or through answered prayer. Usually some combination of these was pivotal in the process by which they became followers of Christ. One Syrian refugee shared,

> I was living in Syria, and before I came here, I didn't know anything about Christ. Everyone kept his religion to himself, and we never talked about it, ever. I came to the church for help. I heard there was an evangelical church giving food portions. I came on Sunday at prayer time to get it, and the pastor invited me to stay and pray. I came again to hear more. I learned something about myself and my heart and it made me very happy. I decided that I would pray, I didn't know what to pray. I didn't know if I was going in the right direction or the wrong direction, but I chose to go the right direction.

While early on she could not articulate exactly what she believed, she took a step of faith to follow Christ. Because of consistent teaching at the church over a year, she was much clearer about what she believed by the time her story was recorded. "I decided to follow Christ for the love, for peace, for brotherhood. It was the love, the idea that you should love your enemy, that was very important. We don't have that kind of love. He's the true savior, and I have peace." Connecting supernatural and mystical experiences and correct beliefs is important and often requires time. As noted earlier, Robin Lane Fox writes that conversion in the early church was a process which may have started with a supernatural or mystical encounter with Christ but was almost always followed up with teaching.[16]

While there may be numerous reasons why they abandoned their traditional faith, what were the triggers that facilitated their encounter with Christ? In the Indian stories, 20 percent chose to follow Christ as a result of reading the Bible or hearing Scripture being taught or preached. Among the Syrian refugee stories, 33.3 percent became followers of Christ by either hearing the Bible being taught or preached, or by reading the Bible themselves. No one of this 20 percent in India nor the 33.3 percent in Lebanon mentioned supernatural experiences as part of their conversion process.

In contrast, 66.6 percent in Lebanon and 80 percent in Bangalore first encountered Christ supernaturally, either through a dream, a vision, healing, answered prayer, or a miracle. This experience then caused them to want to find out more about Christ. Most chose to follow him almost immediately after their encounter. It is important to note that in most of these cases, the individuals and their families had been in contact with Christians, may have heard about Christ, and heard the word of God being read, taught, or preached. However, it was their supernatural experience that was pivotal in causing them to decide to follow Christ.

A critical question is what did they understand and know about the gospel and Christ at the point when they chose to follow Christ? This knowledge was assessed by reviewing how they described what had happened to them. Among the Syrian refugees, there was no standard way in which they described what they had experienced. For most of them, their Christian faith was very new, and they did not have the Christian vocabulary yet to articulate their experience. To describe what had happened, they used terms such as "believed," "chose to go in the right direction," "came to faith," "brought me to faith," "gave my life to him," "began to have more faith to get closer to Christ," "my heart changed and I knew Jesus was the only way," "convinced that Jesus is alive," "growing in my knowledge of Christ," "began to see a clear picture of right and wrong," "I have now followed Christ," and "decided on a new life."

For the slum dwellers in Bangalore, the situation was different. They were being ministered to by one specific indigenous mission organization, unlike in Lebanon where numerous evangelical churches and mission agencies were addressing the physical and spiritual needs of the refugees. For 35 percent of the slum dwellers, the concept of accepting Christ as savior from their sins was based on an awareness of sin and the realization of the need for forgiveness.

---

16. Fox, *Pagans and Christians*, 330.

For the remaining 65 percent, the term "accepting Christ as my savior" was indicative of a change that had taken place where they no longer worshiped other gods and had decided to worship only the living God revealed in Christ. That phrase was learned later since they did not necessarily understand what the term meant or how it related to their encounter with Christ when they changed their allegiance from their traditional deities to Christ, which was evident when they described how they became followers of Christ. It was a learned response and their standardized way of describing whom they now worshiped.

What was evident in both contexts was that a smaller percentage of those interviewed (and mainly in India) understood the issue of sin, the need for forgiveness, and accepting forgiveness offered through Christ at the point when they decided to follow him. For the rest, even though they lacked this understanding initially, their lives changed, and none were in doubt that they had abandoned their traditional deities and were now followers of Christ only. Their identity and social location had changed. But it was over time that their understanding of Christ as savior deepened. By the time they told their stories, 28 percent of the Syrian refugees referred to Christ as savior and giver of eternal life and as having paid for their sins. Of the slum dwellers in Bangalore, 20 percent described Christ as savior and one who forgives their sin.

A number of theologians and missiologists believe that conversion is more than just a punctiliar event – a decision that can be dated. Orlando Costas writes that conversion is a process rather than a single event. While there is a point of initiation to this journey, conversion is a lifelong process, "a plunge into an eschatological adventure where one is confronted with ever new decisions, turning points, fulfillments, and promises which will continue until the ultimate fulfillment of the Kingdom."[17] So in essence what Costas is suggesting is that conversion is not just the moment of justification (regeneration) but encompasses the whole process of salvation, including sanctification, culminating with glorification. The 1978 International Consultation on Gospel and Culture of the Lausanne Movement also affirmed this understanding of conversion, that it is not just a crisis event but a process as well, with public and social implications, which is evident in the stories of both the Syrian refugees and the Indian slum dwellers.[18]

The history and literature on conversion identifies that there are different types of conversion experiences. Context, culture, religion, and life experiences

---

17. Orlando Costas quoted in Stott, "Conversion as a Complex Experience," 182.
18. Stott, *Making Christ Known*, 73–113.

influence how a person becomes a follower of Christ. The 1988 Consultation on Conversion and World Evangelization of the Lausanne Movement differentiated between "insider" and "outsider" conversions.[19] The conversion experiences of the Hindus and Muslims who told their stories for this book would be categorized as "outsider" conversions because they had little or no prior knowledge of Christ or of fundamental Christian truths.[20] As was evident in most of the stories, in order to change their allegiance and become followers of Christ, they needed to change their worldview, give up the rituals and spiritual practices of their traditional faith, and learn what it means to follow Christ and be part of the people of God. This change required behavioral, attitudinal, and relational changes and is what Joshua Iyadurai refers to as a *transformative religious experience*, which is divine in its origin and power.[21] Such changes require time and are a process. The 1978 Consultation on Gospel and Culture highlighted the radical nature of conversion using the language of death and resurrection, which requires a break from the past and then making a new beginning.[22]

The 1988 Lausanne Consultation Report stated that conversion involved a change in allegiance from the gods to Jesus Christ.[23] The understanding is that conversion is not just about forgiveness of sin but is a change in allegiance from the deities they had worshiped to worshiping Christ the Lord. Theologians Matthew Bates and Scot McKnight argue that the true climax of the gospel is the enthronement of Jesus and not just a reconciled relationship with God through a forgiveness of sins made possible by the sacrifice of Christ.[24] Bates draws extensively from ancient literature on the meaning of the Greek word *pistis* (faith) and writes that *pistis* has a much broader meaning than "to believe" (i.e. acknowledging the truth of something). The range of meanings includes

---

19. Stott, *Making Christ Known*, 223–224.

20. This outsider categorization is an important point. Many educated Hindus and Muslims would have attended Christian schools (originally established by missionaries) or have been exposed to the wider world and Christianity through their education. The poor would have had limited educational opportunities or attended government schools which in Syria and India would not have exposed them to Christianity.

21. Iyadurai, *Transformative Religious Experience*.

22. Stott, *Making Christ Known*.

23. Quoted in Stott, *Making Christ Known*, 94.

24. Bates, *Salvation by Allegiance Alone*; McKnight, "Forward," in Bates, *Salvation by Allegiance Alone*; Kelly M. Kapic in his review of Bates' *Salvation by Allegiance Alone* asks the question whether there is a need for a stronger word than "faith," which unfortunately has been reduced to cognitive assent. Kapic, "Do We Need a Stronger Word for 'Faith'?"

fidelity, faithfulness, commitment, and pledged loyalty.[25] McKnight in the "Foreword" to Bates' book writes, "The gospel is the power-releasing story of how Jesus became king and the only adequate response is allegiance alone."[26] He goes on to state that in antiquity, a gift (grace) implicated a person to reciprocate with an appropriate gift. A gift (grace) imposed an obligation on the receiver. He further writes, "Grace can both be one-hundred percent gift and at the same time summon the gifted person with an obligation, a heartfelt and intentional duty, to respond in gratitude and behavior in accordance with the new social bond created by the gift-giver's gift."[27] So in essence conversion is not just about experiencing forgiveness or changing one's divine allegiance, but is transformed behavior, attitudes, and relationships which are in response to the gift of reconciliation with God and of life from God. It is a commitment to live in a new way, in obedience to Christ and his word.

McKnight refers to Dietrich Bonhoeffer's book *The Cost of Discipleship* and the concept of "costly grace."[28] Contrasting this to what is commonly understood about what it means to believe, McKnight writes, "'believe' meant mental acceptance and a single act of reception, and never meant what the term also means in the whole Bible: the kind of faith that is also faithfulness."[29] Conversion is therefore not just a mental acceptance of a truth or a prayer inviting Christ into one's life, but it is a change in allegiance in whom they worship – a renouncing of and turning away from their traditional deities and submitting to Christ the King. This change in allegiance from their traditional deities to the living God is the predominant motif of conversion in the Old Testament.

---

25. Bates, *Salvation by Allegiance Alone*, Kindle Location 2–3.

26. McKnight, "Forward," in Bates, *Salvation by Allegiance Alone*, Kindle Location 43.

27. McKnight, "Forward," Kindle Location 69.

28. Bonhoeffer, *Cost of Discipleship*, 45–60, cited in McKnight, "Forward," Kindle Location 85. Bonhoeffer writes:

> Cheap grace means grace as a doctrine, a principle, a system. It means forgiveness of sins proclaimed as a general truth, the love of God taught as the Christian "conception" of God. An intellectual assent to that idea is held to be of itself sufficient to secure remission of sins. (Bonhoeffer, *Cost of Discipleship*, 45)

> "Costly grace" is the gospel which must be sought again and again, the gift which must be asked for, the door at which a man must knock. Such grace is costly because it calls us to follow, and it is grace because it calls us to follow Jesus Christ. It is costly because it costs a man his life, and it is grace because it gives a man the only true life. It is costly because it condemns sin, and grace because it justifies the sinner.

Bonhoeffer, *Cost of Discipleship*, 47–48.

29. McKnight, "Forward," in Bates, *Salvation by Allegiance Alone*, Kindle Location 92.

This type of conversion is exactly what the stories of the Syrian refugees and Indian slum dwellers show. In almost all the stories in both locations, there is clear evidence of a change in allegiance from the deities and gods they worshiped to Christ. As mentioned earlier, with a change in allegiance were changes in behavior and attitudes, relationships healed, and spiritual hunger. The stories also indicated that the process of conversion is not just about *becoming* a citizen of the kingdom of God through forgiveness of sin and rebellion – namely justification by faith – but also *being* a citizen of the kingdom by continually submitting to the authority of Christ as Lord and King. One Syrian refugee spoke about what it means to follow Christ. "Loving him with all my heart and resting in him. Sharing and being a witness to those around me. Knowing God will open doors even unexpectedly, and trusting him to lead me in the right direction."

"Outsider" conversions are primarily a process, and evangelism has to consider the context of the individual and community. Life experiences, challenges, crises, and frustrations of being poor were critical factors in motivating them to seek a God who cares and answers prayer. As discussed earlier, John Stott states that understanding the context and presence in that context are a prelude to evangelism. He writes, "True evangelism can never take place in a vacuum. It presupposes a context from which it must not be isolated."[30] So the process of conversion starts well before the moment of justification by God. The beginning of the process is when the poor start searching for a God who is real and not distant, and Christ reveals himself as such a God, as is seen repeatedly in most of the stories that were told.

Both Engels (figure 2.2) and Gray (figure 2.3) in their models show that conversion in any context (both "insider" and "outsider") is usually some kind of a linear process. While these models highlight conversion being a process where seekers grow in their understanding of sin and of Christ, the stories recorded here show that it is rarely a standardized linear progression. The model most extensively used by missiologists to understand conversion is by Paul Hiebert (figure 2.1). His model provides a framework to understand when and how conversion is an event or a process. The conversion experiences of Muslims and Hindus recorded here would fit the mold of "well-formed centered sets" in Hiebert's model. As they move toward Christ, the process may include supernatural encounters with Christ, interactions with Christians, worship, prayer, and reading and hearing the Bible. Somewhere along the process, the seeker crosses a boundary and becomes a member of the kingdom of God – at

---

30. Stott, *Down to Earth: Studies in Christianity and Culture*, 21.

which point justification and regeneration take place. The stories indicate that there is no predetermined point in the process or in their understanding of who Christ is, indicating where and when that boundary is. It varied across the testimonies of the poor.

Social science research and theories of conversion also affirm that conversion is a process. Lewis Rambo states that conversion is contextual and cannot be separated from the network of relationships and ideologies within which people live.[31] Therefore, changes in religious allegiance and affiliation have a social impact on the community's fabric of relationships. As a result, Rambo describes the conversion process as being interactive and cumulative and this takes time.[32] This process was seen in numerous stories recorded here of both Hindus and Muslims, where the decision to convert resulted in opposition or persecution by some members of the community because the change in religious allegiance was seen as a threat to the status quo and established relationships within the community, clan, or family. Some of the poor described how they had to adjust their behavior to negotiate continued relationships with members of their larger family or clan. Others spoke about how their conversion had made it possible for other members of their immediate and extended families to become followers of Christ. The conversion process is also cumulative, because each experience, encounter, and decision led to a deeper, clearer, and fuller understanding of who Christ is and what he has done.

Rambo describes the process of conversion as crisis, quest, encounter, interaction, commitment, and consequences.[33] The crisis, quest, and encounter stages in the process can be seen in the lives of the refugees and slum dwellers as their poverty created crises caused them to seek a God who is compassionate, often resulting in an encounter with Christ. This encounter was then complemented by interactions with Christians, which enabled them to make sense of their experience. Sometimes the commitment to follow Christ preceded their interaction with Christians, while as others understood their experience from a biblical perspective, they made a commitment to follow Christ. The final stage in the process, according to Rambo, is the consequences. For a little less than half in both groups, the consequences included opposition or persecution. For all, the consequences included changes in behavior, attitudes, and transformed relationships.

---

31. Rambo, *Understanding Religious Conversion*, 168–169.

32. Rambo, "Conversion: Toward a Holistic Model of Religious Change," 48.

33. Rambo, *Understanding Religious Conversion*, 168–69.

Henri Gooren describes five stages in the process of conversion. The first stage is *pre-affiliation*, which is the worldview and social context of potential members of a group. In this study, the socioeconomic contexts were the chronic poverty in the slums in Bangalore and the event-based poverty of the Syrian refugees. As noted in chapter 3, poverty in each context creates its own culture and worldview, which were deeply intertwined with Hinduism and Islam respectively. Their pre-affiliation context of poverty was instrumental in them seeking Christ. Gooren's second stage is *affiliation*, where the seeker is wanting to become part of a community that worships Christ.[34] As the research by Woodberry among Muslims and Hilderbrand among Buddhists shows, seekers of Christ are attracted to faith communities where the reality of Christ is lived out.[35] However, membership in this group was not yet a central part of the identity of the Christ seekers. Because many of them were unable to continue in their traditional community as a result of their change in religious affiliation, being accepted into a new faith community which worships Christ was key to their spiritual survival. In this study, the new followers of Christ found a faith community and spiritual home in either the local church in Lebanon or in prayer groups in the Bangalore slums.

Gooren's third stage is *conversion*, which involves a radical change of one's worldview and identity. Alan Kreider quotes the work of Thomas Finn on the early church who writes, "the task of conversion was to reshape an entire way of living and system of values."[36] The fourth stage is *confession*, where they are accepted into the new faith community and participate actively, including sharing the reality and experience of their new-found faith with friends and relatives.[37] Confession is seen in the stories of the converts in both locations, where many brought other members of the family to the meetings of the faith community that they were now a part of.

The story from one of the Syrian refugees summarizes so many of the elements of the process of conversion. It includes disillusionment with existing faith, a crisis because of circumstances, a miraculous encounter with the reality of God in Christ, an explanation about the work of Christ which helped with

---

34. Gooren, "Conversion Narratives," 94.

35. Woodberry, Shubin, and Marks, "Why Muslims Follow Jesus: The Results of a Recent Survey of Converts from Islam"; Hilderbrand, "What Led Thai Buddhist Background Believers."

36. Thomas Finn quoted in Kreider, *Change of Conversion and the Origin of Christendom*, xiv–xv.

37. Gooren, "Conversion Narratives," 94.

understanding experiences, further teaching, and finally acceptance into a new community of faith through baptism.

> My wife and children went to the [church] center for sustenance [to get food aid that was being provided]. We were happy about the worship, and it broke down almost all Islamic barriers [against Christians and Christianity]. I was, at the time, fed up in my heart because of my violent religion and was seeking Christianity. We were introduced to a Christian pastor who wanted to visit our house. He came and talked with us about salvation in Christ. I recall one time I asked about being baptized, but he rejected the idea and asked why I wanted that. I told him I was convinced that Jesus is alive! He saved my daughter from a fire in the house while she was sleeping; the curtains were falling on her with the flames. I watched this happen and was amazed by the peace my daughter had and her faith in Christ. She told me she prayed before going to sleep, and Jesus was with her. The second thing I can't forget is that not even one hair on my daughter's head burned. The pastor then led me through the plan of salvation. My wife and I, our two children, and my brother were saved. We are discipled and were later baptized.

Why Did They Choose to Follow Christ?

Missiology has very little on understanding why the poor choose to follow Christ. Any study of the conversion narratives of the poor has to start with the context within which the poor live, out of which come their existential questions. As with any other ethnic and socioeconomic group, their context influences their worldview and spirituality, and their perception and understanding of who Christ is. "Confession of Jesus Christ takes place in particular historical and cultural contexts."[38] The concept of *domain specificity* in the social sciences confirms the relationship between context and culture and perception. "We react to a piece of information not on its logical merits, but on the basis of which framework surrounds it, and how it registers with our social-emotional system."[39]

---

38. Migliore, *Faith Seeking Understanding*, 197.
39. Taleb, *Black Swan*, 53.

Understanding the contexts and life experiences of the refugees and slum dwellers (their social-emotional systems) will provide insights to explain why they chose to follow Christ, because it is the contexts of poverty that are the frameworks through which they interpret life and life experiences and seek for a God who understands their poverty and despair. Were there specific factors which influenced their decision to leave their traditional faith and follow Christ? As Rambo points out, a personal crisis creates a push away from their traditional faith. To resolve this crisis, there has to be something new that attracts them and satisfies their quest.

The context of the Syrian refugees was the reality of their displacement and the resulting consequences. While they had not been destitute in their homes in Syria, they had descended into devastating poverty because of the conflict (event-based poverty). They were now living in deplorable housing conditions with limited access to water and proper sanitation, no proper access to health care, and little or no schooling for their children. They were dependent on food supplements for survival and had limited and insecure livelihood opportunities, and many of them were involved in begging, child labor, or prostitution as means for survival. They had lost most of their possessions, had few material assets, and had no security for the future. The hardest part was that they were despised and marginalized by the majority of the Lebanese host population and had very few human rights protecting them.

An important element in understanding why these refugees became followers of Christ is in understanding what had disillusioned them about their traditional faith. Some of the refugees spoke about how the conflict had disturbed their understanding of Islam and caused them to question their traditional beliefs. For some, they interpreted the war in Syria as religious violence between the different sects of Islam and were turned off by it. Others felt overwhelmed with evil and did not know how to respond. Some found in Christ something that they had missed in their traditional faith but were yearning for – such as experiencing peace and love.

> I had always felt overwhelmed by evil.

> We used to be so scared of dying and facing a judgmental God.

> I was always taught to fear Allah. I lived in constant fear of Allah. He was the one that punishes us, kills us; our ability to choose is taken away.

All of these reasons were strong drivers pushing them away from their traditional faith toward Christ. One refugee woman summarized her experience.

> I am not living in fear. My Lord is the savior. He will never leave
> me and my children. If later someone in my family comes here and
> sees my life, maybe they will change. The Lord changes people. . . .
> Our hearts were always heavy. Now I rejoice. In our religion,
> everything was hitting you. Now peace and joy are part of [our]
> faith. Jesus is my joy and peace.

In the midst of their new experience of poverty, rejected by most Lebanese, and in the context of the hatred, violence, and brutality they had witnessed in Syria, almost half of the refugees interviewed were attracted to the love of Christ. A fifth of the refugees in this study were attracted to Christ because of the peace he gives in the midst of turmoil and uncertainty. As they had witnessed the brutality of the struggles for power and wealth in Syria, some (14 percent) were attracted by the different value system that they saw in Christ and his sacrifice.

While the majority of the Muslim refugees were attracted to a God who is different from the deity and religion that they had traditionally followed, a smaller percentage became followers of Christ because Christ is savior and forgives their sins. The assurance of the forgiveness of sins was something they were never sure of in their traditional faith. Of those interviewed, 14.2 percent said that they were attracted to Christ because "He is the only savior," because "Jesus loved us and was crucified and died for our sins on our behalf," and because "he is the only One who died for us on the cross. He alone can give eternal life." Twenty-eight percent referred to Christ as their salvation, savior, one who forgives their sins, their intercession, and their Redeemer.

> I heard that God would save us and forgive us in Christ. I cried
> and cried, and I felt something washing me clean on the inside. I
> went forward, and when I went forward, my husband asked me
> if I wanted to be a church member, and I said, "I don't know, but
> something has cleaned me on the inside."

The context of the slum dwellers in Bangalore was one of chronic poverty, which in most cases was also generational. All of them had migrated to Bangalore from rural areas or small towns, looking to improve their lives. Being poor, they had settled in the urban slums, living in poor quality housing in unhealthy neighborhoods. Most had insecure livelihoods and were involved in menial work or as daily laborers, resulting in substance abuse and addictions. They barely earned enough to meet their daily needs, with very little to spare. The majority were unskilled, and about half were either illiterate or had very low levels of literacy. The women particularly were vulnerable to domestic violence, depression, and suicide. The nutritional status of the women and children was poor. Slum dwellers do not have access to basic services – especially proper medical care. They have no social or financial safety nets. All of them are politically marginalized and voiceless, unable to advocate for improvements to the settlements where they live. Being slum dwellers, they are socially ostracized.

The Hindu slum dwellers in this study felt ostracized and marginalized because of their poverty and having no one to help them cope. As a result, many of them turned to their deities for help.

> Because my husband went to jail. [She did not have the financial ability or the political patronage that would have helped gain freedom for her husband.].

> Because of my sickness.

> Because I did not get a second child, there was no peace in my life.

> I was suffering from TB (tuberculosis). I could not get well. . . . There was no peace in the family.

> We had financial problems, no peace in the family.

> Because of my father's illness.

> Because of my husband drinking alcohol.

> We lost everything, even our jobs. There was no peace in the family, and we had financial problems.

When in spite of *pujas*, rituals, and supplications, their traditional deities did not respond, they became disillusioned and turned away from their gods. A quarter of them wanted peace in their family life in the midst of the challenges of poverty. They were unable to find this peace in their traditional faith. All of them saw God (and Jesus Christ) as almighty, the one who helps them because he is healer, provider, life-giver, sustainer, peace-giver, and deliverer (35 percent), and is real (20 percent). These attributes are in contrast to their traditional deities who were either unable or unwilling to help them.

About 20 percent of the slum dwellers said that Christ for them was savior, one who forgives their sin, which was their motivation to follow Christ.

> [The COME missionary] shared from James 1:13–14 – that from our desires we commit sin [and these were] put on God. These verses touched me, and I thought that Jesus only can wash my sins, forgive, and will give eternal life. So after hearing from him,

> God talked to me, and I bitterly cried and accepted him as my
> personal savior Jesus Christ.

The poor had few resources to meet their daily needs and were attracted to Christian spiritual songs, Bible stories about Jesus, and messages from the word of God through which they found comfort, strength, and hope that helped them cope with their challenges. One person said, "I love hearing God's word and singing spiritual songs," which helped him understand that God is real and that he does hear him and care for him. The word and worship also helped them express their faith and trust in Christ and submit to his lordship, which is similar to the experience of African-American slaves. The Bible and songs were foundational to their spirituality. Though most of them were illiterate, the Bible was the source of images to process their experiences and then express them in their spirituals. Albert Raboteau explains that when reading the Bible, there is a sense of "sacred time" when past events in the Bible are seen as being in the present time.[40]

For the slum dwellers, there was a sense of powerlessness resulting from their poverty where they felt they were trapped in their circumstances and did not see a way out. In the theologizing of the African-American slaves, their awareness of being trapped in poverty and oppression was mitigated by cries to God for deliverance. From their spirituals, it is apparent that many of the slaves did not believe that society and their circumstances could be changed. So instead, they sought the consolation of God in their circumstances and looked forward in hope to being delivered from this world. For the poor in the slums of Bangalore, the worship songs expressed not only their cry to God for help but was also their acknowledgement of who God is. Singing spiritual songs was their way of worshiping Christ. The stories from the Bible, especially those about Jesus, encouraged them because in these stories they saw that God cares and provides.[41]

---

40. Raboteau, *Slave Religion*, 250.

41. In the devotional aspects of the *Bhakti* movement of Hinduism, *Bhajans* (literally "sharing"), songs of a religious and spiritual nature, are often sung. The content includes legendary epics from their tradition and expressions of devotion to their deity. The devotion expressed in *bhajans* is extoling the qualities of their deity. Devotional songs in Islam are mainly within the Sufi tradition and are usually songs of praise to Allah, Mohammad, and other religious leaders. They also express yearnings for union with the divine. In many major Islamic traditions, music and singing are not allowed. What is different in Christian songs is that most of the time the devotion they express to Christ is in response to what he has done for people and the hope he gives for the present and the future. The songs are of a personal nature rather than only extolling the virtues of a deity.

Considering the corruption and opulent lifestyles of the politicians and many of the religious leaders that they would regularly witness, 20 percent of the slum dwellers were attracted to the sacrifice of Christ and his lifestyle (10 percent). They found in Christ something different from what they saw in the world around them and were drawn to it.

There is a strong connection between poverty and spirituality. The 2009 Gallup global survey on poverty and spirituality concluded that religion has a functional role in the lives of those in the poorest countries as it helps them cope with the daily struggles of providing for themselves and their families.[42] Tomas Rees, in his multicountry study, found that personal insecurity evidenced by income inequality was an important determinant of religiosity.[43] Scott Schieman in his North American study on socioeconomic status (SES) and beliefs about God in everyday life found that individuals from poorer communities professed higher levels of divine involvement and control in their everyday lives compared with individuals from a higher socioeconomic status.[44] The poor being ostracized and marginalized because of their poverty sought a higher power who would help them and enable them to cope.

This connection between poverty and spirituality is repeatedly confirmed throughout the stories recorded here, as most of the poor had been religious but had become dissatisfied with their traditional faith. What they were seeking was the reality of God in the midst of their poverty. Richard Shaull, who had studied liberation theologians in Latin American and their work with the base communities, observed in the 1960s the following about the Pentecostal churches in similar poor communities across the continent. He writes:

> For men and women whose approach to life and the world is essentially religious, Pentecostalism addresses them in their language and offers them what they most long for: a rich and rewarding experience of the closeness and power of God who gives them life and joy and hope. An experience that permeates their whole being and transforms what has become the supreme burden of their daily life: their struggle to survive.[45]

---

42. Cited in Crabtree, "Religiosity Highest in World's Poorest Nations," 3.

43. Rees, "Is Personal Insecurity a Cause," 1–26.

44. Schieman, "Socioeconomic Status and Beliefs," 25–51.

45. Shaull, "Pentecostal Appeal to the Poor," 51–52.

Many Pentecostal churches in the Majority World seem to have understood the motivations of some of the poor as to why they seek God.[46] Korean Pentecostal missiologist Wonsuk Ma writes, "Pentecostalism is a religion *of* the poor and not *for* the poor."[47] This point is probably best illustrated by sociologist Christian Lalive who described Chilean Pentecostal churches in the 1960s. They understood what the poor sought spiritually and responded accordingly.[48]

> The large painting which adorns Pentecostal sanctuaries depicts a restless sea surrounding an island upon the rocks of which a Bible lies open, illuminated by a ray of light from heaven. . . . The symbolism is obvious. In a deeply evil world of misery and perdition, the Christian communities stand like islands of peace and repose. The task of the elect is to give refuge to the drowning, without a thought for how the angry sea might be calmed.[49]

46. The literature on the Pentecostals and their work among the poor in Latin America referred to here is dated. It is important to note that the Pentecostal churches in Latin America have grown beyond their initial work among the poor. Today, they are very much a church of the middle class, while still having a strong impact in poor communities. However, their experience among the poor (though dated) is a critical historical perspective about the motivations of the poor and what attracts many of them to Christ.

47. Ma, "When the Poor Are Fired Up," 29, emphasis original.

48. Because of the influence of liberation theology, it has always been assumed that the poor want liberation. The experience of liberation theologians and the Pentecostals side by side in Brazil provides some interesting insights. John Burdick is critical and sometimes negative in his assessment of liberation theology. He writes:

> I did not doubt that many people were having their consciousness raised by the Church. Yet I found myself puzzling over the implications of Brazilian field reports sent by parish priests to the Church's Commission on CEBs [*Comunidades Eclesiales de Base* – base communities], which made clear that in any given town those who participated actively in the Catholic Church comprised only a very small minority.

Burdick, *Looking for God in Brazil*, Kindle Location 12. Burdick goes on to state that in any given town in a predominantly Catholic country, there were more Pentecostals in the town than there were Catholics involved in CEBs. He wondered why "hadn't the CEB swept all these other people off their feet?" Burdick, Kindle Location 21. Burdick called this the paradox of numbers. For a mass movement that was supposed to transform Brazilian society and politics, studies in a number of archdioceses showed no more than 3–4 percent of the adults were involved in CEBs, while the Pentecostals made up 8–10 percent of the local population. Burdick, Kindle Location 111. While liberation theology experienced through the CEBs was attractive to some, the Pentecostal experience apparently addressed other issues to which many of the poor responded.

49. Lalive, "Pentecostal 'Conquista' in Chile," 24. It is important to note that Pentecostals were not preaching an other-world, escapist gospel. Pentecostals have struggled to find a theology of social engagement without compromising their tradition. For a detailed discussion, see Satyavrata, *Pentecostals and the Poor*. However, records show that the Pentecostals in Latin

This is similar in African Pentecostalism. One of the distinctives of African Pentecostal theology is the *experience* of the Holy Spirit in all aspects of daily life. Allan Anderson at the University of Birmingham in his review of African Pentecostal theology writes, "God's salvation is seen in different manifestations of God's abiding presence through the Spirit in everyday life, seen by Pentecostal believers as divine revelations that assure them that 'God is there' to help in every area of human need."[50]

There is a growing awareness that context is important in evangelism as it influences the local community's perception of God and determines what is important to them spiritually. The contexts of the poor influence how and why they seek God. The 2010 Cape Town Commitment recognized the uniqueness and complexity of different contexts and encouraged a holistic approach to communicate the love of God and the saving grace offered through Christ.[51]

The challenge for traditional evangelical missiology and missional practice particularly is that it has defined the gospel in a very specific way – as the forgiveness of sins through the death and resurrection of Christ – and conversion as a punctiliar event. Steven Lawson in his new book *New Life in Christ* adds a corollary where he refers to the elusive search to find fulfillment which can only be found in new life in Christ.[52] His assumption is that forgiveness and fulfillment are the only motivations for people turning to Christ and becoming his followers.

America did end up having a social impact. Brazilian sociologist Cecilia Mariz writes that both the Pentecostal and liberation theologies promote similar practices such as biblical reflection leading to praxis, developing networks of solidarity; attitudes; and values such as the human worth of the individual and overcoming the dualism of faith and life that enable the poor in their midst to overcome the problems of poverty. Mariz, *Coping with Poverty*, 34–36, 81–100, 131–48. Michael Bergunder at Heidelberg University in his analysis of the Pentecostal Movement in Latin America refers to the social transformation that resulted when individuals became involved with Pentecostal churches. It was not just a religion of escapism from the problems of society. The status of women in their domestic life changed. There was behavior change with the resulting economic benefits to the family when alcohol, drugs, and tobacco were renounced, and there was social engagement in communities when they had the opportunity. While they may have been less politically engaged than other communities, this began to change as their numbers grew and they became aware of their importance in society. Michael Bergunder, "Pentecostal Movement and Basic Ecclesial Communities in Latin America," 163–86. Kamsteeg in his study of Pentecostalism in Chile refers to it as having an accent of liberation theology. Kamsteeg, "Prophetic Pentecostalism in Chile," 23–24.

50. Anderson, "Intercultural Theology, Walter J. Hollenweger and African Pentecostalism," 141.

51. Lausanne Movement, *Cape Town Commitment: A Call to Action*.

52. Lawson, *New Life in Christ*.

Most of the poor in this study responded to the good news that God revealed in Christ, that he is loving, compassionate, almighty, and real. He is not distant, and he responds to their cries for help. He protects and provides. These were their motivations to become followers of Christ. For most, their understanding of sin came later as they gained an awareness of the righteousness of God. In effect, they were encountering the kingdom of God and Christ the King, just as Jesus had announced in Matthew 24:14 and Mark 1:15 – that the kingdom of God has drawn near. This broader understanding of the gospel is slowly gaining traction among evangelical missiologists. The 1988 Manila Manifesto refers to the proclamation of the kingdom of God (and not just the forgiveness of sins) as part of the gospel.[53] The Cape Town Commitment provides a more comprehensive understanding of the gospel when it says that it is God reconciling the world (all of creation) to himself through Jesus Christ.[54]

A critical question that must be asked is did the refugees and slum dwellers become followers of Christ only for utilitarian reasons – because of the benefits they received such as answered prayer and miracles? Would they continue to follow Christ if he did not answer prayer, or they did not experience miracles? This issue was not explored with the poor in this study. However, in previous research done by this author in a slum in Bangalore among similar participants, this question was asked. Their responses were the following:

> Whatever God does in my life is OK. God's joy is greater than the problems. The prayers God has answered allow me to trust in him and rest in peace.

> We are going through a financial crisis and the peace of God is helping me.

> I will believe regardless of what happens. We have been married for eight years and have no child. Even if we have no child, we have joy and peace. When I used to worship [the goddess] Yellamma, there were a number of accidents that almost killed me. Now there aren't any.

> Even when there are problems, God gives me peace when I pray.

---

53. Lausanne Movement, "The Manila Manifesto."

54. Lausanne Movement, *Cape Town Commitment: A Call to Action*.

I aborted three and a half months ago. In the midst of difficulties, I have peace.

Even in suffering we will not leave Jesus. We have two daughters and wanted a son. When the third daughter was born, I will still not leave Him. I know God hears me.[55]

It would seem from these responses and from those in this book that while answered prayers and miracles were often part of the motivation and process of becoming followers of Christ, there was more substance to it. What they sought was a God who would be with them in the midst of their struggles and problems – who would give them peace and hear their prayers, even if for some reason they are not answered. They had felt that the deities they had worshiped were distant and uncaring, and thus they turned away from them. This is very similar to the spiritual experiences of the African-American slaves who saw Jesus as "an ever-present and intimate friend" who was with them in the midst of the horrors of slavery. George Faithful describes this experience as Jesus providing the slaves with "strength in weakness and hope in the midst of suffering."[56]

To summarize, forgiveness from sin motivated some to become followers of Christ. However for the majority, their contexts of poverty influenced their decision. The Syrian refugees who had experienced violence and been displaced were disillusioned by the brutality, hatred, and evil of the conflict, which they saw as an intrareligious conflict within Islam. In sharp contrast, they were attracted to the teachings about love and forgiveness they were hearing at church and the love and charity they were experiencing from Christians in the churches. They were attracted to the love of Christ and the peace he gives. For the slum dwellers in India, the overwhelming motivation for changing their allegiance to Christ was the fact that he is almighty and their healer, provider, life-giver, sustainer, peace-giver, and deliverer, and is real. In addition, the Hindu slum dwellers were attracted to the songs and Bible stories, as they helped them articulate their faith and their feelings and gave them strength and hope in their circumstances. The poor in both contexts were also attracted to the sacrifice of Christ and his sacrificial lifestyle.

---

55. Rupen Das, Unpublished research.

56. Faithful, "Recovering the Theology of the Negro Spirituals," 5.

Their Perception of God Revealed in Christ

The faith of the poor that the stories reveal is that they did not yearn for life after death. For some, that understanding came after their conversion. Instead they wanted a God who is real in the midst of the challenges and evils of life. Since their encounter was with the person of Christ, who did they perceive Christ to be, and what was their understanding of what he has done for them?

For about a quarter of those interviewed in both locations (28 percent in Lebanon and 20 percent in India), Christ forgives their sin. They viewed him as savior. Both Islam and Hinduism have concepts of sin, and each offers atonement through their prescribed rituals and practices for purification to win favor with their deity.[57] It was surprising that more of those who told their stories did not speak about Christ as savior. A smaller number among the refugees (14.2 percent) acknowledged that Christ is God and that he is the Son of God. About a fifth (19 percent) of the refugees said that Christ was their Lord, leader, or captain.

The predominant characteristics of God in Christ that attracted the Muslim refugees were that he is loving (42.8 percent), that he gives peace (19 percent), and that he sacrificed his life (14.2 percent), qualities they had not experienced in their traditional faith. For them (42 percent), Christ was everything. The refugees used words like "father," "mother," "my life," and "everything in my life." One said, "Our life is nothing without Christ." Like a father and mother, Christ took care of them and provided for them. When they had lost everything and had no support, he sustained them – because they felt that their lives were nothing without Christ. When asked what Christ means to them, 23 percent said that he was their hope and gave them joy, peace, love, life, and everything good. Considering their circumstances, these are remarkable perceptions of Christ.

The Muslim refugees already understood God to be great because of their traditional faith, and as a result they did not mention the greatness of God.[58] By contrast the Hindu slum dwellers saw God in Christ as almighty (100 percent), eternal (45 percent), the true God (40 percent), the only One God (15 percent), and one who provides for their needs (35 percent), qualities that they did not see in the pantheon of deities of their traditional faith. Of the slum dwellers, 20 percent spoke about God being real to them in Christ. Interestingly, there

---

57. In Islam God is known as *Ar-Rahman* and *Ar-Rahim*, meaning God is merciful and that he forgives sin.

58. One of the key affirmations of the Islamic faith is the *takbir*, the proclamation *Allahu Akbar*, literally meaning "God is greater" or "God is the greatest."

was only one mention that Christ is a loving God. When they spoke about what Christ means to them, there were also single mentions that he is deliverer, that he does miracles, and that there is happiness in his name.

There is a paucity of literature on how the poor perceive God and Christ. While Protestant, Catholic, and independent churches have been concerned about addressing poverty and injustice, they have not listened to what the objects of their charity, the poor themselves, have to say. Liberation theologians attempt to listen to the voices of the poor, through a structured and limited way. However as described in chapter 4, liberation theologians dilute the voices of the poor with input from others who have also viewed the phenomena of poverty in a particular location. Gustavo Gutiérrez in his article "Theology from the Experience of the Poor" states that the emphasis of liberation theology is on how God views the poor, and as a result what the church's priorities should be. Because of the destitution, marginalization, and oppression of the poor, God has a preferential option for the poor. Gutiérrez does not address the issue of how the poor perceive God and what their spiritual priorities are.[59]

Ernesto Cardenal, a liberation theologian, enables the poor *campesinos* in Nicaragua to describe their spirituality. In the *Gospel in Solentiname*, the *campesinos* were not seeking a savior for their sins. But as they read the Bible, they were trying to understand how they fit into the larger narrative of God. This understanding would then enable them to experience the presence of God.[60] As also noted in chapter 4, Tim Limburg, working among the poor in rural Appalachia, writes that the spiritual priorities of the poor were different since what the poor struggled with were issues of oppression, exploitation, land ownership, and a system that supports injustice. It was from within this context that the poor cried out to God for healing and a "liberating Word from God."[61] Their expectation and perception was that God would hear them and answer.

One of the few bodies of literature that collates the perceptions of God by some of the poor and oppressed are the spirituals of the African-American slaves. Their perceptions were very similar to those of the poor in this present study. George Faithful writes that the slaves adored God as the heavenly Father of believers. Even though most had been separated from their families and sometimes felt "like a motherless child" (quoting some spirituals[62]), they still

---

59. Gutierrez, "Theology from the Experience of the Poor," 26–33.

60. Cardenal, *Gospel in Solentiname*.

61. Limburg, "Gospel to the Poor," 23.

62. The quotations in this paragraph and the next are from African-American spirituals that Faithful cites.

looked to God as a loving Father because he kept his promises, he provided, and he took away their sin.[63] This feeling is similar to what some of the Syrian refugees felt, as noted above. The African-American slaves also perceived Christ as one who suffered like them with "nowhere to lay his head." Some of the refugees and slum dwellers were attracted to the sacrificial life and lifestyle of Jesus seen in the Gospels. He also gave the slaves hope and promised them victory and a future; "he will lead us to glory," and some spirituals refer to him as a "mighty man" and King Emmanuel. One day he would free them from physical and spiritual bondage. Christ was perceived as almighty and powerful and was a healer and miracle worker in this life, someone who empowered the lowly, just as the slum dwellers perceived Christ. Interestingly, Faithful writes that the spirituals spoke about Christ setting an example of how to live and how to die "with a free good will."[64]

Like for many of the refugees and slum dwellers, Christ was savior for the African-American slaves because he had been crucified for them: "Were you there when they crucified my Lord?"[65] For the slaves, Jesus was "an ever-present and intimate friend" with whom they could identify. Faithful summarizes by saying, "Jesus provided the spiritual singers' central paradigm for strength in weakness and hope in the midst of suffering."[66] This paradigm is no different from what the refugees and slum dwellers who yearned for the deity they worshiped. They had now found strength and hope in Christ.

When describing what it means to follow Christ, the poor spoke about having a new identity and living out that identity. One Syrian refugee described this identity as follows.

> To worship Christ is in the way that he walked, in the way that he taught his disciples who were with him, that we are his servants, just as his disciples were.

---

63. Faithful, "Recovering the Theology of the Negro Spirituals," 5.

64. Faithful, 5.

65. Conversion was an important part of the spirituality of the slaves. They saw Christ as savior as they were convicted of sin. Raboteau writes:

> The experience of conversion was essential in the religious life of the slaves. For the only path to salvation lay through that "lonesome valley" wherein the "seekers" underwent conversion, an experience which they treasured as one of the peak moments in their lives. The typical conversion experience was preceded by a period of anxiety over one's salvation which lasted for days or even weeks.

Raboteau, "Secret Religion of the Slaves."

66. Raboteau.

To summarize, while about a quarter of the poor who were interviewed in both locations perceived Christ as savior, the majority saw him as someone who understood their desperation in the midst of their poverty and responded to their cries for help. They spoke of him as loving, one who gives them peace, almighty so that he can provide for them and heal them, one who sustains them, and one who gives them joy, life, and "everything good" in the midst of their circumstances. In contrast to the deities they had worshiped, they saw God in Christ as present with them in their poverty, accessible, and responsive to their cries for help. A smaller percentage in each location were attracted by the sacrifice and sacrificial lifestyle of Christ.

Were There Differences in Perceptions of Christ between the Two Groups?

The culture and religion of the two groups were very different. One was Hindu and experiencing chronic and generational poverty, while the other was Muslim and experiencing event-based poverty. These differences should have influenced their perception of who God is and what their spiritual priorities were. So, what were the similarities and differences in the conversion experiences of the two groups?

One similarity is that 28 percent of the Muslim refugees and 20 percent of the Hindu slum dwellers were attracted to the fact that Christ would forgive their sin. The concept of sin is a fundamental part of both religions, and each offers ways to atone for sin and win the favor of their deity. However, it was surprising that more of them did not identify the grace of God and that he offers forgiveness as what attracted them to Christ.

A fairly high percentage in both communities – 80 percent of the slum dwellers and 66.6 percent of the Syrian refugees – decided to worship Christ because of supernatural experiences such as answered prayers, healing, miracles, dreams, and visions. These percentages are similar to what other research on the conversion experiences of non-Christians from Muslim, Hindu, and Buddhist backgrounds indicates.[67] This correlation may indicate the epistemology of non-Western cultures where truth is perceived and understood through lived experience and the senses rather than primarily

---

67. Woodberry and Shubin, "Why I Chose Jesus"; Woodberry, Shubin, and Marks, "Why Muslims Follow Jesus"; Iyadurai, *Transformative Religious Experience*; and Hilderbrand, "What Led Thai Buddhist Background Believers."

through reasoning and a cognitive process of understanding truth.[68] There is very little research on understanding the epistemology of conversion of those from non-Christian backgrounds (ethno-epistemology).

The major difference between the communities was in their perception of *who* God is in Christ. For the Muslim refugees, the predominant characteristics of God were that he is loving (42.8 percent) and gives peace (19 percent), qualities they felt they had not experienced in their traditional faith. For another 14.2 percent, the fact that Christ sacrificed his life for them was a radical concept. Unlike the Muslim refugees who already understood God to be great because of their traditional faith and who did not necessarily focus on his greatness in their new-found faith, the Hindu slum dwellers saw God in Christ as almighty, eternal, and one who provides for their needs, qualities that they did not see in the deities of their traditional faith. Interestingly, the Hindu slum dwellers did not mention the love of God.

The question that needs to be asked is whether the conversions based on supernatural encounters with Christ were because of the converts non-Western culture, or whether they were because of their poverty. While the majority of them apprehended and understood truth through lived experience rather than responding to a reasoned and logical presentation on sin and forgiveness, the distinction was in *why* they responded to Christ. In both communities, there was a sense that their traditional faith did not help them cope with the reality of their poverty and enable them to meet their basic needs. The Syrian refugees were instead attracted to the love of God, the peace that he gives, and the fact that he answers prayer. For another 23 percent, in the midst of their destitution Christ gave them joy, peace, love, everything good, and life and was their

---

68. The current study only refers to ethno-epistemology and will not discuss it in detail. The only reason ethno-epistemology is mentioned is to identify a possible reason why many people in these two communities may encounter Christ differently and respond to experience rather than a reasoned presentation about sin and forgiveness. Ethno-epistemology is a highly controversial issue and cannot be easily separated into Eastern and Western approaches to philosophy and epistemology. It would be important to differentiate between philosophical traditions and the epistemology of ordinary people. However, ethno-epistemology is a growing field of study. In 1992, Goldman referred to the ethno-epistemology of ordinary people as "epistemic folkways" consisting of prereflective, untutored, and uncritical epistemic concepts, intuitions, judgments, and norms of everyday people. Goldman, *Liaisons: Philosophy Meets the Cognitive and Social Sciences*. A few of the others who have done descriptive studies of intuitions, judgments, standards, and goals of folk epistemic practices are Code, *What Can She Know?*; Coetze and Roux, eds., *African Philosophy Reader*; Eze, ed., *African Philosophy: A Reader*; Radin, *Primitive Man as Philosopher*; and Waters, ed., *American Indian Thought*. One of the criticisms of many of the studies of the ethno-epistemology of ordinary people is that they amount to a compilation of anecdotal evidence and are not critical evaluations using epistemic norms and concepts.

hope. In contrast for 100 percent of the poor slum dwellers, Christ was God almighty, eternal God (45 percent), and healer, provider, life-giver, sustainer, peace-giver, and deliverer (35 percent). What is evident is that it isn't their non-Western epistemology of dreams, visions, and miracles that convinced them to follow Christ. Rather, it was through these supernatural encounters and lived experiences that they came to know a God who is accessible, caring, and compassionate, a God who responded to their poverty and dire circumstances. What they responded to was the reality of God in their daily lives.

In comparing the two contexts, there were no significant differences between the poor in the slums of Bangalore and the Syrian refugees in Lebanon in how they became followers of Christ based on the fact that they experienced different types of poverty – chronic poverty versus event-based poverty. Neither were there any significant differences in their conversion process based on the fact that one community was Hindu and the other Muslim. The common factor between the two communities was that they were poor.

8

Immanuel: The God That the Poor Seek

> Where the retrospective bond with the apostles is concerned, the historical church will ask about continuity. But where the future its apostolate serves is concerned it will be open to leap forward to what is new and surprising. Here 'the most characteristic thing is not the old things that are preserved but the new ones that take place and come into being.'[1]
>
> *Jürgen Moltmann*

Catholic theologian Ivan Illich writes about the purpose of missiology.

> Missiology studies the growth of the Church into new peoples, the birth of the Church beyond its social boundaries; beyond the linguistic barriers with which she feels at home; beyond poetical images in which she taught her children. The Church is led to marvel about the ever-new images in which her venerable knowledge can be meaningful for the first time . . . missiology therefore is the study of the Church as surprise.[2]

"Ever new images" and the "church as surprise" probably best describe my own journey as I tried to listen to the poor in their often surprising encounters with Christ. When I first started listening to the spiritual yearnings of the poor, what they said pushed me beyond my theological comfort level where I had assumed that God works only in the specific ways I had been taught. Questions began to

---

1. Moltmann, *Church in the Power of the Spirit*, 360. The quotation within is from A. A. Ruler, *Theologie van het Apostolaat* (Nijkerk: Callenbach, 1954), 20.

2. Illich, *Mission and Midwifery*, 7.

flood my mind. Can a person become a follower of Christ, a Christian, without fully understanding sin and the saving grace of God offered in Christ? Isn't it wrong to follow Christ because he had answered prayers or had done a miracle for me? Aren't we supposed to follow Christ and worship him for who he is and not because he answers prayers and provides for me? What if he stopped answering my prayers – would I still follow him? Is the good news that Jesus, the apostles, and the early church proclaimed only about forgiveness of sin and reconciliation with God, or is it that the reign of God had dawned with the coming of Christ?

What I saw emerging among the poor was a raw and unvarnished faith with echoes from the Old Testament and the early church where God's presence was real and tangible. Why was this new for me, and why was I surprised? Isn't the biblical narrative one of God dwelling with his people in creation – a God who, at the beginning of the New Testament, identified himself as *Immanuel?*

The motivation for this book was to try to see God and his work of redemption through the eyes of some of the poor. Jürgen Moltmann writes about a theology of hope where the starting place is despair, either because of the loss of faith in any type of utopian or religious ideals, or an ignorance of or unwillingness to accept the eschatological promise of Christ. Yet the despair is evidence of a human yearning for there to be something else, something transcendent, that will sustain and give meaning and shape to life on earth. Moltmann writes, "Thus despair, too, presupposes hope. 'What we do not long for, can be the object neither of our hope nor of our despair' (Augustine). The pain of despair surely lies in the fact that a hope is there, but no way opens up toward its fulfillment."[3] The poor we interviewed despaired because the deities they worshiped had failed them. The object(s) of their faith and trust turned out to be impotent and uncaring. What they longed for was a God who would hear their prayers and help them, who would be with them in the midst of their poverty, a God who understands their despair and struggles. The failure of their deities to respond and being unaware of the eschatological promise of Christ drove them into despair. They finally found hope in the God revealed in Christ because he was real to them in very tangible ways. This hope and reality is what attracted them to Christ and enabled them to survive and cope with their poverty. The gospel for them was not an other-world reality or only an expectation of life after death. God in Christ known as *Immanuel,* present in the midst of their destitution, was good news for them.

---

3. Moltmann, *Theology of Hope,* 23.

So, Is There Anything New and Surprising?

Having spent a good part of my career ministering to the needs of the poor and marginalized through humanitarian agencies, I have come to realize that one of the basic tenets of good practice is to listen to what the beneficiaries of the aid program consider their physical needs to be. Our teams, of course, would complement what they said with a professional needs and gap analysis. As I reviewed the missionary conferences of the past two hundred years and their struggles to understand the mission of God, I found that the conferences that focused on mission strategies to address poverty and social injustice ignored the spirituality of the poor and what the poor yearned for. We all assumed that they approached God the same way that the nonpoor did, and that they were seeking forgiveness and fulfillment – to fill a God-shaped hole in their lives[4] – namely, Jesus's promise that he had come to give life and give it to the full (John 10:10).

If the voices of the poor in the Majority World had been heard, missiologists, missionaries, and church leaders would have realized that the poor were encountering the inaugurated eschatology of the kingdom of God that is now here but not yet in its fullness, and this is what attracted them to Christ. They had encountered the reality of God's salvation and comforting presence in the midst of their poverty. A few of them spoke about eternity and heaven, but rarely did any of them speak about social justice and transformation. For them eternity starts now. Even though many had not understood it theologically, they had sought the inaugurated kingdom and presence of the King in their present lives and circumstances.

It seems that the poor intuitively knew that the unjust socioeconomic and political systems that kept them trapped in poverty were so deeply entrenched that they were powerless to bring about change. Maybe this explains why the 2009 Gallup study and the research of Tomas Rees and Scott Schieman show that religion has a functional role in the lives of those in the poorest

---

4. The concept of a God-shaped hole originates with Blaise Pascal, who in 1670 wrote it in *Pensée VII* (425). Blaise Pascal, *Pensées*, 80.

> What else does this craving, and this helplessness, proclaim but that there was once in man a true happiness, of which all that now remains is the empty print and trace? This he tries in vain to fill with everything around him, seeking in things that are not there the help he cannot find in those that are, though none can help, since this infinite abyss can be filled only with an infinite and immutable object; in other words, by God himself.

In evangelical circles, the concept gained popularity through books such as DeBartolo, *God-Shaped Hole*.

countries.[5] Religion helped them cope with the daily struggles of providing for themselves and their families because they saw no way out of their poverty and marginalization. Philip Yancey makes an insightful comment: "Christians in affluent countries tend to pray, 'Lord, take this trial away from us!' I have heard prisoners, persecuted Christians, and some who live in very poor countries pray instead, 'Lord, give us the strength to bear this trial.'"[6]

The poor, like other human beings, are made in the image of God.[7] Yet poverty warps and disfigures the psychology of the poor. Fell and Hewstone in their research describe how disparaging and humiliating language results in negative stereotyping which leads to the poor perceiving themselves as diminished human beings.[8] Paulo Freire adds a further dimension to the psychology of poverty. He writes that poverty and oppression are so destructive, they rob the poor of being able to liberate themselves to escape the clutches of poverty. Instead they become passive. Because of this, he warns, "Attempting to liberate the oppressed without their reflective participation in the act of liberation is to treat them as objects that must be saved from a burning building."[9] If the process is not handled properly, the oppressed become oppressors instead of striving for liberation.[10]

Community development practitioners have failed to understand that social injustice is so deeply entrenched in the socioeconomic and political systems of society that the poor are unable to extricate themselves from it by their own efforts. When these practitioners empower the poor to stand up for their rights, more often than not they set them up to fail, especially in societies that only have a veneer of democracy.[11] The Bible nowhere exhorts the poor to seek social justice or to rebel against oppression, probably because of the

---

5. Gallup study cited in Crabtree, "Religiosity Highest in World's Poorest Nations"; Rees, "Is Personal Insecurity a Cause"; Schieman, "Socioeconomic Status and Beliefs."

6. Yancy, *Reaching for the Invisible God*, 53.

7. Gen 1:26–27.

8. Fell and Hewstone, *Psychological Perspectives on Poverty*.

9. Freire, *Pedagogy of the Oppressed*, 52.

10. Freire, 29–30.

11. Movements for socioeconomic and political justice among the poor, oppressed, or marginalized that have achieved any degree of success *peacefully* have done so because there were individuals among the elite and powerful who actively supported them and pushed for political change. For example in the fight against apartheid, white church leaders and certain political leaders openly opposed apartheid. There were at least 139 white South African anti-apartheid activists. The situation was similar in the Civil Rights movement in the US in the 1960s. "The white Southerners who fought US segregation," BBC News (12 March 2019). A key political ally was the US attorney general Robert Kennedy.

understanding that the powerful will oppose anyone who challenges their power, authority, and control. Instead the exhortation to ensure social justice is directed at the wealthy, the elite, those in power. In the Old Testament, the exhortation was to the nation of Israel as a whole. Ultimately, it is God himself who defends and vindicates the poor and marginalized and brings judgment on the oppressors.

> Speak up for those who cannot speak for themselves,
>> for the rights of all who are destitute.
> Speak up and judge fairly;
>> defend the rights of the poor and needy. (Prov 31:8–9)
> Learn to do right; seek justice.
>> Defend the oppressed.
> Take up the cause of the fatherless;
>> plead the case of the widow. (Isa 1:17)

This is what the LORD says: Do what is just and right. Rescue from the hand of the oppressor the one who has been robbed. Do no wrong or violence to the foreigner, the fatherless or the widow, and do not shed innocent blood in this place. (Jer 22:3)

> He has shown you, O mortal, what is good.
>> And what does the LORD require of you?
> To act justly and to love mercy
>> and to walk humbly with your God. (Mic 6:8)

This is what the LORD Almighty said: "Administer true justice; show mercy and compassion to one another. Do not oppress the widow or the fatherless, the foreigner or the poor. Do not plot evil against each other." (Zech 7:9–10)

Ensuring social justice is not just an Old Testament mandate. Jesus starts his ministry by stating:

> "The Spirit of the Lord is on me,
> because he has anointed me
> to proclaim good news to the poor.
> He has sent me to proclaim freedom for the prisoners
> and recovery of sight for the blind,
> to set the oppressed free,
> to proclaim the year of the Lord's favor." (Luke 4:18–19)

While proclaiming the inauguration of the kingdom of God, he quotes two Old Testament passages[12] to say that nothing of what is required had changed – social justice and compassion are still the values that govern the kingdom of ancient Israel and now the kingdom of God. Social justice and compassion are only possible if the wealthy and powerful align their values with those of the kingdom of God. The tragedy is that they are rarely willing to yield their power and privilege.

The first thing we have learned is that if we had taken the time to listen to the poor, we would have seen the world through their eyes. The poor know that they are snared in the swamp of poverty. They see no way out, and no one is willing to help them, regardless of what the politicians promise. These reasons are why many of them are looking for a God who is real, is with them, and is a deliverer. Looking for divine help, they despair because their traditional deities have failed them. They find the help they need in the God revealed in Jesus Christ.

Veteran missionary Lesslie Newbigin warns that there is no "pure gospel unadulterated by cultural accretion," and pursuing it is an illusion.[13] In the passion to share the gospel with a world that desperately needs an answer to the meaninglessness of life and the evil and injustice embedded in the social institutions of society, what is presented as a life-changing message is that God has forgiven our sins through Jesus Christ. While that is good news for many, it rings hollow for the poor and marginalized who feel that they are the ones who have been sinned against. They are the ones whose rights have been denied, who do not have access to equal opportunities because of discrimination, and who often cannot access basic services like health care and education because they are ignored, neglected, and marginalized.

The biblical book of Job has one of the oldest descriptions of how the poor are sinned against and exploited by the rich. David Pleins contrasts the book of Job with the standard explanation for poverty found in Proverbs, that poverty is caused by laziness and personal moral failure. Instead Pleins states that in Job, "poverty is the product of exploitation."[14]

Job indicts the wealthy for their mistreatment of the poor (Job 24:2–14). They rob the poor, even widows and orphans, of their land and their livestock,

---

12. Isa 61:1–2; 58:6.

13. Newbigin, *Foolishness to the Greeks*, 4.

14. Pleins, *Social Visions of the Hebrew Bible*, 501. Also see Das, *Compassion and the Mission of God*, 44–86.

the only source of livelihood they have (vv. 2–3). They physically abuse and terrify them (v. 4). They force the poor to forage for food and gather what little they can from the wastelands to feed their children (vv. 5–6). The poor are forced to sleep outside with no clothes and little covering in the drenching rain, trying to find what little shelter they can from the rocks (vv. 7–8). Defenseless infants and children are taken away as collateral for unpaid debts (v. 9). The poor have few clothes, work hard, and still go hungry (v. 10). While producing olive oil and wine for the wealthy, the poor suffer from thirst (v. 11). The poor groan under their pain and suffering and no one hears them (v. 12); and at night they are robbed and killed (v. 14).

With only slight variations, at least three thousand years later this passage is still the reality of the destitute, those living in extreme poverty, child laborers, illegal migrants, and victims of human trafficking and modern-day slavery.[15] If the gospel is to be good news, what would Jesus mean to them? This question touches the fundamental question that has divided the church over the past hundred years – what is the gospel?

John Stott noted that the salvation Christ gives involves both being saved *from* and being saved *for.* He describes salvation as "freedom from sin in all its ugly manifestation and liberation into a new life of service, until finally we attain 'the glorious liberty of the children of God.'"[16] This freedom is not just from personal sins and failure, but also from the sins that ensnare the poor in poverty. That is why Jesus's proclamation at the synagogue in Nazareth (Luke 4:18–19) is actually good news to the poor. He promises that the oppressed would have freedom. As noted in so many of the stories recorded in this book, the victims of the war in Syria who had been condemned to destitution, and those living in unjust sociopolitical systems in India, were able to experience the reality of God's deliverance in specific areas of need when no one else would or could help them. As they experienced the reality of a God who can deliver them from the immediate problems they faced, they changed their allegiance to worship this God they had encountered in Christ. This seemingly small

---

15. In 2015, two-thirds of the world lived on less than $10 per day (about $300 per month) and 10 percent on less than $1.90 per day (designated as extreme poverty). The levels of poverty have dramatically fallen because of one single factor – the millions of poor in China and India who moved out of poverty into the lower middle class. The levels of extreme poverty across the world, other than in India and China, have not changed nor have the levels of poverty in the rest of the Majority World. The COVID-19 crisis of 2020 has pushed the levels of poverty and extreme poverty higher across the world. Roser and Ortiz-Ospina, "Global Extreme Poverty."

16. Stott, *Christian Mission in the Modern World*, 151.

experience of God's deliverance is a foretaste of the complete deliverance in store for them when the kingdom is revealed in all its magnificence and fullness.

There are two dimensions to their motivation to change their allegiance from the deities they worshiped to Christ. The first is the *push* or what within their context drove them away from their existing belief system. The second is the *pull* or what attracted them to their new faith that helped them cope with the harsh realities of poverty.

In his model of poverty, Robert Chambers identifies marginalization as evidenced by vulnerability, powerlessness, and voicelessness as being both a cause and a symptom of poverty. Marginalization has a profound impact on the well-being (or ill-being) of the community, and influences how they cope with the challenges they face. The sense of powerlessness creates a deep-rooted feeling that they cannot change society. It would seem that they are more aware than the nonpoor of how deeply entrenched corruption and unjust socioeconomic and political systems are because they affect their daily lives.

These issues are what Walter Rauschenbausch, Reinhold Niebuhr, and Walter Wink refer to as the parts of social order which are unjust and inherently evil.[17] They oppress and marginalize individuals and whole communities. Jayakumar Christian writes that there are clusters of power that are social, economic, bureaucratic, political, and religious in nature which render themselves absolute to keep the poor powerless.[18] It was this sense of powerlessness that motivated the majority of the poor in this study to seek Christ. It provided them the push away from their existing belief system and deities.[19]

Some of the Muslim refugees spoke of how the violence in Syria and the inadequacy of their traditional religious beliefs overwhelmed them and how they felt paralyzed. They had a sense of powerlessness, and they could do nothing about it. Some had felt overwhelmed by evil and fear as the conflict touched their daily lives; others were scared of dying and facing the judgment of God. Yet others were disillusioned by their traditional faith as they saw the

---

17. Rauschenbausch, *Theology for the Social Gospel*; Niebuhr, *Moral Man and Immoral Society*; and Wink, *Engaging the Powers*.

18. Christian, *God of the Empty-Handed*.

19. It is interesting to note that the idea of social transformation and addressing social injustice comes from the nonpoor, especially activists, facilitators, and community development professionals who work with the poor. There is very little literature on whether the poor, who know the reality and complexity of social injustice firsthand, want transformation or believe that it is possible.

war in Syria as an intra-Islam conflict. Their reasons for leaving their traditional faith were imbedded in their motivation to follow Christ.

The Hindu slum dwellers spoke about the challenges of poverty and not having the financial and social resources to respond. They could not afford the quality of doctors or medical treatment required, and many had no job security because they were day laborers. One person spoke about a husband who was jailed. Being poor, she could not afford to help him nor had the political patronage to get him out. Some spoke about husbands who became alcoholics because of the desperation of their poverty. Like with the Muslim refugees, part of their motivation for converting to worship Christ lay in the fact that their traditional deities had remained silent to their prayers and cries for help, which was the push away from their existing belief system.

What attracted them to Christ was that he is a God who heard their prayers, cared about their needs, and was present with them. This pull was not a feel-good escapism but the experience of the reality of God in the midst of their poverty and destitution. One refugee spoke about what attracted him to Christ. "What attracts me to Christ is that he is present at all times. Once we invite him and ask him to be in our hearts, he is present." He was articulating the biblical concept of *Immanuel*, that God was present with him in his suffering. Other Muslim refugees spoke about a God who is loving and gives them peace. Their understanding of "savior" was something very tangible in this life, of one who saved them from the destructive effects of poverty and forced displacement. The understanding of "savior" as one who forgives their sins and saved them from eternal damnation came later.

> Because really, with the pain that I was in, he was the only savior. No one came to me and said, "I will save you from what you're in." No one said, "I will come and save you." No one but Christ touched me with his touch, as I was sick, and unable to work, and my life was falling and going backward [getting worse]. And in that time Christ came and gave me strength, and I am working, and I feel that I am very close to him, and I have a strong drive to move forward, to get closer to him. May I be at his side to be one of his disciples.

As their lives changed, they found freedom from fear and had hope for the future. Some had seen dramatic answers to prayer. While for others, even though the circumstances of their lives hadn't changed and life was still hard, they felt they could endure the poverty and displacement of being refugees.

One refugee commented, "My life was very hard. But then I came here and found hope, and God was glorified. Now I can live in peace."

The Hindu slum dwellers repeatedly spoke about how their prayers to their traditional deities were not answered but how Christ had answered them. The predominant quality of God that they were attracted to was that he is almighty. Because of his power, he can heal and provide for them. Their lives changed as a result. Addictions that were ruining the family were broken, and they were able to save money. Family relationships were healed. They saw their prayers of desperation answered.

David Bosch writes that contextualization of the gospel falls into one of two categories. One category starts with the local context for Christian reflection and practice by the poor and the nonpoor together. These are the liberation theologies. The other is inculturation, which uses the different philosophical and cultural frameworks of the local population to contextualize the gospel.[20]

Even though the context of the refugees and slum dwellers in this book was mired in social injustice, poverty, and marginalization, their spiritual journeys did not resonate with a liberation theology. The poor in this book did not start with a socioeconomic and political analysis of the local context. They were not seeking social justice but were seeking a transcendent reality that would enable them to cope with the challenges of poverty. The nonpoor, on the other hand, in order to walk with the poor, need to understand the influence of the socioeconomic contexts on the philosophical frameworks and worldviews of the poor, as well as their spiritual priorities. They need to be careful not to impose their solutions as outsiders on the poor. They need to understand what it is that the poor seek, realizing that the particular contexts of poverty will influence who they perceive and understand Christ to be.

The second new thing we have learned is that the poor in this book understood the good news of Jesus Christ from within their social, economic, and political context. Context identified their spiritual priorities. The reality of poverty, marginalization, war, and violence "pushed" them away from their traditional deities who seemed silent and impotent. What attracted them to Christ was that Christ is Immanuel, a God who is with them, who provides for them, delivers them, and comforts them. Contextualization in traditional missions has focused on language, culture, and religion. The contexts of the poor create their own unique culture, out of which rise their existential questions.

The question of how conversion actually happens has plagued the church for centuries. As reviewed in chapter 2, political events, theological beliefs,

---

20. Bosch, *Transforming Mission,* 420–56.

social dynamics, and religious contexts determined the process of conversion and judge when conversion actually occurs. The three main orientations that have characterized conversions or initiation into the body of Christ throughout church history are socialization, liturgical acts, and personal decision.

Regardless of the orientation, John Stott distinguishes between the internal work of the Holy Spirit bringing life and the outward act of conversion. He writes that the point when a person is justified and regenerated is the work of the Holy Spirit. In contrast, conversion is what an individual does when they repent and believe.[21] Regeneration is unconscious, while conversion is normally conscious. Regeneration is an instantaneous and a complete work of God, while conversion (repentance and faith) is usually, though not always, a process rather than an event.[22]

This regeneration is what was seen among the poor quoted in this book. At some point in their searching for a deity who hears their prayers, God in a moment of his choosing intervened, and regeneration took place. Some were conscious of it, while others were not. With regards to conversion, the process started with making decisions to change their allegiance from their traditional deities (repentance – a turning away from) and then choosing to follow Christ (an act of faith). Justification, which is a legal process, is God's act of removing the guilt and penalty of sin and declaring the person righteous through the atoning sacrifice of Christ.[23] Regeneration as a result of justification happens at a point in time. Conversion, on the other hand, is *how* human beings respond to this work of God. As seen in the review of the literature in chapter 2, conversion is influenced by culture, context, history, and personality.

Hinduism and Islam are holistic in nature and influence every aspect of a person's life. Therefore, any change in behavior, attitude, relationships, and ritual practice to reflect a new allegiance takes time. In such contexts, the only evidence of genuine conversion to Christ is changed lives as a result of the regeneration that Christ brings. What this change looks like may vary from person to person. In the initial stages, they may not be able to articulate what they believe, other than the fact that they had encountered a God who is powerful. It took time for the poor to understand who Christ is. While the mystical or supernatural encounter with Christ experienced by many of the participants was life changing, who they understood Christ to be took time.

---

21. Stott, *Christian Mission in the Modern World*, 169–70.

22. Stott, 171–74.

23. Stott, 153–54.

This process is not new in church history. As early as in the sixth century, Pope Gregory the Great understood that conversion from the pagan religions is a process. He wrote to Augustine through the Abbot Melitus:

> The temples of the idols in that nation ought not to be destroyed; but let the idols that are in them be destroyed. . . . For if those temples are well built, it is requisite that they are converted from the worship of devils to the service of the true God; that the nation, seeing that their temples are not destroyed, may remove error from their hearts, and knowing and adoring the true God, may they more familiarly resort to the places to which they have been accustomed.[24]

It takes time to abandon places of worship (which many have emotional connections with) and familiar rituals and then adopt new ones. Regeneration by the Holy Spirit is required to change attitudes and behavior as people grow in their understanding of their new faith and allegiance. Gregory understood that the key to conversion was that idols be destroyed and their ideology removed from hearts, which often takes time.

This understanding is an integral part of the apostle Paul's instruction throughout his letters, to young believers from pagan backgrounds to abstain from immorality, act righteously, realign relationships, abstain from certain religious practices, and adopt new ones that reflect their worship of Christ. These behaviors are the continuing work of conversion that is part of their change in spiritual allegiance. Conversion as a crisis event that is punctiliar emerged from within a Christianized culture in the Western world. They were "insider" conversions involving people who had some notion of sin and the concept of a God who judges.

The experience and understanding of who Christ is by the refugees and slum dwellers was progressive, though not in a linear or standardized format as described by Engel's scale and Gray's matrix. It is best illustrated by Hiebert's centered set (figure 2.1), where a person is centered on Christ and continues to move toward him, though all do not necessarily travel the same route. At some point, people cross a boundary of faith when they are justified and regeneration takes place as they continue their journey toward Christ. Orlando Costas best summarized this movement when he described conversion as complex, without a fixed number of experiences. Initiation into what he calls

---

24. Gregory the Great, quoted in Venerable Bede, *Eccelsiastical History of the English Nation*, Book I, Ch. XXX.

an "eschatological adventure" involves "ever new decisions, turning points, fulfillments, and promises which will continue until the ultimate fulfillment of the kingdom."[25]

The third thing that we learned in this study is not something new but a reaffirmation of what many throughout Christian history have said – that conversion of those especially from non-Christian backgrounds is a process. The poor may encounter the reality of God without fully understanding sin, who Christ is, and what he has done. The pivotal moment in their conversion was when they abandoned their allegiance to their traditional deity to worship Christ, because they had found a God who was concerned for them. As they experienced regeneration, the Holy Spirit over time revealed Christ more fully to them and made them aware of their sinfulness.

New Testament scholar Dean Flemming studied contextualization in the New Testament. Following is a summary of his points:

- In the New Testament there is no one formulation of the gospel, and the gospel is applied and explained in a number of different ways that made sense to specific audiences. However, Flemming urges the discerning of limits and cautions against syncretism.
- Different images and metaphors are used to communicate the gospel in different contexts.
- The coherent narrative of the gospel is the life, death, and resurrection of Jesus Christ. This is the metanarrative of the gospel story, and people locate their personal story within this larger metanarrative.
- There is no such thing as a pure, culture-free gospel.[26]

Flemming's findings in the New Testament confirm the experience of the refugees and slum dwellers quoted in this book. The good news that the poor responded to was the reality and relevance of the life, death, and resurrection of Jesus Christ in their daily lives – an inaugurated eschatology. Each conversion story was unique as God met each person in his or her place of need, and not as the result of a standard formulaic process. The conversion experiences of the poor have deep roots in historical Christianity, especially in the experiences of the early church and of converts from Islam, Hinduism, and Buddhism. Finally, the refugees and slum dwellers understood Christ to be good news from within the cultures of poverty in which they lived.

---

25. Costas, "Conversion as a Complex Experience," 182.

26. Flemming, *Contextualization in the New Testament*, Kindle Location 3782–5234.

Andrew Walls writes that in the very early Jewish-dominated church, conversion was understood as repentance, a turning away from sin in the light of the laws given by God dealing with the worship of the true God – just as John the Baptist had preached. The call for repentance (conversion) in the Gospels was for the Jews as they continued to focus on "messianic renewal and restoration of Israel."[27] However, with the growing focus on pagan Gentiles who had no understanding of the Messiah, the Hope of Israel, there was a linguistic and conceptual translation in evangelism. Christ was presented to the Gentiles using the Greek word *kyrios*, Lord, rather than as Messiah, since *kyrios* was the title used by the Greeks for the divinities of cults. Christ is Lord of lords.[28] These were outsider conversions, where conversion involved a change in allegiance as to whom they worshiped, rather than as a result of confession of sin.

The research by Woodberry among the Muslims, Iyadurai of Hindus, and Hilderbrand of Buddhists shows that conversion of people from these religious backgrounds often involves a mystical or supernatural encounter with Christ. These encounters convinced them that the God revealed in Christ is real, leading ultimately to their conversion. If conversion is an encounter with the living God revealed in Christ, where does the issue of the forgiveness of sin come in, something that is at the very core of most evangelistic thinking and practice?

The answer is in understanding what is meant by sin. There are at least nine Hebrew words,[29] four Greek nouns,[30] five Greek adjectives,[31] and three Greek verbs[32] that have been translated as "sin" in the English language. The meanings of the words include evil, offense, wicked, perverse, crooked, twisted, stray, transgress, quarrel, acting in ignorance, depraved, worthless, unjust, unrighteous, lawless, disobedient, and much more. In summary, sin is anything that is contrary to God's nature.[33]

---

27. Walls, "Converts or Proselytes?," 4.

28. *Kyrios kyriōn* or *kurios ton kurieuinton* (1 Tim 6:15).

29. Transliteration of Hebrew words from *Strong's Exhaustive Concordance*: *ra'* [#7451], *chatta'ah* [#2403], *rasha* [#7563], *avon* [#5771], *pesha* [#6588], *asham* [#816], *taah* [#8582], *pasha* [#6586], *shagah* [#7686], *asebeia* [#763].

30. Transliteration of Greek nouns from *Strong's Exhaustive Concordance*: *hamartia* [#266], *paraptoma* [#3900], *parabasis* [#3847], *hamartema* [#265].

31. Transliteration of Greek adjectives from *Strong's Exhaustive Concordance*: *poneros* [#4190], *kakos* [#2556], *adikos* [#94], *anomos* [#459], *enochos* [#1777].

32. Transliteration of Greek verbs from *Strong's Exhaustive Concordance*: *hamartano* [#264], *planao* [#4105], *parabaino* [#3845].

33. *Strong's Exhaustive Concordance*: *ra'* [#7451].

Most contemporary evangelism focuses on verses like Romans 3:23, "for all have sinned and fall short of the glory of God." The understanding of sin that is often communicated is that all of humanity has fallen short of God's standards of righteousness and have disobeyed or transgressed the laws of God. So, the forgiveness sought is for having disobeyed God's laws. However, one of the Hebrew words, פֶּשַׁע transliterated *pesha,* means not only transgression but also rebellion, which is often connected with idolatry.[34] Idolatry throughout the Bible is rebellion against God who is Creator of all and is forbidden (Lev 19:4). Idolatry is not just the worship of a graven image but of any god or ideology other than the true God.

While some of the poor in the study understood the word "sin" to mean disobedience against God's laws, the majority by changing their allegiance to the living God were acknowledging the idolatry (rebellion) they had been involved in. They were now putting their trust (faith) in the true God revealed in Jesus Christ. Their conversion consisted of repentance, a turning away from idols and their traditional deities, and putting their trust (faith) in Christ. Some were able to articulate this, while others communicated what they believed by their changed allegiance and whom they now worshiped.

Jürgen Moltmann adds another dimension to understanding sin. He writes that there are two sides to sin. One side is where the individual seeks to be god. The other side is hopelessness, resignation, inertia, and melancholy. The context of Moltmann's writing is either a Christianized or a secular society where people *choose* to not believe the hope that God offers in Christ and as a result they despair. He quotes the early church father John Chrysostom, "It is not so much sin that plunges us into disaster, as rather despair."[35] Moltmann writes, "Despair is the premature, arbitrary anticipation of the non-fulfillment of what we hope for from God."[36] The disappointment of the refugees and slum dwellers was with the deities they had worshiped. They were not aware of the hope the Christ offers. Because of their ignorance, they lived in sin. Moltmann calls this situation a sin of omission.[37]

So, a supernatural encounter with the person of Christ does not preclude the issue of sin in the conversion experiences of the poor. The biblical narrative is about the reign of God and the coming of his kingdom here on earth. Because he is not only King but also Creator, the source of all life, he will not tolerate

---

34. *Strong's Exhaustive Concordance: pesha* [#6588].

35. John Chrysostom quoted in Moltmann, *Theology of Hope,* 23.

36. Moltmann, *Theology of Hope,* 23.

37. Moltmann, 23.

worship of anything in the created universe. All allegiance belongs to him. The sin that entangled the refugees and slum dwellers was the despair arising from worshiping traditional deities rather than the almighty God revealed in Jesus Christ. By their decision to change their allegiance, they understood the dark core of sin is idolatry, the giving of glory to anything other than the Creator. All other sins such as disobedience, depravity, or any other form of lawlessness arise from their idolatry and despair. This view is in contrast with the prevailing understanding that sin is a personal moral failure and that it can be set right by seeking forgiveness through Christ, when sin is actually a betrayal of our Creator, the King, who through unimaginable suffering reconciled us to himself.

Edward Rommen writes that there has been an almost exclusive focus on the *message* about Christ. There is little understanding about ethno-epistemology and how context influences people's understanding of God, and who they perceive Christ to be. The majority of the poor in the two non-Western contexts of poverty in this study encountered Christ through lived experience because of needs arising out of poverty, rather than through a reasoned understanding of God's redemptive work through Christ. As Rommen points out, contextualization also needs to facilitate an encounter with the *person* of Christ in ways that are relevant to the population.[38] Based on his pastoral experience, Catholic priest Terrance Klein affirms Rommen's observation when he writes, "Before faith is a question of content, a debate about revealed facts, it is an undeniable encounter with a person. . . . At that moment we are not asked to accept facts about the person. We are asked to accept the person."[39]

The final thing we learned from this study is that the conversion of most of the refugees and slum dwellers was the result of an encounter with the person of Christ. Gordon Smith writes, "People are converted not because they have come to terms with 'spiritual laws' or questions that might be asked 'when they get to heaven,' or even 'evidence that demands a verdict' – but because they experience the transforming grace of God through an encounter with the risen and ascended Christ."[40]

---

38. Rommen, *Come and See*, xii–xiii.

39. Klien, "Faith Is Not a Debate about Facts."

40. Smith, "Conversion and Redemption," 219–20.

What Does This Study Tell Us about the Poor and the God They Seek?

We started with the question of what the poor think about God and why they turn to him, when it would seem that they have not only been forgotten by the world but by God himself. In listening to the stories of the poor, there are four thing that we learned.

The first is that if we had taken the time to listen to the poor, we would have seen the world through their eyes. The poor know and understand their destitution. Because they live on the margins of society, they are powerless and don't have the influence to bring about change. With no support and no one to help them, they look beyond themselves and their world for a deity who is real, is with them, and hears their prayers. Looking for divine help, they despair because their traditional deities have failed them. They find hope and help in the God revealed in Jesus.

The second thing that we have learned is that the socioeconomic and political contexts of the poor influence what they understand the good news of Jesus Christ to be. Contextualization in traditional missions has focused on language, culture, and religion. The various contexts of the poor create their own unique cultures, out of which rise their existential questions and spiritual priorities.

The third thing that we learned is not something new but a reaffirmation of what many Christians throughout history have understood – that the conversion of those from predominantly non-Christian backgrounds is a process. The poor may encounter the reality of God without fully understanding sin and the saving work of Christ. Their conversion happened when they abandoned their allegiance to their traditional deity in order to worship Christ, because they had found a God who is concerned for them. Now with the Holy Spirit at work because of regeneration, over time they began to understand Christ more fully and became aware of their sinfulness.

Fourth, we learned that the conversion of most of the refugees and slum dwellers was the result of an encounter with the person of Christ.

In the end, this book is not about the poor but about the God that the poor seek. Looking at who God is through the eyes of the poor, I saw things that had not seemed important to me from my position of privilege and comfort. I realized the poverty of my own spirituality.

The God that the poor seek is not *Christus Victor*, the conquering hero who through his death and resurrection saves us from our sin by overcoming the powers of darkness – the devil, sin, the law, and death.[41] They cannot relate to the sense of triumphalism in the midst of the destitution of their daily lives. Instead they found themselves drawn to the God who was crucified and knows their suffering.

So much of our Western theology is based on God being absolutely transcendent, far beyond anything that our minds can even conceive, much less comprehend. Because he is beyond time and space, and the origin of all that exists, he is immutable. This view reflects the influence of Plato's concept of the separation of the material world from the spiritual realm on the early church fathers and the development of Western theology.[42] This chasm between the material and physical realms kept God distant.

The question is how does a transcendent, immutable, holy, and morally righteous God relate to a constantly changing and flawed world?[43] Irenaeus of Antioch never questioned the divine attributes of God. Being a pastor rather than an academic or a philosopher, he focused on the anthropomorphic attributes of God, stating that Jesus the Son and the Holy Spirit are the "hands of God." Justo Gonzales writes that Irenaeus' purpose in using such imagery was to show that God is not distant but relates directly with the world.

> While Justin [Martyr], Clement [of Alexandria], Origen, and the entire tradition which springs from them tend to separate God from the world using the second person of the Trinity – the Word, Logos, or Son, as the link between the two – Irenaeus speaks of a God whose hands enter into the world in the work of creation and in the leading of history.[44]

---

41. Swedish Lutheran theologian Gustaf Aulén in his book *Christus Victor* presents the three theories of atonement in Christianity. He argues that theologians have concluded incorrectly that the early church fathers believed in the ransom theory of atonement. Instead Aulén argues that the church fathers believed that the crucifixion was not a payment of ransom to the devil, instead it represented the liberation of humanity from the bondage of sin, death, and the devil. It was a rescue or liberation of the human race from slavery, sickness, and sin. Aulén and Hebert, *Christus Victor.*

42. These church fathers include Clement of Alexandria and Origen.

43. Justo Gonzales writes about the three centers of learning centered around Alexandria, Carthage, and Antioch which embodied three distinct schools of theology. Each struggled with different images of God based on the religious challenges they faced in their context. Origen in Alexandria and Justin Martyr conceived of God as transcendent and immutable, and the only way he could relate to the flawed world was through an intermediary – the Logos or Word. This view raised serious questions as to whether this intermediary is mutable or immutable in order to relate to both the world and God. Gonzales, *Christian Thought Revisited*, 24–26.

44. Gonzales, *Christian Thought Revisited*, 28.

God's presence not only permeates his creation but he is deeply involved with what happens to the human beings he created and the history of the world that shapes their lives.

Ernesto Cardenal found that the poor *campesinos* in Nicaragua were able to comprehend such a God because as farmers they saw him work in nature all around them. They did not necessarily find a place for God in their lives but realized that they are part of the larger narrative of God. Just as God cared for his creation, he would care for them. For the refugees and slum dwellers, God was not silent and distant; they came to know him as *Immanuel,* God with us.

So, who is the God that the poor seek? Jürgen Moltmann writes:

> In concrete terms, God is revealed in the cross of Christ who was abandoned by God. . . . The epistemological principle of the theology of the cross can only be this dialectic principle: The deity of God is revealed in the paradox of the cross. This makes it easier to understand what Jesus did: it was not the devout, but the sinners, and not the righteous but the unrighteous who recognized him, because in them he revealed the divine righteousness of grace, and the kingdom. He revealed his identity amongst those who had lost their identity, amongst the lepers, sick, rejected, and despised, and was recognized as the Son of Man amongst those who had been deprived of their humanity.[45]

The God that the poor seek is not physically and emotionally distant but is the crucified God who understands their suffering because he has experienced it. They recognize him in Jesus Christ, the man of sorrow, who although he is almighty, great, and powerful, yet is loving enough to respond to their desperate prayers.

---

45. Moltmann, *Crucified God,* 27.

Appendix I

Using Translators as Recorders of the Stories

Prior to Recording the Stories

In order to understand the perspective of an "insider" as much as possible and in preparation for recording the stories of the poor, I conducted a pilot by recording the stories of eight individuals in a slum in Bangalore, thus getting an initial idea of the types of experiences and perceptions that form the conversion experiences of the poor in that context. The focus of these conversations was on how and why they had become followers of Christ and some of the consequences of their decisions. The eight individuals were from specific slums where the local ministry COME was actively involved in visiting the slum dwellers and praying with them and establishing prayer meetings and fellowships. The individuals were identified by representatives of COME as people who had turned away from Hinduism and had become followers of Christ. This change of allegiance was attested by changes in their lives and lifestyles, as well as a consistency in their worship of Christ as evidenced by attending prayer meetings, worship services, and teaching sessions, and their hunger for the teachings of the Bible.

In order to understand how to listen to the voices of the poor, I drew on my experience of conducting the field research and writing *Profiles of Poverty: The Human Face of Poverty in Lebanon*[1] using methods and tools drawn from Robert Coles' work *Children in Crisis* and Robert Chambers' participatory rural appraisal (PRA). This experience enabled me to discern the optimal level of mediation and providing some minimal structure while recording the stories that would enable the poor to speak freely about their experiences and perceptions. By focusing on the *how, what,* and *why,* evaluative judgments were

---

1. Das and Davidson, *Profiles of Poverty*.

suspended while the stories were recorded which allowed for the phenomena of conversion to be described by the poor themselves.

Using Translators as Recorders of the Stories

The stories of the poor were told in four different languages in two countries. For two reasons, I made use of interpreters to record these stories:

- Though the primary researcher and author of this study, I do not have language fluency in the four native languages of the various participants in the two countries and therefore needed to use interpreters.
- Based on experience during the pilot project in Bangalore, and extensive conversations with refugees in Lebanon, I observed that a foreigner or outsider conducting the interview using an interpreter changes the dynamics of the relationship with the interviewee and influences the type of responses provided. Therefore it is better for the interview to be conducted by a local person who is bilingual, familiar with the context, and known to the interviewees.

An important question to consider is whether the issue of using an interpreter is critical to research methodology and the results derived. Researchers who do their own translation do not necessarily produce better results, just different ones.[2] Bogusia Temple and Alys Young point out that there is a significant amount of research on ethnic minority communities in Britain which make no reference to language issues and in which the findings are presented as if the interviewees spoke fluent English and that language issues were irrelevant.[3] The "discussion of epistemological and methodological issues around translation across languages has been neglected in cross-cultural social science research."[4]

So the question that Temple and Young ask is whether it matters if the act of translation is discussed. Drawing on the debates on epistemological

---

2. Temple and Young, "Qualitative Research and Translation Dilemmas," 168.

3. Temple and Young, 163. None of the following questions were addressed in this research: What language was the data collected in? At what stage were the interviews translated and transcribed? What translation and transcription issues were there? For example an opening quote could be from a woman speaking English, or it could be from an interview in another language that has been translated, presumably by the researcher. What is the researcher's relationship to the interviewees, and were they given a chance to define their own household patterns?

4. Temple and Young, 174.

issues,[5] they state that in approaches to knowledge, there needs to be an acknowledgement of the location of the researchers within the social world and the fact that this location influences how they perceive knowledge. Translators then form part of the process of the production of knowledge. Temple and Young write:

> There is no neutral position from which to translate and the power relationships within research need to be acknowledged. . . . Researchers working with people who speak/sign different languages rarely address the implications of their relative positions within language hierarchies . . . methodological and epistemological challenges arise from the recognition that people using different languages may construct different ways of seeing social life.[6]

The implication is that translation does not involve a one-to-one translation of words but an understanding of what is being communicated, sometimes referred to as dynamic equivalence. Sherry Simon writes:

> The solutions to many of the translator's dilemmas are not to be found in dictionaries, but rather in an understanding of the way language is tied to local realities, to literary forms and to changing identities. Translators must constantly make decisions about the cultural meanings which language carries and evaluate the degree to which the two different worlds they inhabit are "the same." These are not technical difficulties; they are not the domain of specialists in obscure or quaint vocabularies. . . . In fact the process of meaning transfer has less to do with *finding* the cultural inscription of a term than in reconstructing its value.[7]

One option that Temple and Young suggest is using the translators as key informants and recording information in the third person. They refer to Edwards who argues that by treating the translators as key informants rather than neutral transmitters of messages, it is then possible to begin to discuss the

---

5. See M. Hammersley, *The Politics of Social Research* (London: Sage, 1995); L. Stanley and S. Wise, *Breaking Out Again: Feminist Ontology and Epistemology* (London: Routledge, 1993); and I. M. Young, *Intersecting Voices: Dilemmas of Gender, Political Philosophy, and Policy* (Princeton, NJ: Princeton University Press, 1997).

6. Temple and Young, "Qualitative Research and Translation Dilemmas," 164.

7. Sherry Simon quoted in Temple and Young, 165, emphasis original. Original source Simon, *Gender in Translation: Cultural Identity and the Politics of Transmission* (London: Routledge, 1996).

differences in perspectives.[8] It is critical that the perspective of the translators is understood. "Without talking to interpreters about their views on the issues being discussed the researcher will not be able to begin to allow for differences in understandings of words, concepts and worldviews across languages."[9]

Temple and Young conclude:

> The lack of a one-to-one relationship between language and meaning does not absolve the researcher from investigating the role of language in cross language research. Instead, it indicates that the boundaries around languages are permeable. Although the conversation with people who use other languages is difficult, it is possible, and probably essential, if we are to move on from the objectifying gaze on difference.[10]

A number of factors influence the quality of translation when a researcher uses translators. Maria Birbili identifies three – the competence of the translators, their autobiography, and the position the translators hold in relation to the researcher.[11] However, there are a number of challenges when translating from another language. The first is gaining conceptual equivalence. If there is no direct "lexical equivalence," then the effort needs to be made "towards obtaining conceptual equivalence without concern for lexical comparability."[12] A second issue is to make the participants' words accessible and understandable. A decision needs to be made whether to use a literal or free translation of the words used – each have their benefits and drawbacks. Birbili concludes by stating that translation related decisions need to be made explicit.[13]

In the light of the above, the study reported in this book analyzed the content of interviews and did not use narrative analysis because of the challenges of doing the research in multiple languages. Second, I used translators who were bilingual in both English and the local language – in this case Kannada, Telugu, Tamil, and Arabic – as the primary recorders of the stories. Third, the translators were thoroughly briefed about the project so that

---

8. Temple and Young, 170–171 citing R. Edwards, "A Critical Examination of the Use of Interpreters in the Qualitative Research Process," *Journal of Ethnic and Migration Studies* 24 (1998): 197–208.

9. Temple and Young, 170–71.

10. Temple and Young, 174.

11. Birbili, "Translating from One Language to Another," 2.

12. Birbili, 2.

13. Birbili, 4.

they understood why the stories were being recorded. Fourth, the translators were well known to the researcher so that their "autobiography" could be taken into account if certain translations were problematic or unclear. Fifth, I was in constant dialogue with the translators to ensure conceptual equivalence was being gained. One of the things that Birbili suggests is to pilot the process or pretest questions. As mentioned above, I did this which enabled me to refine the process.

Selection of Participants

Two different types of poverty contexts using time-based categorization of poverty were chosen.[14] One was a slum in Bangalore, India, where the people are *chronically* poor. And the other was Syrian refugees who were experiencing *event-based* poverty in Lebanon.[15]

The stories of twenty slum dwellers in Bangalore and twenty-one refugees in Lebanon were recorded for a total of forty-one participants.[16] The twenty slum dwellers were drawn from those who are involved in prayer groups that COME has established in many of the slums of Bangalore. Each prayer group consists of fifty to seventy-five individuals, all from Hindu backgrounds who had either chosen to follow Christ or were actively seeking him. This interest in Christ among Hindus in the slums of Bangalore is part of the growth of Christianity in India from 2.5 percent to 5.8 percent over the past few decades, with the majority of those choosing to follow Christ being from Hindu backgrounds and a few from Muslim backgrounds.[17] A high percentage of the new believers in Christ were from poor and marginalized communities. In Lebanon, the twenty-one Syrian refugees were drawn from the hundreds of Muslims who are turning up in evangelical churches across the country wanting to know more about Christ, and the churches have doubled or tripled in size with new followers of Christ over the past few years. This interest in Christ among Syrians and Muslims from other countries in the region is part of a larger move of the Holy Spirit specifically among refugees in the Middle East

---

14. Hulme, Shepherd, and Spray, *Chronic Poverty Report*.

15. These contexts and the frameworks and categorizations to understand and analyze poverty are discussed in the introduction.

16. The choice of numbers was based on Baker and Edwards, "How Many Qualitative Interviews Is Enough?"

17. "India," *Operation World*, 2018. However, the census figures still remain at 2.5 percent.

and in Europe.[18] Because of the political and social sensitivities of conversion from Hinduism and Islam to Christianity, there is very little documentation of this phenomena in the public domain other than occasional media reports. The physical and social contexts of the slum dwellers and refugees are described in chapters 5 and 6.

The selection criteria for the participants was that they were recognized as being poor and by their own admission were now followers of Christ, which was attested by the church or indigenous missionaries in each context. Other indicators used in the selection were regular attendance at a church service or prayer meeting and having ceased to worship any idols or other gods. For those in the slums in Bangalore, the fact that they lived in a slum where the poorest in Bangalore live indicated that they were poor.[19] In Lebanon, the interviewees were selected from among those refugees to whom the churches were ministering. The churches had done a needs-assessment and had identified the vulnerable refugees in the community. So, for this study that assessment of vulnerability was accepted.

In Lebanon, four people who were fluent in English and Arabic and involved in ministering to Syrian refugees recorded the stories of the refugees spread across various parts of Lebanon. The refugees were involved in three churches – in Zahle in the Bekaa valley, in the Beruit suburb of Mansourieh, and in the city of Beirut. Two refugees were involved with ministries that were not church based. Each of these churches had holistic assistance programs for the Syrian refugees, addressing their physical, social, and spiritual needs. They ensured that there was no conditionality in any of the assistance they provide and that none of the refugees were required to attend any evangelistic meetings or take any Christian literature. They also did not discriminate according to religion. Anyone in need, regardless of their faith, received assistance. However, there were significant numbers of Muslims choosing to come to the churches, many of whom were not receiving any assistance from the churches.

---

18. The author as part of his work with Canadian Baptists has witnessed firsthand this move of the Holy Spirit among the refugees in Lebanon, Syria, Turkey, and in various countries in Europe. See also Garrison, *Wind in the House of Islam.*

19. See chapter 6 for an analysis of the types of poverty in the urban slums of Bangalore.

Table 1. Demographics of the Syrian Refugees Whose Stories Were Recorded

Lebanon (21 interviewees)	
Gender • Male • Female	 7 14
Age (years) 20–29 30–39 40+	 6 12 3
Married	20
Present occupation • Mason • Carpenter • Volunteer at church • Housewife • Teacher • Wall painter • Machine operator • Curtain installer • Part-time house cleaner • Sewing and crafts • Unemployed	 1 1 6 4 3 1 1 1 1 1 1
Religious background (Sunni Muslim)	21
Any others in the family who also follow Christ • Yes • No	 14 7
Migrants (displaced) from elsewhere	21
Number of years as a refugee 2 3–4 5+	 3 11 6

The majority of the refugees interviewed were in their twenties and thirties, and all but one were married. All were working at subsistence level. Since it is illegal for Syrian refugees to work in Lebanon, even those who were working as teachers and machine operators were being paid illegally, well below minimum wage. All were displaced from various parts of Syria, and most had been refugees in Lebanon for at least three years. All of those interviewed had been

Sunni Muslims. The majority (two thirds) of those who had become followers of Christ had at least one other member of their family who were also followers of Christ. So the decision to convert was not just an individual decision but often also included a spouse and/or child. A number of women said that their husbands were also "praying," implying that they were still seeking but had not yet encountered Christ.

In Bangalore, India, one staff member of the indigenous mission organization COME recorded the stories of the slum dwellers who lived in four slums in the city where COME had ministries. These slums were Mathikere near BEL circle in Yeswahtpur, Kogilu Layout in Yelahanka, Rachanahalli in Tanisandra, and Nayandahalli on the Mysore Road.

Table 2. Demographics of Slum Dwellers Whose Stories Were Recorded

Bangalore, India (20 interviewees)	
Gender • Male • Female	 5 15
Age (years) 15–19 20–29 30–39	 2 11 7
Married	17
Present Occupation • Day laborer (*coolie*) • Sweeper • Student • Housewife • Domestic servant • Supervisor • Driver • Small business	 10 2 1 2 2 1 1 1
Religious background (Hindu)	20
Any others in the family who also follow Christ • Yes • No	 16 4
Migrants from elsewhere	18
Number of years living in the slum	Between 2–25

While the majority of the slum dwellers whose stories were recorded were female, many of the spouses of the married women were also followers of Christ but were not available to be interviewed. Fourteen lived in extreme poverty while working as day laborers, domestic servants, and street sweepers. The husbands of the two housewives also worked as day laborers. Only four out of the twenty were considered poor (the student, supervisor, micro business owner, and driver), but not destitute and living in extreme poverty. Sixteen of the interviewees had other members of the family (spouse and/or children) who were also followers of Christ. This meant that the decision to convert was not just by an individual, but the majority of the family choosing to affiliate themselves with another God and to worship him. While the adults may have individually decided to follow Christ, some of the children may not have, but were involved in activities with other children (Sunday school) or with the adults and other families (worship services, prayer meetings).

Appendix II

Analysis of the Content of the Stories

The following questions were asked or issues explored when analyzing the content of the stories.

1. How Participants Became Followers of Christ

Bangalore, India – Slum dwellers	#	%
Became followers of Christ primarily through hearing the word taught or preached or by reading the Bible	4	20
Became a follower of Christ through an initial supernatural encounter	16	80
Lebanon – Syrian Refugees		
Became followers of Christ primarily through hearing the word taught or preached or by reading the Bible	7	33.3
Became a follower of Christ through an initial supernatural encounter	14	66.6

2. Describing Their Encounter with Christ

While all the Syrian refugees attested that something had profoundly changed in them, there was no standard way in how they described what had happened. This diversity is partly explained by the different ways each of them encountered God and his truths.

For seven of the participants (35 percent) from the slums in Bangalore, the concept of accepting Christ as savior from our sins was based on an awareness of sin and the realization of the need for forgiveness. For the remaining 13 participants (65 percent), the term "accepting Christ as my savior" was indicative of a change that had taken place where they no longer worshiped other gods and had decided to only worship and follow the living God revealed in Christ. They did not necessarily understand what the term meant or how it related to their encounter with Christ. But it was their standardized way of describing in retrospect who they now worshiped.

3. What Disillusioned Them about Their Traditional Faith

For the Syrian refugees, the war had disturbed their traditional faith and beliefs. There was no one reason why they turned away from Islam. It was often a combination of the following: for some it was the religious violence they witnessed. Others felt overwhelmed with evil and did not know how to respond. Others found in Christ something that they had been missing in their traditional faith and were yearning for – such as peace and love.

The majority of the slum dwellers in India turned away from their traditional deities because they were disillusioned that in spite of the rituals and prayers, their deity did not respond. A quarter of them wanted peace in their family life in the midst of the challenges of poverty.

What Disillusioned Slum Dwellers in Bangalore with Their Traditional Faith	#	%
Disillusioned that in spite of rituals and prayers, their deity did not respond.	15/20	75
Wanting peace in their family life in the midst of challenges.	5/20	25

4. Did They Experience Any Harassment or Persecution, and Were There Any Social Consequences for Them for Following Christ?

Lebanon – Syrian Refugees	#	%
No harassment or social consequences for following Christ	10/21	47.0
Mild to severe opposition for following Christ	9/21	42.8
Bangalore, India – Slum Dwellers		
No harassment or social consequences for following Christ	11/20	55.0
Mild to severe opposition for following Christ	9/20	45.0

5. What Attracted Them to Christ?
Slum Dwellers, Bangalore

Twenty (100%) of the slum dwellers in Bangalore said that they were attracted to Christian worship because of the "spiritual songs" and "God's word or message" and stories from the Bible, especially the Jesus story. One person stated the reason for this attraction. "I love hearing God's word and singing spiritual songs." They felt that hearing the word of God, Bible stories, and spiritual songs made them feel closer to God/Christ.

Additional reasons they gave for what attracted them to Christ were the following:

4 (20%)   Gave his life for me

2 (10%)   Lifestyle of Jesus

Some mentioned Christ as being a loving God, deliverance, happiness in his name, miracles. Smaller numbers were attracted to the sacrifice of Christ 4 (20%) and Jesus's lifestyle 2 (10%).

Reason Slum Dwellers Were Attracted to Christ	#	%
Spiritual songs, God's word, messages, stories from the Bible – especially the Jesus story	20/20	100
The sacrifice of Christ (he gave his life for me)	4/20	20
Jesus's lifestyle	2/20	10

Syrian Refugees

Reason Syrian Refugees Were Attracted to Christ	#	%
God's love	9/21	42.8
Peace he gives	4/21	19.0
The sacrifice of Christ	3/21	14.2

This question of what attracted the poor to Christ is at the heart of this study. For the Syrian refugees, the love of God and the peace he gives were among the main reasons why they were attracted to Christ. Three (14.2 percent) said that they were attracted to Christ because of his sacrifice.

6. What Does Christ Mean to Them?

Syrian Refugees	#	%
Father, mother, my life, everything in my life, our life is nothing without Christ	9/21	42
My salvation, savior, forgives my sins, my intercession, my Redeemer	6/21	28
Joy, peace, love, everything good, life, my hope	5/21	23
Lord, leader, captain	4/21	19
He is God, Son of God	3/21	14.2

Slum Dwellers in Bangalore	#	%
Almighty God	20/20	100
Eternal God	9/20	45
Healer, provider, life-giver, sustainer, peace-giver, deliverer	9/20	45
True God	8/20	40
God being real	4/20	20
Forgives my sin, savior	4/20	20
Only One God	3/20	15
Friend, anointed one, Creator, Father; one who is going to come back	3/20	15

7. How Had Their Life Changed?

Their decision to follow Christ was not just a mental assent to a set of propositions. They changed as people. All of them without exception spoke about how their lives had been changed.

Syrian Refugees

In Lebanon, the refugees spoke about life still being hard. However, they now had joy and peace in the midst of conflict and very difficult circumstances. They spoke about the different way they now handled their difficult circumstances – even though materially very little had changed. Many spoke about how their attitudes had changed. Some said that they felt they had moved from the "darkness" of their previous religion.

A lot of things changed. The difference is that now I have something good to look for in tomorrow. Tomorrow is a sweeter day.

Our lives changed. Our hearts were always heavy. Now I rejoice. In our religion, there were always demands on you of what to do and what not to do. Now peace and joy are part of the faith. Jesus is my joy and peace. What was black is now made white.

I changed as a person. I had lived in fear. My personality was fearful. I was full of hate. Maybe I would have been a killer. Maybe I would have killed my brother or neighbor. Today I cannot think about anyone, even for one minute and say, "I am going to kill you." Jesus doesn't teach us to think about killing; he teaches us to think about love.

I was baptized and became a Christian. All of us were living in darkness. I am able to speak about Jesus with a new spirit. I can ask anything. If I ask anything according to his will, he will give it to me.

Everything changed of course. I can face the world with peace. People ask how God allows bad in the world, but it is the opposite. He made man and the world good.

Spiritually, I am not talking about material things, there is a big change. The person who was living in Islam lived like this [hands over eyes]. I was living in darkness. Now I am born again spiritually.

My life was very hard. But then I came here and found hope, and God was glorified. Now I can live in peace.

As a result, there is a great change in the family. A new purpose in life. More discipline and perpetual hope.

My physical circumstances haven't changed, but the way I handle them has. I am no longer worried about tomorrow. Before I was always so nervous and would take it out on my kids. Now I am full of his peace. I used to think God was against me, but now I know he is working for me. I feel his presence at work in our family. I am a new creation.

I don't try to fix everything or stay up at night worrying (about family in Syria and needs), but I pray and I put my head down to sleep. And throughout the day I pray and feel his presence and peace.

My family life has completely changed. My marriage is much happier because we have Jesus bringing us together. I have a peace like I have never experienced before. I don't worry about my future.

I feel joy and peace in my life in spite of all the difficulties. I used to get depressed quickly before. Now I have more hope. I also have more wisdom. He opens new doors for me. He has made me stronger as a person. He got a lot of weakness out of my heart.

I used to have a lot of hatred and not forgive easily. I now forgive and love others easily.

My financial situation has gotten worse. But I have changed. I have joy and peace in my life. Without Jesus in my life I would have left my husband and kids. Everyone is shocked at my peace.

In spite of my financial pressure, I have peace. Our family changed. I raise my kids on God's word now. We have more love for one another.

Slum Dwellers, Bangalore

In India, the decision of slum dwellers to worship Christ and follow him resulted in immediate behavior changes. They spoke of addictions (chewing tobacco and alcohol) being broken. Others stopped practicing witchcraft. All stopped worshiping idols. Some spoke of changes in attitude and behavior (stopped quarreling and fighting). One person even said that as a result of the changes in their lives, the family had been able to save money and have now been able to buy a small piece of land. Others spoke of being healed.

My life changed after I started worshiping Jesus. He healed me from my sickness. We stopped quarreling and fighting; we stopped doing *pujas*, and I'm not angry anymore.

A lot has changed in my life. I did not commit suicide; controlled my quarreling; not angry or doing *pujas*.

Bibliography

Abadie, Alberto. "Poverty, Political Freedom, and the Roots of Terrorism." *The American Economic Review* 96, no. 2 (2006): 50–66.

Anderson, Allan. "Intercultural Theology, Walter J. Hollenweger and African Pentecostalism." In *Intercultural Theology: Approaches and Themes*, edited by Mark J. Cartledge and David Cheethem, 128–44. London: SCM, 2011.

Anderson, B. Y. Sulome. "Syria's Refugee Children Have Lost All Hope." *Foreign Policy* (29 June 2016). https://foreignpolicy.com/2016/06/29/syrias-refugee-children-have-lost-all-hope/.

Anderson, Gerald H., ed. *Theology of the Christian Mission*. London: SCM, 1961.

Askew, Thomas A. "The 1888 London Centenary Missions Conference: Ecumenical Disappointment or American Missions Coming of Age?" *International Bulletin of Missionary Research* 18, no. 3 (1994): 113–18.

———. "The New York 1900 Ecumenical Missionary Conference: A Centennial Reflection." *International Bulletin of Missionary Research* 24, no. 4 (2000): 146–50.

Aulén, Gutaf, and A. G. Hebert. *Christus Victor: A Historical Study of the Three Main Types of the Idea of Atonement*. London: SPCK, 1931.

Baker, Sarah Elsie, and Rosalind Edwards. "How Many Qualitative Interviews Is Enough?" Southampton: National Centre for Research Methods, 2012.

Barth, Karl. *God in Action*. Edinburgh: T&T Clark, 1936.

———. *Karl Barth's Table Talk*. Edited by John D. Godsey. London: Oliver & Boyd, 1965.

Bate, Stuart C. "Method in Contextual Missiology." *Missionalia* 26, no. 2 (1998): 150–85.

Bates, Matthew W. *Salvation by Allegiance Alone: Rethinking Faith, Works and the Gospel of Jesus the King*. Grand Rapids, MI: Baker Academic, 2017.

Batson, D. C., P. Schoenrade, and L. W. Ventis. *Religion and the Individual: A Social-Psychological Perspective*. New York: Oxford University Press, 1993.

Bauer, C. J. "Conversion: From Puritanism to Revivalism." *Journal of Religion* 58 (1978): 227–43.

Bede, Venerable. *The Ecclesiastical History of the English Nation*. A.M. Sellar (ed.) London: George Bell & Sons, 1907.

Bergunder, Michael. "The Pentecostal Movement and Basic Ecclesial Communities in Latin America: Sociological Theories and Theological Debates." *International Review of Mission* 91, no. 361 (2002): 163–86.

Berkhof, Louis. *Systematic Theology*. Grand Rapids, MI: Eerdmans, 1941.

Bevans, Steven B. "Book Review: Come and See: An Eastern Orthodox Perspective on Contextualization." *International Bulletin of Mission Research* 38, no. 1 (2013): 44.

Bevans, Stephen B., and Roger P. Schroeder. *Constants in Context: A Theology for Mission Today*. Maryknoll, NY: Orbis, 2004.

Beyerhaus, Peter, et. al. "Frankfurt Declaration on the Fundamental Crisis in Mission." Theological Convention of Confessing Fellowships. 4 March 1970. Frankfort / Main, Germany. http://institut-diakrisis.bekenntnisbruderschaft.de/fd.pdf. (see also: https://www.ikbg.net/pdf/fe.pdf)

Bhagwati, Jagdish, and T. N. Srinivasan. "Trade and Poverty in the Poor Countries." *American Economic Review* 92, no. 2 (2002): 180–83.

Billings, J. Todd. "John Calvin's Soteriology: On the Multifaceted 'Sum' of the Gospel." *International Journal of Systematic Theology* 11, no. 4 (2009): 428–47.

Birbili, Maria. "Translating from One Language to Another." *Social Research Update*, no. 31 (2000): 1–6.

Boesen, Jacob Kirkeman, and Tomas Martin. *Applying a Rights-Based Approach: An Inspirational Guide for Civil Society*. Copenhagen: The Danish Institute for Human Rights, 2007.

Boff, Leonardo, and Clodovis Boff. *Introducing Liberation Theology*. Maryknoll, NY: Orbis, 2008.

Bonhoeffer, Dietrich. *The Cost of Discipleship*. New York: Macmillan, 1963.

Bonino, Jose Miguez. "Doing Theology in the Context of the Struggle of the Poor." *Mid-Stream* 20, no. 4 (1981): 369–373.

Bosch, David J. "Church Growth Missiology." *Missionalia* 16, no. 1 (1988): 13–24.

———. *Transforming Mission: Paradigm Shifts in Theology of Missions*. Maryknoll: Orbis, 1991.

Brown, Peter. *Poverty and Leadership in the Later Roman Empire: The Menahem Stern Jerusalem Lectures*. Hanover: University Press of New England, 2002.

———. *Through the Eye of a Needle: Wealth, the Fall of Rome, and the Making of Christianity in the West, 350–550 AD*. Princeton: Princeton University Press, 2012.

Brueggemann, Walter. "How the Early Church Practiced Charity." *The Christian Century* (June 2003): 30–31.

Bulkeley, Kelly. *Visions of the Night: Dreams, Religion, and Psychology*. SUNY Series in Dream Studies CN - BF1091. B94 1999 154.6/3. Albany: SUNY Press, 1999.

Burdick, John. *Looking for God in Brazil: The Progressive Catholic Church in Urban Brazil's Religious Arena*. Berkeley: University of California Press, 1996.

Bush, Luis. "The Meaning of Ethne in Matthew 28:19." *Mission Frontiers* (Sept/Oct 2013): 31–35.

Calvin, John. *Institutes of the Christian Religion*. Edinburgh: Calvin Translation Society, 1845.

Cardenal, Ernesto. *The Gospel in Solentiname*. Maryknoll: Orbis, 2010.

Carey, George. "A Biblical Perspective." In *Entering the Kingdom: A Fresh Look at Conversion*, edited by Monica Hill, 9–21. Middlesex: MARC Europe, 1986.

Cartledge, Mark J., and David Cheetham. *Intercultural Theology: Approaches and Themes*. London: SCM, 2011.

Centre for Education and Documentation (CED). "Vulnerability Assessment of Urban Marginalised Communities: A Pilot Study in Bangalore Slum Areas." Mumbai: CED, 2011. http://www.ced.org.in/docs/inecc/member_reports/VA-rep-urban-marginalised.pdf.

Chambers, Robert. "Paradigms, Poverty and Adaptive Pluralism." IDS Working Paper 344, Brighton: Institute of Development Studies, 2010.

———. "Paradigm Shifts and the Practice of Participatory Research and Development." In *Power and Participatory Development: Theory and Practice*, edited by Nici Nelson and Susan Wright, 30–42. London: Intermediate Technology, 1994.

———. *Rural Development: Putting the Last First*. London: Longman, 1983.

———. "Voices of the Poor and Beyond: Lessons from the Past, Agenda for the Future." Lecture delivered on the occasion of the 60th Dies Natalis of the International Institute of Social Studies, The Hague. 11 October 2012. https://www.iss.nl/en/media/robertchambershonoraryfellow.

———. *Whose Reality Counts? Putting the First Last*. London: ITDG, 1997.

Chang, Eunhye, J. Rupert Morgan, Timothy Nyasulu, and Robert J. Priest. "Paul G. Hiebert and Critical Contextualization." *Trinity Journal* 30, no. 2 (2009): 199–207.

Chilman, Catherine S. *Growing Up Poor*. Washington: U.S. Government Printing Office, 1966.

Christian, Jayakumar. *God of the Empty-Handed: Poverty, Power and the Kingdom of God*. Monrovia: MARC, 1999.

Cidade, Elívia Camurça, James Ferreira Moura, Bárbara Barbosa Nepomuceno, Verônica Morais Ximenes, and Jorge Castellá Sarriera. "Poverty and Fatalism: Impacts on the Community Dynamics and on Hope in Brazilian Residents." *Journal of Prevention & Intervention in the Community* 44, no. 1 (2 January 2016): 51–62.

Code, Lorraine. *What Can She Know? Feminist Theory and the Construction of Knowledge*. Ithaca: Cornell University Press, 1991.

Coetze, P. H., and A. P. J. Roux, eds. *The African Philosophy Reader*. New York: Routledge, 1998.

Coles, Robert. *Children of Crisis: Selections from the Pulitzer Prize-Winning Five-Volume Children of Crisis Series*. Boston: Little, Brown, 2003.

———. *Children of Crisis Volume I: A Study of Courage and Fear*. New York: Little, Brown, 1967.

Costas, Orlando E. *Christ Outside the Gate: Mission beyond Christendom*. 2nd ed. Maryknoll: Orbis, 1982.

———. "Conversion as a Complex Experience." In *Down to Earth: Studies in Christianity and Culture*, edited by R. T. Coote and J. R. W. Stott, chapter 11. Grand Rapids: Eerdmans, 1980.

Coward, Barbara E., Joe R. Feagin, and J. Allen Williams. "The Culture of Poverty Debate: Some Additional Data." *Social Problems* 21 (1973): 621–34.

Crabtree, Steve. "Religiosity Highest in World's Poorest Nations." *Gallup Global Reports* (21 August 2012). https://news.gallup.com/poll/142727/religiosity-highest-world-poorest-nations.aspx.

Cumming, Joseph. "Muslim Followers of Jesus?" *Christianity Today* (20 November 2009). https://www.christianitytoday.com/ct/2009/december/main.html.

Das, Rupen. "Becoming a Follower of Christ: Exploring Conversion through Historical and Missiological Lenses." *Perichoresis* 16, no. 1 (2018): 21–40.

———. *Compassion and the Mission of God: Revealing the Hidden Kingdom*. Carlisle: Langham Global Library, 2016.

———. "Impact of the Local Church Showing Compassion: Lessons from the Syrian Crisis." *SEEDBED: Practioners in Conversation* 29, no. 1 (2015): 43–50.

———. *The Poor and Poverty in Islam: Compassion and Social Justice*. Riga: Scholars, 2018.

———. "Refugees: Exploring Theological and Missiological Foundations." *Journal of European Baptist Studies* 16, no. 2 (2016): 33–37.

———. "The World of the Poor: How Development Professionals Understand and Assess Poverty." In *The Poor and Poverty in the Religions: Religious Responses to the Problem of Poverty*, edited by Rupen Das and William H. Brackney, 1–53. Santa Barbara: Praeger, 2018.

Das, Rupen, and Brent Hamoud. *Strangers in the Kingdom: Refugees, Migrants and the Stateless*. Carlisle: Langham Global Library, 2017.

Das, Rupen, and Julie Davidson. *Profiles of Poverty: The Human Face of Poverty in Lebanon*. Beirut: Dar Manhal al Hayat, 2011.

Das, Rupen, and William H. Brackney, eds. *Poverty and the Poor in the World Religions: Religious Responses to the Problem of Poverty*. Santa Barbara: Praeger, 2018.

Davidson, Ivor, and Murray E. Rae, eds. *God of Salvation: Soteriology in Theological Perspective*. Ashgate E-Book. Surrey: Ashgate, 2011.

DeBartolo, Tiffanie. *God-Shaped Hole*. Naperville: Sourcebooks Landmark, 2002.

Department for International Development (DfID). *Sustainable Livelihoods Guidance Sheets*. London: DfID, 1999.

Dobschutz, Ernst von. "Proselytes." *Christian Classics Ethereal Library* (2004). http://www.ccel.org/s/schaff/encyc/encyc09/htm/iv.v.xlii.htm.

Donovan, Vincent. *Christianity Rediscovered*. Maryknoll, NY: Orbis, 1978.

Downton, J. V. "An Evolutionary Theory of Spiritual Conversion and Commitment: The Case of Divine Light Mission." *Journal for the Scientific Study of Religion* 19 (1980): 381–96.

Dunbar-Odem, Donna. *Defying the Odds: Class and the Pursuit of Higher Literacy*. Albany: State University of New York Press, 2007.

Ecumenical Missionary Conference New York, 1900. New York: American Tract Society, 1900.

Ediger, Gerald. "Conversion in Anabaptist and Mennonite History." *Direction: A Mennonite Brethren Forum* 9, no. 4 (1980): 16–23.

Engel, James F., and Wilbert Norton. *What's Gone Wrong with the Harvest? A Communication Strategy for the Church and World Evangelism*. Grand Rapids, MI: Zondervan, 1975.

Erikson, Erik. *Childhood and Society*. New York: W. W. Norton, 1950.

Eze, Emmanuel Chukweze, ed. *African Philosophy: A Reader*. Oxford: Blackwell, 1996.

Faithful, George. "Recovering the Theology of the Negro Spirituals." *Saint Louis University Credo Ut Intelligam* 1, no. 1 (2007): 1–11.

Farah, Warrick. "Emerging Missiological Themes in MBB Conversion Factors." *International Journal of Frontier Missiology* 30, no. 1 (2013): 13–20.

———. "Factors Influencing Arab Muslims to Embrace Biblical Faith That Inform Adaptive Evangelism in Islamic Contexts." Fuller Theological Seminary, 2015. https://www.academia.edu/37787197/_Dissertation_Factors_Influencing_Arab_Muslims_to_Embrace_Biblical_Faith_That_Inform_Adaptive_Evangelism_in_Islamic_Contexts.

Farmer, Paul. *Pathologies of Power: Health, Human Rights, and the New War on the Poor*. Berkeley: University of California Press, 2005.

Farquhar, John Nicol. *The Crown of Hinduism*. Ithaca, NY: Cornell University Library, 1915.

Feagin, Joe R. "Poverty: We Still Believe That God Helps Those Who Help Themselves." *Psychology Today* 6 (1972): 101–29.

Feinberg, Paul D. "An Evangelical Approach to Contextualization of Theology." *Trinity World Forum* 7, no. 3 (1982): 7.

Fell, Ben, and Miles Hewstone. *Psychological Perspectives on Poverty*. York: Joseph Rowntree Foundation, 2015.

Fernandes, Napson. "Over 30% of Children in Bangalore Slums Are Underweight." Pocket News Alert (2015). http://www.pocketnewsalert.com/2015/11/Over-30-percent-of-children-in-Bangalore-Slums-are-underweight.html.

Fleming, Bruce C. E. *Contextualization in Theology: An Evangelical Perspective*. Pasadena, CA: William Carey Library, 1980.

Flemming, Dean. *Contextualization in the New Testament: Patterns for Theology and Mission*. Leicester: Apollos, 2005.

Fong, Bruce W. "A Critique of the Homogeneous Unit Principle in Light of a Practical Theology Perspective." University of Aberdeen, 1992. https://www.proquest.com/openview/be1e8ed81aa3418a50f836021c4aae18/1?pq-origsite=gscholar&cbl=51922&diss=y.

Frank, Arthur W. *Letting Stories Breathe: A Socio-Narratology*. Chicago: University of Chicago Press, 2010.

Freire, Paulo. *Pedagogy of the Oppressed*. New York: Seabury, 1970.

Friedman, Thomas L. *The World Is Flat: A Brief History of the Twenty-First Century*. New York: Farrar, Straus & Giroux, 2006.

Garrison, David. *A Wind in the House of Islam: How God Is Drawing Muslims around the World to Faith in Jesus Christ*. Monument, CO: WIGTake Resources, 2014.

Gebauer, Jochen E., and Gregory R. Maio. "The Need to Belong Can Motivate Belief in God." *Journal of Personality* 80, no. 2 (2012): 465–501.

Gibbs, Eddie. *I Believe in Church Growth*. Grand Rapids: Eerdmans, 1981.

Glasser, Arthur F. "Church Growth at Fuller." *Missiology* 14, no. 4 (1986): 401–20.

———. "The Conciliar Debate." In *Entering the Kingdom: A Fresh Look at Conversion*, edited by Monica Hill, 84–97. Middlesex: MARC Europe, 1986.

———. "An International Perspective." In *Entering the Kingdom: A Fresh Look at Conversion*, edited by Monica Hill, 22–38. Middlesex: MARC Europe, 1986.

Goheen, Michael W., ed. *Reading the Bible Missionally: Words upon the Word*. Grand Rapids: Eerdmans, 2016.

Goldman, A. *Liaisons: Philosophy Meets the Cognitive and Social Sciences*. Cambridge: MIT Press, 1992.

Gonzales, Justo L. *Christian Thought Revisited: Three Types of Theology*. 2nd ed. Maryknoll: Orbis, 1999.

Gooren, Henri. "Conversion Narratives." In *Studying Global Pentecostalism: Theories and Methods*, edited by Michael Bergunder, A. F. Droogers, Allan Anderson, and Cornelius van der Laan, 93–112. Berkeley: University of California Press, 2010.

Graber, J. A., and J. Brooks-Gunn. "Models of Development: Understanding Risk in Adolescence." *Suicide and Life-Threatening Behavior* 25 (1995): 18–25.

Graham, Billy. *How to Be Born Again*. Waco: Word Books, 1977.

Grant, Tobin. "Religion and Inequality Go Hand-in-Hand." *Christianity Today* (September 2011). https://www.christianitytoday.com/news/2011/september/religioninequality.html.

Gray, Frank. "The Gray Matrix – Tracking its History (1977–2015) ver1.0" (2015). http://thegraymatrix.org/wp-content/uploads/2019/10/GrayMatrix_Tracking-its-History.pdf.

Green, Gene L., Stephen T. Pardue, and K. K. Yeo, eds. *So Great a Salvation: Soteriology in the Majority World*. Carlisle: Langham Global Library, 2017.

Green, Joel B. *Salvation*. St. Louis: Chalice, 2003.

Grenier, Paola. "Jubilee 2000: Laying the Foundations for a Social Movement." In *Globalizing Civic Engagement: Civil Society and Transnational Action*, edited by John D. Clark, 86–108. London: Routledge, 2003.

Groenewald, Thomas. "A Phenomenological Research Design Illustrated." *International Journal of Qualitative Methods* 3, no. 1 (2004): 1–26. http://www.ualberta.ca/~iiqm/backissues/3_1/html/groenewald.html.

Groody, Daniel G. *Crossing the Divide: Foundations of a Theology of Migration and Refugees – Monograph 15*. Oxford: Crowther Centre Monographs, 2010.

Groody, Daniel G., ed. *The Option for the Poor in Christian Theology*. Notre Dame: University of Notre Dame Press, 2007.

Gross, Edward N. *Is Charles Kraft an Evangelical? A Critique of Christianity and Culture*. Published privately by the author. Printed by Christian Beacon Press, 1985.

Grudem, Wayne A. *Systematic Theology: An Introduction to Biblical Doctrine*. Grand Rapids: Zondervan, 1994.

Gutiérrez, Gustavo. *The Power of the Poor in History: Selected Writings*. Edited and translated by Robert R. Barr. Maryknoll: Orbis, 1983.

———. "Theology from the Experience of the Poor." *CTSA Proceedings* 47 (1992): 26–33.

———. *A Theology of Liberation*. Maryknoll: Orbis, 1988.

———. *The Truth Shall Make You Free: Confrontations*. Edited and translated by Matthew J. O'Connell. *Collier's Weekly* (1 November 1990). Maryknoll: Orbis, 1990.

———. *We Drink from Our Own Wells: The Spiritual Journey of a People*. Maryknoll: Orbis, 1984.

Hall, Douglas John. *The Cross in Our Context: Jesus and the Suffering World*. Minneapolis: Fortress, 2003.

Hamilton, Michael S. "The 'Religious Affections' of Billy Graham's Evangelism." *Christianity Today* (7 November 2017). http://www.christianitytoday.com/ct/2017/november-web-only/how-billy-graham-preached.html?utm_source=ctdirect-html&utm_medium=Newsletter&utm_term=10383464&utm_content=546868397&utm_campaign=email.

Hamman, A. G., and W. Mitchell, eds. *Early Christian Prayers*. Chicago: Henry Regnery, 1961.

Haney, Jim. "The Meaning of Ethnos in Matthew 28:19." *Mission Frontiers* (Sept/Oct 2013): 33.

Hannerz, Ulf. *Soulside: Inquiries into Ghetto Culture and Community*. New York: Columbia University Press, 1969.

Harper, Douglas. "Proselyte." *Online Etymological Dictionary* (2016). http://www.etymonline.com/index.php?term=proselyte.

Hartnett, Daniel. "Remembering the Poor: An Interview with Gustavo Gutiérrez." *The National Catholic Review* 188, no. 3 (2003): 11–14.

Haushofer, Johannes, and Ernst Fehr. "On the Psychology of Poverty." *Science* 344, no. 6186 (2014): 862–67.

Hebblethwaite, Margaret. *Base Communities: An Introduction*. Mahwah, NJ: Paulist, 1994.

Held, David, and Anthony McGrew. *Globalization / Anti-Globalization: Beyond the Great Divide*. Vol. 19. Cambridge: Polity, 2007.

Henry, Carl. F. H. "The Cultural Relativizing of Revelation." *Trinity Journal* 1 (Fall 1980): 153–64.

———. *The Uneasy Conscience of Modern Fundamentalism*. Grand Rapids: Eerdmans, 1947.

Hesselgrave, David J. *Communicating Christ Cross-Culturally: An Introduction to Missionary Communication*. Grand Rapids: Zondervan, 1991.

———. *Scripture and Strategy: The Use of the Bible in Postmodern Church and Mission*. Pasadena: William Carey Library, 1994.

Hesselgrave, David, and Edward Rommen. *Contextualization: Meaning, Methods, and Models*. Leicester: Apollos, 1987.

Hesselgrave, David J., and Ed Stetzer. *Mission Shift*. Nashville: B&H Academic, 2010.

Hibbert, Richard Y. "Negotiating Identity: Extending and Applying Alan Tippett's Model of Conversion to Believers from Muslim and Hindu Backgrounds." *Missiology* 43, no. 1 (January 2015): 59–72.

Hiebert, Paul G. *Anthropological Reflections on Missiological Issues*. Grand Rapids: Baker, 1994.

———. "Critical Contextualization." *International Bulletin of Missionary Research* 11, no. 3 (1987): 104–12.

Hilderbrand, Kelly Michael. "What Led Thai Buddhist Background Believers to Become Christians: A Study of One Church in Bangkok." *Missiology: An International Review* 44, no. 4 (2016): 400–415.

Hill, Monica. "Entering the Kingdom: Then and Now." In *Entering the Kingdom: A Fresh Look at Conversion*, edited by Monica Hill, 1–8. Middlesex: MARC Europe, 1986.

Hill, Monica, ed. *Entering the Kingdom: A Fresh Look at Conversion*. Middlesex: MARC Europe, 1986.

Hoefer, Herbert E. *Churchless Christianity*. Pasadena: William Carey Library, 2002.

Hollenbach, David. "Gaudium et Spes (1965)." In *Modern Catholic Social Teaching: Commentaries & Interpretations*, edited by Kenneth R. Himes, 266–314. Washington, D.C.: Georgetown University Press, 2005.

Houston, Tom. "The Story of the Lausanne Covenant: Case Study in Cooperation." Lausanne Movement (2013). https://www.lausanne.org/wp-content/uploads/2009/12/Story_of_the_Covenant.pdf.

Hulme, David, Andrew Shepherd, and Paul Spray. *The Chronic Poverty Report: Chronic Poverty Research Centre*. Manchester, UK: The Institute for Development Policy & Management, 2005.

Hunt, Robert A. "The History of the Lausanne Movement, 1974–2010." *International Bulletin of Missionary Research* 35, no. 2 (2011): 81–84.

Hunter, James D. *American Evangelicalism: Conservative Religion and the Quandary of Modernity*. New Brunswick: Rutgers University Press, 1983.

Ibn Warraq, ed. *Leaving Islam: Apostates Speak Out*. New York: Prometheus, 2003.

Ijzendoorn, M. H. Van, C. M. J. L. Vereijken, M. J. Bakermans-Kranenburg, and M. J. Riksen-Walraven. "Assessing Attachment Security with the Attachment Q Sort: Meta-Analytic Evidence for the Validity of the Observer AQS 1188–1213." *Child Development* 75, no. 4 (2004): 1188–1213.

Illich, Ivan. *Mission and Midwifery*. Gwelo, Rhodesia/Zimbabwe: Mambo Press, 1974.

Ilo, Stan Chu. "Poverty and Economic Justice in Pope Francis." *International Bulletin of Mission Research* 43, no. 1 (2019): 38–56.

"India." *Operation World* (2018). https://operationworld.org/locations/india/.

Iyadurai, Joshua. *Transformative Religious Experience: A Phenomenological Understanding of Religious Conversion.* Eugene: Pickwick, 2015.

James, William. *The Varieties of Religious Experience: A Study in Human Nature* (1902). London: Penguin Publishing Group, 1982.

Johnston, James, ed. *Report of the Centenary Conference on Protestant Missions of the World.* London: James Nesbit, 1888.

Jones, E. Stanley. *The Christ of the Indian Road.* Nashville: Abingdon, 1925.

Kallenberg, Brad. "Conversion Converted: A Postmodern Formulation of the Doctrine of Conversion." *Evangelical Quarterly* 67, no. 4 (1995): 335–64.

Kamsteeg, Frans H. "Prophetic Pentecostalism in Chile." *Studies in Evangelicalism* 15 (1998): 23–24.

Kapic, Kelly M. "Do We Need a Stronger Word for 'Faith'?" *Christianity Today* (21 June 2017). http://www.christianitytoday.com/ct/2017/july-august/do-we-need-stronger-word-for-faith.html?utm_source=ctdirect-html&utm_medium=Newsletter&utm_term=10383464&utm_content=531164721&utm_campaign=email.

Keesmaat, Sylvia C., and Brian J. Walsh. *Romans Disarmed: Resisting Empire, Demanding Justice.* Grand Rapids: Brazos Press, 2019.

Kevan, Ernest F. *Salvation.* Grand Rapids: Baker Book House, 1963.

Kirk, J. Andrew. *Liberation Theology: An Evangelical View from the Third World.* Basingstoke: Marshall, Morgan & Scott, 1979.

———. *What Is Mission? Theological Explorations.* Minneapolis, MN: Fortress, 2000.

Klien, Terrance. "Faith Is Not a Debate about Facts. It Is an Encounter with a Face." *America: The Jesuit Review* (2 August 2017). https://www.americamagazine.org/faith/2017/08/02/faith-not-debate-about-facts-it-encounter-face.

Kling, David W. "Conversion to Christianity." In *The Oxford Handbook of Religious Conversion,* edited by Lewis R. Rambo and Charles E. Farhadian, 599–622. Oxford: Oxford University Press, 2014.

Knapp, Robert. "How Magic and Miracles Spread Christianity." *Biblical Archaeology Review* 46, no. 1 (2020): 50–53.

Kraft, Charles H. *Christianity in Culture: A Study in Dynamic Biblical Theologizing in Cross-Cultural Perspective.* 2nd ed. Maryknoll: Orbis, 2005.

———. "Culture, Worldview and Contextualization." In *Perspectives on the World Christian Movement,* edited by Ralph D. Winter and Steven C. Hawthorne, 384–91. Pasadena, CA: William Carey Library, 1999.

Kreider, Alan. *The Change of Conversion and the Origin of Christendom.* Eugene, OR: Wipf & Stock, 1999.

———. *The Patient Ferment of the Early Church: The Improbable Rise of Christianity in the Roman Empire.* Grand Rapids: Baker Academic, 2016.

Krueger, Alan B., and Jitka Malečková. "Education, Poverty and Terrorism: Is There a Causal Connection?" *Journal of Economic Perspectives* 17, no. 4 (2003): 119–44.

Kwan, Simon Shui-Man. *Postcolonial Resistance and Asian Theologies*. London: Routledge, 2014.

Lalive, Christian. "The Pentecostal 'Conquista' in Chile." *The Ecumenical Review* (January 1968): 16–32.

Lane Fox, Robin. *Pagans and Christians*. New York: HarperCollins, 1996.

Laniak, Timothy S. *Finding the Lost Images of God*. Grand Rapids: Zondervan, 2010.

Laughlin, Tabor. "Western vs. Chinese Theology." *ChinaSource* (11 August 2017). http://www.chinasource.org/resource-library/from-the-west-courtyard/western-vs-chinese-theology.

The Lausanne Movement. *The Cape Town Commitment: A Call to Action*. Peabody, MA: Hendrickson, 2013.

———. "Evangelism and Social Responsibility: An Evangelical Commitment." Lausanne Occasional Paper 21, 1982. Lausanne Committee for World Evangelization and the World Evangelical Fellowship. https://www.lausanne.org/content/lop/lop-21.

———. "The Manila Manifesto." *The Lausanne Movement* (1989). https://www.lausanne.org/content/manifesto/the-manila-manifesto.

Lawson, Steven J. *New Life in Christ: What Really Happens When You Are Born Again and Why It Matters*. Grand Rapids, MI: Baker Books, 2020.

Lebanese Society for Educational and Social Development (LSESD). "LSESD Food Aid Response: A Summary of the Survey Data Analysis Conducted from February–July 2014 for Phase IV of the CFGB Zahle Food Aid Project." Beirut: LSESD, 2014.

Lee, Archie C. C. "God's Asian Names: Rendering the Biblical God in Chinese." *SBL Forum*. n.p. [cited Oct 2005]. http://sbl-site.org/Article.aspx?ArticleID=456.

Leeds, Anthony. "The Concept of the 'Culture of Poverty': Conceptual, Logical, and Empirical Problems, with Perspectives from Brazil and Peru." In *The Culture of Poverty: A Critique*, edited by Eleanor B. Leacock, 226–84. New York: Simon & Schuster, 1971.

Leo XIII, Pope. "Rerum Novarum: Encyclical of Pope Leo XIII on Capital and Labor." *The Journal of Ecclesiastical History* 51, no. 3 (1891): 592–651.

Lewis, Oscar. "The Culture of Poverty." In *Explosive Forces in Latin America*, edited by John Tepaske and Sydney N. Fisher, 149–173. Columbus: Ohio University Press, 1964.

———. *Five Families: Mexican Case Studies in the Culture of Poverty*. New York: Basic Books, 1959.

———. *La Vida: A Puerto Rican Family in the Culture of Poverty – San Juan and New York*. New York: Random House, 1966.

Limburg, Tim. "The Gospel to the Poor." *The Reformed Journal* (October 1978): 20–23.

Loewen, Jacob A. "Socialization and Conversion in the Ongoing Church." In *Culture and Human Values: Christian Intervention in Anthropological Perspective*, edited by Jacob A. Loewen, 235–51. Pasadena: William Carey Library, 1975.

Lofland, John, and Norman Skonovd. "Conversion Motifs." *Journal for the Scientific Study of Religion* 20, no. 4 (1981): 373–85.

Lonergan, B. *Method in Theology*. London: Darton, Longman & Todd, 1990.

Luria, A. R. *Cognitive Development: Its Cultural and Social Foundations*. Cambridge: Harvard University Press, 1982.

Luther, Martin. "Sermons of Martin Luther – Day of Christ's Ascension into Heaven." *Bible Explore.com*. http://www.godrules.net/library/luther/129luther_c13.htm.

Ma, Wonsuk. "'When the Poor Are Fired Up': The Role of Pneumatology in Pentecostal/ Charismatic Mission." *The Spirit in the World: Emerging Pentecostal Theologies in Global Contexts* 24 (2009): 40–52.

Majid, Nisar, Guhad Adan, Khalif Abdirahman, Jeeyon Janet Kim, and Daniel Maxwell. *Narratives of Famine: Somalia 2011*. Somerville: Feinstein International Center, 2016.

Mani, Anandi, Sendhil Mullainathan, Eldar Shafir, and Jiaying Zhao. "Poverty Impedes Cognitive Function." *Science* 341, no. 6149 (2013): 976–80.

Manriques, Samuel Palma. "Religion of the People and Evangelism: A Pentecostal Perspective." *International Review of Mission* 82, no. 327 (1993): 365–75.

Mariz, Cecilia L. *Coping with Poverty: Pentecostals and Christian Base Communities in Brazil*. Philadelphia: Temple University Press, 1994.

Markandaya, Kamala. *Nectar in a Sieve*. Calcutta: Signet, 1954.

Markham, Paul N. *Rewired: Exploring Religious Conversion*. Eugene: Wipf & Stock, 2007.

Martorell, Reynaldo. "Undernutrition during Pregnancy and Early Childhood: Consequences for Cognitive and Behavioral Development." In *International Congress Series; Early Child Development: Investing in Our Children's Future*. Washington: World Bank, 1997.

Massey, Joshua. "God's Amazing Diversity in Drawing Muslims to Christ." *International Journal of Frontier Missions* 17, no. 1 (2000): 5–14.

Maxwell, Simon. *The Meaning and Measurement of Poverty. ODI Poverty Briefing*. Vol. 3. London: Overseas Development Institute (ODI), 1999.

McClintok, Wayne. "A Sociological Critique of the Homogenous Unit Principle." *International Review of Mission* 77, no. 305 (1988): 107–16.

McGavran, Donald A. *The Bridges of God*. Rev. ed. New York: Friendship, 1981.

———. *Momentous Decision in Missions Today*. Grand Rapids: Baker Books, 1984.

———. "Will Uppsala Betray the Two Billion?" *Church Growth Bulletin* 5, no. 4 (1968): 233–41.

———. "Wrong Strategy, the Real Crisis in Mission." *IRM* 54 (October 1965): 451–61.

McGavran, Donald A., ed. *Crucial Issues in Mission Tomorrow*. Chicago: Moody, 1972.

McGill, Jenny. *Religious Identity and Cultural Negotiation: Toward a Theology of Christian Identity in Migration*. Eugene: Pickwick, 2016.

McGrath, Alister E. *Christian Theology: An Introduction*. 5th ed. Chichester: Wiley-Blackwell, 2011.

McGuire, Meredith B. *Religion: The Social Context*. Belmont: Wadsworth Thomson Learning, 2002.

McIntyre, John. *The Shape of Soteriology: Studies in the Doctrine of the Death of Christ*. Edinburgh: T&T Clark, 1992.

McKnight, Scot. "Forward." In Michael W. Bates. *Salvation by Allegiance Alone: Rethinking Faith, Works and the Gospel of Jesus the King*. Grand Rapids: Baker Academic, 2017. Kindle Location 34–98.

———. *Kingdom Conspiracy: Returning to the Radical Mission of the Local Church*. Grand Rapids: Brazos, 2014.

———. *Turning to Jesus: The Sociology of Conversion in the Gospels*. Louisville: Westminster John Knox, 2002.

Migliore, Daniel L. *Faith Seeking Understanding: An Introduction to Christian Theology*. Grand Rapids: Eerdmans, 2004.

Misra, G., and K. A. Mohanty. "Consequences of Poverty and Disadvantage: A Review of Indian Studies." In *Psychology of Poverty and Disadvantage*, edited by K. A. Mohanty and G. Misra, 121–48. New Delhi: Concept, 2000.

Moltmann, Jürgen. *The Church in the Power of the Spirit*. New York: Harper & Row, 1977.

———. *The Crucified God*. London: SCM, 1974.

———. *Theology of Hope*. Minneapolis: Fortress, 1993.

Mood, Carina, and Jan O. Jonsson. "The Social Consequences of Poverty: An Empirical Test on Longitudinal Data." *Social Indicators Research* (May 2015): 1–20.

Moreau, A Scott. "Contextualization." In *The Changing Face of World Missions*, edited by Michael Pocock, Gailyn Van Rheenen, and Douglas McConnel, 321–48. Grand Rapids: Baker, 2005.

———. *Contextualization in World Missions: Mapping and Assessing Evangelical Models*. 2nd ed. Grand Rapids: Kregel Academic, 2012.

Mother Teresa. *In the Heart of the World: Thoughts, Stories and Prayers*. Edited by Becky Benenate. Novato: New World Library, 1997.

Moynihan, Daniel Patrick. "The Negro Family: The Case For National Action." Washington DC, Office of Policy Planning and Research, U.S. Department of Labour: 1965.

———. *On Understanding Poverty: Perspectives from the Social Sciences*. New York: Basic Books, 1969.

Muldoon, James. "Introduction: Conversion of Europe." In *Varieties of Religious Conversion in the Middle Ages*, edited by James Muldoon, 1–12. Gainesville: University Press of Florida, 1997.

Mullainathan, Sendhil. "The Psychology of Poverty." *Focus* 28, no. 1 (2011): 19–22.

Mullens, Lincoln A. *The Chance of Salvation: A History of Conversion in America*. Cambridge: Harvard University Press, 2017.

Murray, J. "Liberation for Communion in the Soteriology of Gustavo Gutierrez." *Theological Studies* 59, no. 1 (1998): 51–59.

Narayanasamy, N. *Participatory Rural Appraisal: Principles, Methods and Applications*. New Delhi: Sage Publications India, 2009.

Narayan-Parker, Deepa, Raj Patel, and D. Narayan. *Voices of the Poor: Can Anyone Hear Us?* Vol. 1. New York: Oxford University Press, 2000.

National Association of Evangelicals. "What Is an Evangelical?" NAE (n.d.). https://www.nae.net/what-is-an-evangelical/.

Newbigin, Lesslie. "Conversion." *Religion and Society (Bangalore)* 13, no. 4 (1966): 30–42.

———. *Foolishness to the Greeks: The Gospel and Western Culture*. Grand Rapids: Eerdmans, 1986.

———. *The Gospel in a Pluralistic Society*. Grand Rapids: Eerdmans, 1989.

Newbigin, Lesslie, and Geoffrey Wainwright. *Signs amid the Rubble: The Purposes of God in Human History*. Grand Rapids: Eerdmans, 2003.

Nicholls, Bruce J. *Contextualization: Theology of Gospel and Culture*. Vancouver: Regent College Publishing, 1979.

———. "Strategy Paper: The Relationship of Proclamation to Service." In *Go Forth and Tell: Report on the All India Congress on Missions and Evangelism*. Devlali: AICOME, 1977.

Niebuhr, H. Richard. *Christ and Culture*. New York: Harper, 1951.

Niebuhr, Reinhold. *Moral Man and Immoral Society: A Study of Ethics and Politics*. New York: Scribner, 1932.

Niles, D. Preman. *From East and West: Rethinking Christian Mission*. St. Louis: Chalice, 2004.

Noble, K. G., M. F. Norman, and M. J. Farah. "Neurocognitive Correlates of Socioeconomic Status in Kindergarten Children." *Development Science* 8, no. 1 (2005): 74–78.

Noble, Tim. *Keeping the Windows Open: The Theological Method of Clodovis Boff and the Problem of the Alterity of the Poor*. Prague: International Baptist Theological Seminary, 2009.

Olsen, Roger E. *Reformed and Always Reforming: The Postconservative Approach to Evangelical Theology*. Grand Rapids: Baker, 2007.

———. "What Is an 'Evangelical' and Does It Matter?" *Patheos* (28 July 2017). http://www.patheos.com/blogs/rogereolson/2017/07/what-is-an-evangelical-and-does-it-matter/.

Ormerod, Neil, and Shane Clifton. *Globalization and the Mission of the Church*. Ecclesiological Investigations. Vol. 6. London: T&T Clark, 2009.

Padilla, C. René. "The Unity of the Church and the Homogeneous Unit Principle." In *Exploring Church Growth*, edited by Wilbert R. Shenk, 289–302. Grand Rapids: Eerdmans, 1983.

Pascal, Blaise. *Pensees* (1660). Christian Classics Ethereal Library. https://ccel.org/ccel/pascal/pensees/pensees.

Paul VI, Pope. "Constitution on the Sacred Liturgy SACROSANCTUM CONCILIUM." Vatican City: Vatican, 1963.

———. *Evangelii Nuntiand.* The Vatican: Libreria Editrice Vaticana, 1975.

———. "Evangelica Testuficatio: On the Renewal of the Religious Life According to the Teaching of the Second Vatican Council." Rome: Vatican, 1971, 1–20.

———. "Populorum Progressio: Encyclical of Pope Paul VI on the Development of Peoples: 26th March 1967." Rome: Vatican, 2007.

Payne, Ruby K. *Framework for Understanding Poverty: A Cognitive Approach.* Highland: aha! Process, 2013.

Peace, Richard V. "Conflicting Understandings of Christian Conversion: A Missiological Challenge." *International Bulletin of Missionary Research* 28, no. 1 (2004): 8–10.

Perkins, John M. *Let Justice Roll Down.* Grand Rapids: Baker Books, 1976.

———. *A Quiet Revolution: The Christian Response to Human Need, a Strategy for Today.* Waco: Word, 1976.

Phan, Peter C. "The World Missionary Conference, Edinburgh 1910: Challenges for Church and Theology in the Twenty-First Century." *International Bulletin of Missionary Research* 34, no. 2 (2010): 105–8.

Pikkert, Pieter. "Protestant Missionaries to the Middle East: Ambassadors of Christ or Culture?" Pretoria: University of South Africa, 2006.

Piper, John. *Desiring God.* Sisters: Multnomah, 2003.

Pleins, J. David. *The Social Visions of the Hebrew Bible: A Theological Introduction.* Louisville: Westminster John Knox, 2001.

Portes, Alejandro. "Social Capital: Its Origins and Applications in Modern Sociology." *Annual Review of Sociology* 24, no. 1 (1998): 1–24.

Powell, Mark Allen. "The Forgotten Famine: Personal Responsibility in Luke's Parable of 'The Prodigal Son.'" In *Literary Encounters with the Reign of God*, edited by Sharon H. Ringe and H. C. Paul Kim, 265–74. London: T&T Clark, 2004.

Prince, Andrew James. *Contextualization of the Gospel: Towards an Evangelical Approach in the Light of Scripture and the Church Fathers.* Eugene: Wipf & Stock, 2017.

Raboteau, Albert J. "The Secret Religion of the Slaves." *Christianity Today* (1992). http://www.christianitytoday.com/history/issues/issue-33/secret-religion-of-slaves.html.

———. *Slave Religion: The "Invisible Institution" in the Antebellum South.* Oxford: Oxford University Press, 1980.

Radin, Paul. *Primitive Man as Philosopher.* 2nd ed. New York: Dover, 1957.

Rafiq, Sobia. "Need Assessment: Slum Homes." Selco Foundation Urban Community Lab (2015). https://www.slideshare.net/SobiaRafiq2/06uclneedassessmentslumhomes.

Rajamanicham, S. *The First Oriental Scholar: Robert de Nobili, Alias Tattuva Podagar, The Father of Tamil Prose.* Palayamkottai, India: De Nobili Research Institute, St. Xavier's College, 1972.

Ramachandran, H., and S. V. Subramanian. "Slum Household Characteristics in Bangalore: A Comparative Analysis 1973 and 1992." In *Living in India's Slums,* edited by Hans Schenk, 79–112. New Delhi: Manohar, 2001.

Rambo, Lewis R. "Conversion: Toward a Holistic Model of Religious Change." *Pastoral Psychology* 38, no. 1 (1989): 47–63.

———. *Understanding Religious Conversion.* New Haven: Yale University Press, 1993.

Rambo, Lewis R., and Charles E. Farhadian, eds. *The Oxford Handbook of Religious Conversion.* Oxford: Oxford University Press, 2014.

Rauschenbausch, Walter. *A Theology for the Social Gospel.* New York: MacMillan, 1917.

Rees, Tomas James. "Is Personal Insecurity a Cause of Cross-National Differences in the Intensity of Religious Belief?" *Journal of Religion and Society* 11 (2009): 1–26.

Richardson, Don. *Peace Child: An Unforgettable Story of Primitive Jungle Treachery in the 20th Century.* Ventura: Regal, 2005.

Roach, Jack L., and Orville R. Gursslin. "An Evaluation of the Concept 'Culture of Poverty.'" *Social Forces* 45, no. 3 (1967): 383–92.

Rodman, Hyman. "The Lower-Class Value Stretch." In *Poverty in America,* edited by Louis A. Ferman et al., 270–85. Ann Arbor: University of Michigan Press, 1968.

Romero, Oscar. *The Violence of Love.* Maryknoll: Orbis, 2003.

Rommen, E. *Come and See: An Eastern Orthodox Perspective on Contextualization.* Pasadena: William Carey Library, 2013.

Roser, Max, and Esteban Ortiz-Ospina. "Global Extreme Poverty." *Our World in Data* (2019). https://ourworldindata.org/extreme-poverty.

Sachs, Jeffrey. *The End of Poverty.* Leicester: Penguin, 2005.

Satyavrata, Ivan. *Pentecostals and the Poor: Reflections from the Indian Context.* Baguio City: Asia Pacific Theological Seminary Press, 2017.

Schieman, Scott. "Socioeconomic Status and Beliefs about God's Influence in Everyday Life." *Sociology of Religion* 71 (February 2010): 25–51.

Schreiner, Thomas. "Saved by 'Allegiance' Alone? On a New Attempt to Revise the Reformation." *The Gospel Coalition* (3 March 2017). https://www.thegospelcoalition.org/article/book-review-salvation-by-allegiance-alone.

Schreiter, Robert J., and Edward Schillebeeckx. *Constructing Local Theologies.* Maryknoll: Orbis, 1985.

Scribner, Sylvia, and Michael Cole. *The Psychology of Literacy.* Cambridge: Harvard University Press, 1981.

Second Vatican Council, The. "Decree on the Missionary Activity of the Church: Ad Gentes." Vatican City: Vatican, 1965. https://www.vatican.va/archive/hist_councils/ii_vatican_council/documents/vat-ii_decree_19651207_ad-gentes_en.html.

The Secretaries to the Conference, ed. *Conference on Missions Held in 1860 at Liverpool.* London: James Nesbit, 1860.

———. *Proceedings of the General Conference on Foreign Missions.* London: John F. Shaw, 1879.

Sepulveda, J. "Future Perspectives for Latin American Pentecostalism." *International Review of Missions* 87, no. 345 (1998): 189–203.

Shaull, Richard. "Foreword." In *Pedagogy of the Oppressed*, 9–15. New York: Seabury, 1968.

———. "The Pentecostal Appeal to the Poor." *Church and Society* 86, no. 4 (1996): 51–52.

Shetty, P. S. "City Studies on Nutrition: Bangalore, India." *The Southeast Asian Journal of Tropical Medicine and Public Health* 23, no. 3 (1992): 54–58.

Shivaraj B. M., Vinay Kiran B. S., and Ranganath T. S. "Prevalence of Hypertension and Diabetes Mellitus at Selected Urban Slums in Bangalore, India: A Cross Sectional Study." *International Journal of Community Medicine and Public Health* 3, no. 1 (2016): 74–77.

Sinha, Rekha, and Udai Prakash Sinha. *Ecology and Quality of Life in Urban Slums: An Empirical Study*. New Delhi: Concept, 2007.

Small, Mario Luis. *Villa Victoria: The Transformation of Social Capital in a Boston Barrio*. Chicago: University of Chicago Press, 2004.

Small, Mario Luis, David J. Harding, and Citable Link. "Introduction: Reconsidering Culture and Poverty." *Annals of the American Academy* 629 (May 2015): 6–27.

Smith, Alex G. "Strategic Approaches for the Buddhist World." Tokyo, 2010. https://www.ggcn.org/wp-content/uploads/tokyo2010/resources/Tokyo2010_C_Alex_Smith(3).pdf.

Smith, David. "The Church Growth Principles of Donald McGavran." *Transformation* 2, no. 2 (1985): 25–30.

Smith, Gordon T. "Conversion and Redemption." In *The Oxford Handbook of Evangelical Theology*, edited by Gerald McDermott, 209–20. Oxford: Oxford University Press, 2010.

———. *Transforming Conversion: Rethinking the Language and Contours of Christian Initiation*. Grand Rapids: Baker Academic, 2010.

Smith, James K. A. *Desiring the Kingdom: Worship, Worldview, and Cultural Formation*. Grand Rapids: Baker Academic, 2009.

Smith, Jeffrey. *The Concept of Religion Reflected in the Early Negro Spiritual*. Bloomington: iUniverse, 2008.

Society for Participatory Research in Asia. *Bengaluru Study Report 2014*. New Delhi: Society for Participatory Research in Asia, 2014.

Stackhouse, John G., ed. *What Does It Mean to Be Saved? Broadening Evangelical Horizons of Salvation*. Grand Rapids: Baker Academic, 2002.

Stott, John R. W. *Christian Mission in the Modern World*. Downers Grove: InterVarsity, 1975.

———. *Down to Earth: Studies in Christianity and Culture*, edited by R. T. Coote and J. R. W. Stott. Grand Rapids: Eerdmans, 1980.

———. *The Lausanne Covenant: An Exposition and Commentary*. Minneapolis, MN: Worldwide, 1975.

Stott, John R. W., ed. *Making Christ Known: Historic Mission Documents from the Lausanne Movement, 1974–1989*. Grand Rapids: Eerdmans, 1997.

Strong's Concordance. "7725. shub." *Bible Hub*. http://biblehub.com/hebrew/7725.htm.

Strong's Exhaustive Concordance of the Bible. Peabody: Hendrickson, 2009.

Sugden, Chris. *Radical Discipleship*. London: Marshall, Morgan & Scott, 1981.

Sunquist, Scott W. *Understanding Christian Mission, Participation in Suffering and Glory*. Grand Rapids: Baker Academic, 2013.

Sweet, Leonard, and Frank Viola. *Jesus Manifesto: Restoring the Supremacy and Sovereignty of Jesus Christ*. Nashville, TN: Thomas Nelson, 2010.

Taleb, Nassim Nicholas. *Black Swan: The Impact of Highly Improbable*. New York: Random House, 2010.

Tan, Jonathan Y. "Pope Francis's Preferential Option for Migrants, Refugees, and Asylum Seekers." *International Bulletin of Mission Research* 43, no. 1 (2019): 58–66.

Teasedale, Wayne. *Catholicism in Dialogue: Conversations across Traditions*. New York: Rowman & Littlefield, 2004.

Temple, Bogusia, and Alys Young. "Qualitative Research and Translation Dilemmas." *Qualitative Research* 4, no. 2 (2004): 161–78.

Terry, John Mark, ed. *Missiology: An Introduction to the Foundations, History, and Strategies of World Missions*. Nashville: B&H Academic, 2015.

Terry, John Mark, and J. D. Payne. *Developing a Strategy for Missions: A Biblical, Historical, and Cultural Introduction*. Grand Rapids: Baker Academic, 2013.

Theological Education Fund. *Ministry in Context: The Third Mandate Programme of the Theological Education Fund (1970–77)*. Bromley: Theological Education Fund, 1972.

Thomas, M. M. *The Acknowledged Christ of the Indian Renaissance. Confessing the Faith in India Series*. Bangalore: Christian Institute for the Study of Religion and Society, 1969.

———. "India: Towards an Indigenous Christian Theology." In *Asian Voices in Christian Theology*, edited by Gerald H. Anderson, 11–35. Maryknoll: Orbis, 1976.

Tippett, Alan R. "The Cultural Anthropology of Conversion." In *Handbook of Religious Conversion*, edited by H. N. Malony and S. Southard, 192–205. Birmingham: Religious Education Press, 1992.

———. *Verdict Theology in Missionary Theory*. Pasadena: William Carey Library, 1973.

Tizon, Al. *Transformation After Lausanne: Radical Evangelical Mission in Global-Local Perspective*. Eugene: Wipf & Stock, 2008.

Travasso, Sandra Mary, Divya Rajaraman, and Sally Jody Heymann. "A Qualitative Study of Factors Affecting Mental Health Amongst Low-Income Working Mothers in Bangalore, India." *BMC Women's Health* 14, 22 (2014). https://doi.org/10.1186/1472-6874-14-22.

Travis, John. "The C1 to C6 Spectrum: A Practical Tool for Defining Six Types of 'Christ Centered Communities.'" *Evangelical Missions Quarterly* 34, no. 4 (October 1998): 407–8.

UNESCO, "Statement of Commitment for Action to Eradicate Poverty Adopted by Administrative Committee on Coordination." UNESCO (1998), accessed 10 January 2015, https://www.un.org/press/en/1998/19980520.eco5759.html.

UNHCR, UNICEF, and WFP. *Vulnerability Assessment of Syrian Refugees in Lebanon 2015*. Beirut: World Food Programme, UN Children's Fund, UN High Commissioner for Refugees, 2015.

Ustoff, Werner. "The Cultural Origins of 'Intercultural' Theology." In *Intercultural Theology: Approaches and Themes*, edited by Mark J. Cartledge and David Cheetham, 11–28. London: SCM, 2011.

Valentine, Charles. "The 'Culture of Poverty': Its Scientific Significance and Its Implications for Action." In *The Culture of Poverty: A Critique*, edited by Eleanor B. Leacock, 193–225. New York: Simon & Schuster, 1971.

———. *Culture and Poverty: Critique and Counter-Proposals*. Chicago: University of Chicago Press, 1968.

Van Engen, Chuck. "Is the Church for Everyone? Planting Multi-Ethnic Congregations in North America." *Global Missiology* 1, no. 2 (2004): 1–53.

Vaters, Karl. "Why Millennials Won't Build the Kinds of Churches Their Parents Built." *Christianity Today: Culture and Values*. Pivot: A Blog by Karl Vaters (10 October 2016). www.christianitytoday.com/karl-vaters/2016/october/why-millennials-wont-build-kinds-of-churches-their-parents-.html?paging=off.

Vicedom, Georg E. *The Mission of God*. St. Louis, MO: Concordia, 1965.

Vygotsky, L. S., and M. Cole. *Mind in Society: The Development of Higher Psychological Processes*. Cambridge: Harvard University Press, 1978.

Wagner, C. Peter. *Church Growth and the Whole Gospel: A Biblical Mandate*. New York: Harper & Row, 1981.

———. *Latin American Theology: Radical or Evangelical? The Struggle for the Faith in a Young Church*. Grand Rapids: Eerdmans, 1970.

———. *Our Kind of People: The Ethical Dimensions of Church Growth in America*. Atlanta: John Knox, 1979.

Walls, Andrew F. "Converts or Proselytes? The Crisis over Conversion in the Early Church." *International Bulletin of Missionary Research* 28, no. 1 (2004): 2–6.

———. *The Missionary Movement in Christian History: Studies in the Transmission of Faith*. Maryknoll: Orbis, 1996.

———. "Missiology." In *Dictionary of the Ecumenical Movement*, 689–90. Geneva: World Council of Churches, 2002.

Waters, Anne, ed. *American Indian Thought*. Oxford: Blackwell, 2004.

Webber, Timothy P. *Living in the Shadow of the Second Coming*. Grand Rapids, MI: Zondervan, 1983.

Webster, John. "What's Evangelical about Evangelical Soteriology?" In *What Does It Mean to Be Saved? Broadening Evangelical Horizons of Salvation*, edited by John G. Stackhouse Jr., 179–84. Grand Rapids: Baker Academic, 2002.

Wells, David. *Turning to God: Biblical Conversion in the Modern World*. Milton Keynes: Paternoster, 1989.

Weyers, M., and W. Saayman. "'Belonging before Believing': Some Missiological Implications of Membership and Belonging in a Christian Community." *Verbum et Ecclesia* 34, no. 1 (2013): 1–8.

"Wheaton Declaration." *International Review of Mission* 55, no. 220 (1966): 458–76.

Wheeler, Ray. "The Legacy of Shoki Coe." *International Bulletin of Missionary Research* 26, no. 2 (2002): 77–80.

Whiteman, Darrell L. "Anthropological Reflections on Contextualizing Theology in a Globalizing World." In *Globalizing Theology: Belief and Practice in an Era of World Christianity*, edited by Craig Ott and Harold A. Netland, 52–69. Grand Rapids: Baker, 2006.

———. "Contextualization: The Theory, the Gap, the Challenge." *International Bulletin of Missionary Research* 21, no. 1 (1997): 2–7.

"The White Southerners Who Fought US segregation." *BBC News* (12 March 2019). https://www.bbc.com/news/world-us-canada-47477354.

"William Booth: The First General of the Salvation Army." Christian History. *Christianity Today* (2008). http://www.christianitytoday.com//ch/131christians/activists/williambooth.html.

Wilson, Andrew. "Why Jesus, Not Salvation, Is God's Greatest Gift to Us." *Christianity Today* (22 August 2016). http://www.christianitytoday.com/ct/2016/september/why-jesus-not-salvation-is-gods-greatest-gift-to-us.html.

Wilson, J. Christy. "Muslims Who Came to Christ." *Missionary Monthly* (March 1994).

Wilson, Jonathan R. "Clarifying Vision, Empowering Witness." In *What Does It Mean to Be Saved? Broadening Evangelical Horizons of Salvation*, edited by John G. Stackhouse Jr., 185–94. Grand Rapids: Baker Academic, 2002.

Wimber, John, and Kevin Springer. *Power Evangelism*. Bloomington, MN: Chosen Books, 1986.

Wink, Walter. *Engaging the Powers: Discernment and Resistance in a World of Domination*. Minneapolis: Fortress, 1992.

Woodberry, D., and R. Shubin. "Why I Chose Jesus." *Mission Frontiers* (2001). http://www.missionfrontiers.org/issue/article/muslims-tell…-why-i-chose-jesus.

Woodberry, J. Dudley, Russell G. Shubin, and G. Marks. "Why Muslims Follow Jesus: The Results of a Recent Survey of Converts from Islam." *Christianity Today* (24 October 2007). http://www.christianitytoday.com/ct/2007/october/42.80.html.

Woodberry, Robert D. "The Missionary Roots of Liberal Democracy." *American Political Science Review* 106, no. 2 (2012): 244–74.

"Workshop II Evangelism and the Poor." *Missiology* 10, no. 3 (1982): 349–57.

World Council of Churches. "Revised Report of the Commission on 'Christian Witness, Proselytism and Religious Liberty.'" *Ecumenical Review* 13, no. 1 (1960): 79–89.

World Council of Churches, Commission on World Mission and Evangelism. "Mission and Evangelism: An Ecumenical Affirmation." *International Bulletin of Missionary Research* (April 1983): 65–71.

The World Evangelical Alliance Global Review Panel. *Report to World Evangelical Alliance for Conveyance to Wycliffe Global Alliance and SIL International*, Deerfield, IL: World Evangelical Alliance, 2013.

The World Missionary Conference, 1910: The History and Records of the Conference, Together with Addresses Delivered at the Evening Meetings. Edinburgh, London: Oliphant, Anderson & Ferrier, 1910.

Wright, Christopher J. H. "Implications of Conversion in the Old Testament and the New Testament." *International Bulletin of Missionary Research* 28, no. 1 (2004): 14–19.

———. *The Mission of God: Unlocking the Bible's Grand Narrative*. Nottingham: Inter-Varsity Press, 2006.

Yancy, Philip. *Reaching for the Invisible God: What Can We Expect to Find?* Grand Rapids: Zondervan, 2000.

Yeh, Allen. *Polycentric Missiology: 21st-Century Mission from Everyone to Everywhere*. Downers Grove: IVP Academic, 2016.

Yoder, Michael L., Michael H. Lee, Jonathan Ro, and Robert J. Priest. "Understanding Christian Identity in Terms of Bounded and Centered Set Theory in the Writings of Paul G. Hiebert." *Trinity Journal* 30, no. 2 (2009): 177–88.

Zwemer, Samuel Marinus. *Raymund Lull First Missionary to the Moslems*. Lenox: Hard Press, 2013.

Langham Literature and its imprints are a ministry of Langham Partnership.

Langham Partnership is a global fellowship working in pursuit of the vision God entrusted to its founder John Stott –

to facilitate the growth of the church in maturity and Christ-likeness through raising the standards of biblical preaching and teaching.

Our vision is to see churches in the Majority World equipped for mission and growing to maturity in Christ through the ministry of pastors and leaders who believe, teach and live by the word of God.

Our mission is to strengthen the ministry of the word of God through:
- nurturing national movements for biblical preaching
- fostering the creation and distribution of evangelical literature
- enhancing evangelical theological education

especially in countries where churches are under-resourced.

Our ministry

Langham Preaching partners with national leaders to nurture indigenous biblical preaching movements for pastors and lay preachers all around the world. With the support of a team of trainers from many countries, a multi-level programme of seminars provides practical training, and is followed by a programme for training local facilitators. Local preachers' groups and national and regional networks ensure continuity and ongoing development, seeking to build vigorous movements committed to Bible exposition.

Langham Literature provides Majority World preachers, scholars and seminary libraries with evangelical books and electronic resources through publishing and distribution, grants and discounts. The programme also fosters the creation of indigenous evangelical books in many languages, through writer's grants, strengthening local evangelical publishing houses, and investment in major regional literature projects, such as one volume Bible commentaries like *The Africa Bible Commentary* and *The South Asia Bible Commentary*.

Langham Scholars provides financial support for evangelical doctoral students from the Majority World so that, when they return home, they may train pastors and other Christian leaders with sound, biblical and theological teaching. This programme equips those who equip others. Langham Scholars also works in partnership with Majority World seminaries in strengthening evangelical theological education. A growing number of Langham Scholars study in high quality doctoral programmes in the Majority World itself. As well as teaching the next generation of pastors, graduated Langham Scholars exercise significant influence through their writing and leadership.

To learn more about Langham Partnership and the work we do visit **langham.org**

9 781839 732737